TITLES IN THIS SERIES

The Doctrine of God, Gerald Bray
The Work of Christ, Robert Letham
The Providence of God, Paul Helm
The Church, Edmund P. Clowney

THE
CHURCH

EDMUND P. CLOWNEY

CONTOURS *of*

CHRISTIAN

THEOLOGY

GERALD BRAY
General Editor

InterVarsity Press
Downers Grove, Illinois

Published in the United States of America by InterVarsity Press, Downers Grove, Illinois, with permission from Universities and Colleges Christian Fellowship, Leicester, England.

InterVarsity Press® is the book-publishing division of InterVarsity Christian Fellowship®, a student movement active on campus at hundreds of universities, colleges and schools of nursing in the United States of America, and a member movement of the International Fellowship of Evangelical Students. For information about local and regional activities, write Public Relations Dept., InterVarsity Christian Fellowship, 6400 Schroeder Rd., P.O. Box 7895, Madison, WI 53707-7895.

ISBN 0-8308-1534-1
Printed in the United States of America ♾

Library of Congress Cataloging-in-Publication Data

Clowney, Edmund P.
    The church/by Edmund P. Clowney.
        p.   cm.—(Contours of Christian theology)
    Includes bibliographical references.
    ISBN 0-8308-1534-1
    1. Church.   2. Church—Biblical teaching.   3. Church—History of doctrines.   4. Mission of the church.   I. Title.   II. Series.
    BV600.2.C57   1995
    262—dc20
                                             94-45405
                                              CIP

17   16   15   14   13   12   11
09   08   07   06

Contents

Series Preface

Contours of Christian Theology covers the main themes of Christian doctrine. The series offers a systematic presentation of most of the major doctrines in a way which complements the traditional textbooks but does not copy them. Top priority has been given to contemporary issues, some of which may not be dealt with elsewhere from an evangelical point of view. The series aims, however, not merely to answer current objections to evangelical Christianity, but also to rework the orthodox evangelical position in a fresh and compelling way. The overall thrust is therefore positive and evangelistic in the best sense.

The series is intended to be of value to theological students at all levels, whether at a Bible college, a seminary or a secular university. It should also appeal to ministers and to educated lay-people. As far as possible, efforts have been made to make technical vocabulary accessible to the non-specialist reader, and the presentation has avoided the extremes of academic style. Occasionally this has meant that particular issues have been presented without a thorough argument, taking into account different positions, but when this has happened, authors have been encouraged to refer the reader to other works which take the discussion further. For this purpose adequate but not extensive notes have been provided.

The doctrines covered in the series are not exhaustive, but have been chosen in response to contemporary concerns. The title and general presentation of each volume are at the discretion of the author, but final editorial decisions have been taken by the Series Editor in consultation with IVP.

In offering this series to the public, the authors and the publishers hope that it will meet the needs of theological students in this generation, and bring honour and glory to God the Father, and to his Son, Jesus Christ, in whose service the work has been undertaken from the beginning.

Gerald Bray
Series Editor

Preface

Only courageous – and committed – publishers would present a series of books on biblical doctrines to a reading public so attached to 'feel-good' religion. The secular mind-set is outraged by the very notion that religion can be a matter of fact rather than feeling or opinion. New Testament scholars of the 'Jesus Seminar', having disallowed 80% of the words of Jesus reported in the Gospels, now declare that he never rose from the dead, but that Christians should be undisturbed, since ' "God raised Jesus from the dead" is a statement of faith, not historic fact'.[1]

Evangelicals continue to resist such a view of Christian doctrine, but even they may be surprised by a book on the biblical doctrine of the church, especially one that takes account of the Old Testament form of the people of God. Yet the church, too, is part of God's revelation. If it is to stand against the gates of hell, it must know its own divine charter, its bond to Jesus Christ, and the 'Holy Spiritual' power of its calling. For the church to be the church in the year 2000, it must be more than 'seeker-friendly'; it must be 'Seeker-sent', thrust forth by the Lord to bear his gospel of the cross to the peoples.

I wish to express my deep appreciation to Inter-Varsity Press, and especially to the Theological Books Editor, David Kingdon. He has given time and help far beyond professional thoroughness, as a servant of Christ. My daughter, Rebecca Jones, edited and condensed the entire manuscript, eliminating countless passive constructions. My wife Jean showed her usual patience with me during my many hours at the computer. My students and colleagues over the years have been also my teachers. I appreciate particularly the assistance of Steven Baugh and the gracious responses of Wayne Grudem – even when we disagree.

Edmund P. Clowney

Abbreviations

ASV	American Standard Version.
BAR	*Biblical Archaeology Review.*
DPCM	*Dictionary of Pentecostal and Charismatic Movements*, ed. Stanley M. Burgess and Gary B. McGee (Grand Rapids: Zondervan, 1988).
JTS	*Journal of Theological Studies.*
LXX	Septuagint (Greek version of the Old Testament).
NASB	New American Standard Bible.
NIV	New International Version.
NKJV	New King James Version.
SJT	*Scottish Journal of Theology.*
TDNT	*Theological Dictionary of the New Testament*, ed. G. Kittel & G. Friedrich, trans. and ed. G. W. Bromiley, 10 vols. (Grand Rapids: Eerdmans, 1964–76).
WTJ	*Westminster Theological Journal.*

1

THE COLONY
OF HEAVEN

In the heart of London's financial district, dwarfed by the soaring towers of the city, nestles St Helen's Church, Bishopsgate. How did this ancient church survive the bombs of Hitler, of the Irish Republican Army, and the bulldozers of progress? Sheer glass walls surround it, the faceless centres of banking and business. A programmer peering down at the quaint church from his thirtieth-floor office smiles over his coffee at this lonely monument to an implausible faith.

Christianity, of course, has never lacked prophets of its demise: among the more recent Nietzsche, Feuerbach, Marx, Gide and Sartre.[1] Yet since the Second World War the culture of the West, profoundly influenced by Christianity, has been undercut, not so much by the processes of urbanization and globalization, as by a 'systematic dismemberment, a "trashing" of our culture'.[2] Leaders in education, in the media, and increasingly in government, have attacked Christian faith and values, claiming that they oppose both individual liberty and global unity.

A Tuesday visitor in the nave of St Helen's takes advantage of the quiet to reflect on the church in modern life. A young businessman appears, takes a seat and begins to pray. Fair enough. A small percentage of Britain's diverse population still does this sort of thing. But then another young man appears, and another. Soon they come streaming into the church from the surrounding concrete canyons. Financiers and office staff, men and women, young and old, they crowd in by the hundreds for the lunch-hour Bible exposition, famous at St Helen's for more than a decade.[3] Dick Lucas, pastor of the church, climbs into the pulpit, announces a hymn, then asks his audience to open their Bibles. With startling clarity and force, he explains just what the passage says about Jesus Christ, and why the men and women before him need to know the Lord.

Remarkable as such services may be in a secular age, do they really affect our estimate of the church? It is 'not the New Moon or the Sabbath', but the lunch hour when these people gather. No doubt many are not church members at all. Some will appear for congregational worship on Sunday morning, but office workers cannot create a neighbourhood church. Does the Tuesday-noon gathering at St Helen's only reinforce the impression that the institutional church is indeed a relic, whatever may be the remaining attraction of the gospel message? After bomb damage in 1991 and 1993, St Helen's sought permission to renovate so as to provide more seating. Societies dedicated to preserving period architecture vigorously protested. They wanted the church restored as a monument, not as a centre for gospel proclamation to the city.[4]

The church in an age of pluralism

Once the church was central in European culture. All Christendom assumed that there was no salvation outside the church. The Protestant Reformers never questioned the importance of the church. Failing to reform the church of Rome, they challenged its claims by distinguishing the marks of the true church.

Now, however, the Roman Catholic Church has surrendered its claim to a sacramental monopoly on salvation. Vatican II describes the blessings of new life in Christ, then adds:

> All this holds true not for Christians only but also for all men of good will in whose hearts grace is active

14

invisibly. For since Christ died for all, and since all men are in fact called to one and the same destiny, which is divine, we must hold that the Holy Spirit offers to all the possibility of being made partners, in a way known to God, in the paschal mystery.[5]

Even this sweeping concession still assumes that salvation requires some secret identification with Christ in the 'paschal mystery'. Not so, say radical contemporary theologians. Salvation is not limited to the church, to Christianity, or to Christ.[6] All religions have equal rights for they hold an equal claim to religious truth. An enlightened Christian world citizen, we are told, will avoid Christian terminology that might offend other religions. He or she will speak of God as 'he / she / it'.[7] The only God who might take offence at this neutering is the God of the Bible, noted for his exclusive claims. That God, we are told, died long ago with orthodox theology, and the church is his tomb.

Faced with the revival of heathenism and 'earth religions', should we shelve our concerns about the church and return to Paul's message on the Areopagus, proclaiming to modern pagans the unknown God, Lord of heaven and earth? Many urge just such a change. J. C. Hoekendijk once observed that 'In history a keen ecclesiological interest has, almost without exception, been a sign of spiritual decadence . . .'[8]

To be sure, if the church rather than Christ becomes the centre of our devotion, spiritual decay has begun. A doctrine of the church that does not centre on Christ is self-defeating and false. But Jesus said to the disciples who confessed him, 'I will build my church.'[9] To ignore his purpose is to deny his lordship. The good news of Christ's coming includes the good news of what he came to do: to join us to himself and to one another as his body, the new people of God.

The very threats to the existence of the church in the twenty-first century show again our need of the church. The courage to stand apart, to be unashamed of Christ's claims, is nurtured in the community of those who are baptized into his name. The church may not apply for a union card in a pluralist establishment by signing away its right to proclaim the only Saviour of the world. Together we must make clear that it is to Christ and not to ourselves that we witness. In that witness we are not only

15

individual points of light in the world, but a city set on a hill. In the ethnic hostility that ravages Europe, Africa and the Middle East, the church must show the bond of Christ's love that unites former enemies as brothers and sisters in the Lord. Only so can the church be a sign of his kingdom: the kingdom that will come when Christ comes, and that is already present through his Spirit.[10]

Modern technology and mass media are not in themselves secularistic. They also serve the spread of the gospel. Yet the worlds of business, education and information assume that, while ethical issues remain, religious matters are private concerns, outside the realm of public policy or interest. Individual testimony to Christ's lordship and kingdom wins only a shrug: 'If you have had a religious experience, fine. So did the Jehovah's Witnesses who bothered me yesterday.'

The church, however, as the community of Christ's kingdom, can show the world an ethical integrity it must respect. When Peter describes the impact of Christian righteous deeds in a pagan world, he is thinking not of isolated saints, but of the *people* of God, called out of darkness into God's light.[11] Christian witness that is limited to private religious experience cannot challenge secularism. Christians in community must again show the world, not merely family values, but the bond of the love of Christ. Increasingly the ordered fellowship of the church becomes the sign of grace for the warring factions of a disordered world. Only as the church binds together those whom selfishness and hate have cut apart will its message be heard and its ministry of hope to the friendless be received.

The need of the secular world is greatest at the very points where its criticism of the church is most intense. Only God's truth can set people free; for the church to concede the secular assumption of a chance universe is to deny both Christ's lordship and its own meaning.[12] The church is the community of the Word, the Word that reveals the plan and purpose of God. In the church the gospel is preached, believed, obeyed. It is the pillar and ground of the truth because it holds fast the Scriptures (Phil. 2:16).[13]

Heightened political awareness has again reached the evangelical churches. The left-leaning activism of liberal churches has been overshadowed by the activity of the 'religious right'. Dedicated Christians have blocked access to abortion clinics with their bodies, accepting police brutality and imprisonment. Protests against pornography and government-sponsored lotteries have caught the attention of news media. Americans have taken new interest in the history of European Christian political parties.

Freedom of religion, so fundamental for democratic life, has moved to centre-stage as Christians have become aware of its erosion under secularist pressure. Jesus declared that his kingdom is not of this world.[14] How, then, are his disciples to witness for truth and justice without forfeiting their pilgrim status? Is the church to be an association for the promotion of detached piety, and is all engagement with society to be the task of Christian organizations distinct from the church? If we are to be faithful to the Lord of the church we must first understand his will for the church.

The church and the churches

Our concern for the relation of the church to the world forces us to consider also the relation of the church to the churches. For some, the denominational divisions of the church express a healthy diversity. They see the church as a tree bearing twelve kinds of fruit on different branches,[15] and view organizational uniformity as threatening the organic diversity of free growth. In these days, however, even the most ardent advocate of diversity must plead for some limit to the splintering of the people of God.

The missionary expansion of the church has made the issue of church unity inescapable. In the twentieth century the church has been planted in every major country of the world. 'Receiving' churches have become 'sending' churches. The Presbyterian churches of South Korea, for example, now play a major role in the world mission of the church. Missionary concern was a leading factor in the development of the ecumenical movement. Denominational competition in missionary activity could not be controlled by comity agreements (a colonialist technique of dividing up unevangelized areas into assigned missionary territories). The collapse of European imperialism called for a drastic shift in missionary polity. Sending churches and missions

17

had to take account of the 'younger churches' established in the areas they served. Concern for the visible unity of Christ's church has come to the fore again as heretical sects have rushed in to exploit greater freedom of religion in Eastern Europe.

The ecumenical concern of Christians has been channelled in liberal directions, however, by the ecclesiology of the World Council of Churches (WCC). In the course of the century the ecclesiology of the ecumenical movement traced a full circle. In the early days of the Life and Work movement (one of the confluent streams from which the WCC originated), the motto was, 'Theology divides; service unites.' To an old-fashioned liberal, the peace movement stirred by the First World War offered an obvious and urgent channel for unity in service. But the need for doctrine could not be escaped. In the mid-thirties, confronted with Hitler's nazified German Christian Church, Visser 't Hooft and other neo-orthodox leaders showed the need for a doctrine of the church to answer Hitler. The Faith and Order Conference in Lund in 1952 concluded that 'the doctrine of the church [should] be treated in close relation both to the doctrine of Christ and to the doctrine of the Spirit'.[16]

Theological studies in response to this call during the next ten years, however, did not yield a biblical doctrine of the church that was grounded in renewed understanding of Christology and the doctrine of the Holy Spirit. Rather, the theological assumptions that had shaped ecumenical ecclesiology were applied to these more fundamental doctrines as well. The church had been defined as becoming rather than *being*; it was not a company of the redeemed, but a ministry of redemption. Accordingly, Claude Welch argued that the doctrine of Christ as well as the doctrine of the church must be consistently expressed in terms of becoming, of 'being-in-relation'. The divine and the human in Christ appear, not as two 'natures', but as a polarity resolved in personal relatedness. The incarnate Christ as well as the church exists in *act*, in becoming, not in being.[17]

The ecumenical movement was close to a consensus in ecclesiology, a consensus shaped by the tension of dialectical theology. Faith and Order reports in preparation for the meeting in Montreal in 1963 tried to resolve the contrasting views of the church by setting them in polarity. The tension

18

between the church viewed as 'act' in the Barthian pattern and the church viewed as sacramental institution in catholic theology could be welcomed as the polarity of the eternal and the temporal.

This attempt at consensus, however, carried the seeds of a more radical approach that made it irrelevant. Ecumenical ecclesiology veered sharply to the left, and became, in spite of some protest, a theology of revolution. Papers at the Geneva conference on Church and Society in 1966 called on the church to 'become actively involved in the struggle against the present political, social, and economic organization'. This revolutionary overthrow required Christian 'participation in equivocal situations in which the dividing line between good and evil is not clear-cut'.[18] To discern the will of God the church must see how God is acting in history and plunge into the centre of revolution to join him there. Situational ethics justified the participation of the church in revolutionary violence. 'From within the struggle we discover that we do not bear witness in revolution by preserving our purity in line with certain moral principles, but rather by freedom to be *for man* at every moment.'[19] Liberation theology gained a dominant role in the ecumenical movement in the latter part of the century. It was the Department of Church and Society of the WCC that sponsored the Geneva conference of 1966. That department represents the continuance, within the WCC, of the Life and Work movement that had met in Stockholm in 1925. Geneva 1966 brought the WCC back to the social action commended at Stockholm 1925. The significant shift was that the social action advocated was now the war of liberation rather than the peace of liberalism.

The shift from a dialectical theology to a theology of revolution was not as drastic as it might appear. The dialectical approach defined the church in *act*, not in theory. A truly 'catholic' theology must therefore include a plurality of theories. Ecumenical documents increasingly advocated theological pluralism. Critical scholarship held that the Bible contains many contradictory theologies, and therefore concludes that it cannot provide the norm for any one view of the church and its task.

The theme 'Come, Holy Spirit – Renew the Whole Creation' was chosen for the Seventh Assembly of the WCC in Canberra,

Australia, 1991. The theme was thought appropriate for the last decade of the century because it was appealing to: 1. feminists, who prefer 'Spirit' to male terms for God; 2. environmentalists, who are concerned with the renewal of creation; 3. adherents of non-Christian religions, who are offended by such themes as 'Jesus Christ, the Life of the World' (the theme of the Sixth Assembly), but who, as non-Christians, can dialogue about shared conceptions of 'Spirit'; 4. advocates of liberation theology who identify the Spirit 'with their common focus on human empowerment and social transformation'; 5. Pentecostal, charismatic, and Black churches; 6. Eastern Orthodox churches, who have criticized Christianity in the West for being Christocentric; and 7. 'evangelical traditions, whether conservative or radical', who cherish the Spirit's work of rebirth and renewal.[20]

In short, the WCC found that a theme linking the Spirit and creation picked up on language that is 'a promising and widely shared voice of a lively pluralism around the world'.[21]

Assemblies of the WCC have had little impact, however, in comparison with that of the Second Vatican Council (1962–65), which marked a new effort on the part of the Roman Catholic Church to define ecclesiology. Official publication of the Council documents in October 1966 sparked intense discussion of the nature and mission of the church among Catholic theologians. The revered summary of papal authority, 'Rome has spoken, the case is concluded', has not marked the response to Vatican II. Some explained that little was changed by Vatican II,[22] but many ran for the exit from institutional authority through what looked like the 'open door' policy of the conciliar decrees. Theological fashions in the WCC found advocates in the Roman Church. Edward Schillebeeckx outdid many ecumenical theologians in embracing a chance universe. He insisted on ultimate contingency; the historical future is not known even to God, otherwise it would be 'a large-scale Muppet show!'[23]

Liberation theology was given definitive form by Roman Catholic theologians in Latin America; it brings to a focus the broader spectrum of 'secular theology' advocated within the Roman Church.[24] Richard P. McBrien asks, 'Do we need the Church?' His answer is 'No!' if a 'Ptolemaic, pre-Einsteinian Church' is meant.[25] He judges that Vatican II accomplished a

Copernican revolution of sorts by abandoning the traditional church-centred view of Christianity. It did not, however, bring in the theological relativity that the church needs in order to address the contemporary world. Einstein's theory of relativity in physics still needs its parallel in ecclesiology, argues McBrien. He finds the relativity he seeks in the 'secular' theologians, those who would agree that 'Salvation comes through participation in the Kingdom of God rather than through affiliation with the Christian Church.'[26] 'All men are called to the Kingdom; not all men are called to the church.'[27]

The American Catholic theologian Avery R. Dulles opposes both the theology of liberation and the secular theology that underlies it. In it he finds a loss of the transcendent dimension of the church's life.[28] He opposes the religious pluralism that would grant equal validity to all religions and remove the church from the 'salvation business'.[29] At the same time, Dulles does not wish to see the church reformed as the Protestant Reformers sought to reform it, by a return to the New Testament and to the apostolic church. Rather, reform must restate doctrines in 'creative interaction' with changing cultures.

In his defence of Vatican II, Dulles finds a key in its formulation of tradition. He traces the position of the Council through Yves Congar back to the lay philosopher Maurice Blondel.[30] Tradition is to be defined, not as objective knowledge, handed down from the past (the 'traditional' Catholic position), or as a 'mere method of investigation and discovery' (the liberal Catholic position), but as a tacit understanding shared in the community, into which neophytes are inducted, and which they learn in practice. Not verbal formulations, but the continuing consciousness of the community carries tradition. Tradition thereby gains a critical role as the medium of the continuing but changing doctrine of the church. It is not clear, however, how the Vatican II doctrine, as expounded by Dulles, can defend itself against the more radical demands of those who find in it the opportunity for a 'quantum leap' in the formulation of doctrine to fit the demands of the twenty-first century.[31] When once the objective authority of verbal revelation is relativized, the church, not the Bible, becomes the ultimate standard of truth.

Among evangelicals, particularly in America, radical changes

21

in church structure and practice have accompanied evangelical growth. Reflection on the biblical doctrine of the church has not kept pace with changing practice. Sociologist James Hunter, one of the most perceptive students of American evangelicalism, has discerned among the movement's younger leadership a marked tendency to follow the same disastrous path that was followed by American liberalism.[32] As evangelicalism broke out of the ghetto of fundamentalist isolation, it began to make the same compromises with the secular culture that made liberalism respectable – and redundant.

Evangelical organizations in the United States, Great Britain and around the world have served to unite Christians in Bible-believing churches with one another and with fellow-believers in mainline liberal denominations. In part, this has come about through the establishment of national councils or unions of evangelicals, most of which have become affiliated with the World Evangelical Fellowship. Mission conferences have also created networks of fellowship and service among evangelicals. The Congress on Evangelism in Berlin in 1966 launched a series of gatherings with significant 'Two-Thirds World' participation. A continuation committee, formed at the Lausanne Congress on World Evangelization in 1974, provided another structure for ecumenical evangelicalism.

Largely because of liberal control of the mainline denominations, evangelicalism took shape apart from the organized church. Growing parachurch organizations enabled individual Christians to unite for service apart from denominational structures. Missionary organizations established in the late eighteenth and early nineteenth centuries had formed both within and across denominational boundaries. Though denominations gradually set up boards for foreign missions, independent boards also flourished. Some were defined by a geographical target, e.g. China Inland Mission, Africa Inland Mission and Sudan Interior Mission. Such agencies aimed to focus interdenominational support. Other agencies were defined by their vision for ministry, ranging from 'frontier' missions to Bible translators, campus ministries, educational institutions and relief agencies. The evangelical world, institutionalized primarily in a vast number of parachurch agencies, left church unity to the ecumenical movement. While some denominations readily identified with national evangelical organizations, other conservative churches distanced themselves from them (in the United States, for example, the Southern Baptist Convention, and the Lutheran Church – Missouri Synod).

The growth of Bible churches and the wide acceptance of the dispensational theology of the Scofield Reference Bible strengthened the parachurch tilt of evangelicalism. Many of the churches sharing this doctrinal position formed their own ecclesiastical connection; thousands of others found their identity in a less formal but no less real relationship. Mission agencies with geographical designations did not hesitate to define themselves doctrinally in credal affirmations that were specifically dispensational. In the receiving countries, evangelical missions established denominations that followed the patterns and sometimes adopted the name of the sponsoring mission. Evangelicalism gradually gained a quasi-denominational structure.[33]

Denominational division in the organized church and the quasi-denominational consensus in evangelicalism have caused unfortunate misunderstandings. Denominational churches may each think of themselves as Christ's church on earth, giving little thought to the claims of other denominations, though acknowledging them as true churches. They may look on parachurch groups as irregular, a threat to ecclesiastical order and to church finances. Local churches have sometimes taught that all the offerings of church members should be channelled through the church, with the expenditures regulated by church officers. A variant of this attitude was seen when the General Assembly of the Presbyterian Church, USA, declared in 1935 that it was as necessary to give to the established agencies of the church as to come to the Lord's Table.[34] The Assembly then proceeded to discipline Dr J. Gresham Machen because he refused to resign from the Independent Board for Presbyterian Foreign Missions.[35]

The growth of the evangelical 'mega-church', particularly in the United States and South Korea, raises a new issue in denominationalism. Such a church, with thousands or even hundreds of thousands of members, becomes a virtual denomination, usually under the strong leadership of one senior pastor. Again the problem can arise: the mega-church may conduct its affairs as though it were the church universal, viewing with suspicion or lack of interest those outside its fellowship.

Parachurch groups, for their part, because they do not regard themselves as churches, organize and conduct their operations in any way they see fit, borrowing structures from business corporations, or even from the military. The founder of the organization then becomes the chief executive officer or the commander-in-chief. So common has business organization become in American parachurch organizations that the church itself has taken up the same model.

Are we to suppose, because the New Testament says nothing about mission boards, that there is no New Testament teaching about their order and function?[36] When Christians form organizations to accomplish part of the church's ministry, what responsibility do they have to apply to themselves the teaching of the New Testament regarding church office and discipline? What do the Scriptures teach about the form and function of the church of Christ?

The church and the Spirit

One final question compels us to consider the doctrine of the church: in what way is the church the dwelling-place of the Holy Spirit? The charismatic movement has spread throughout the world, cutting across denominational lines, both uniting and dividing Christians. Every Sunday morning Protestant churches in every continent sing God's praise often using Catholic charismatic songs. In Latin America, particularly, the churches that have grown most rapidly have professed the gifts of tongues, prophecy and healing.

Tension between ardour and order was already part of the struggle of the early church with Montanism; it continued in the sectarian movements of the Middle Ages. Luther and Calvin opposed Anabaptist fervour with heated condemnation. Orthodox believers opposed the 'enthusiasts', concerned about the threat that they posed to the order and doctrine of the church. Today we face the same questions. Are critics of the charismatic movement guilty of seeking to quench the Spirit? What biblical teachings need to be recovered regarding the work of the Spirit? Contemporary issues converge on our need of a deeper understanding of the rich revelation of the church in Scripture.

In the following chapters we will consider the biblical theology of the church as the people of God, as the disciples of Christ, and as the fellowship of the Holy Spirit (chapters 2 to 5). Chapters 6 and 7 treat the 'attributes' of the church as apostolic, one, holy and catholic. Next comes the question as to how the church is to be recognized, the 'marks' of the church (chapter 8). Three chapters then deal with the ministry of the church: its worship, nurture and mission (chapters 9 to 11). The mission of the church leads us to think of the church in relation to the cultures of the world (chapter 12), and its governments (chapter 13). After reviewing the structure of the church and its offices (chapter 14), we turn to two much-debated topics, the ministry of women in the church (chapter 15), and the charismatic gifts of tongues (chapter 16) and of prophecy (chapter 17). Finally, the place of the sacraments in the church is considered (chapter 18).

Quite evidently, this book can provide only a brief survey of these matters, but it seeks to remind us of our Lord's teaching about his church so that by his Word and Spirit he may renew and direct us into a new century, until he comes.

2

THE PEOPLE
OF GOD

Alex Haley's television drama *Roots* proved unforgettable for
millions. The author had researched the history of his own
family as plantation slaves, tracing them back to the very village
in Africa from which their ancestor had been brought in the
hold of a slave ship. Not only African Americans, but Americans
from Europe, the Middle East and Asia began to look into the
story of their own ancestors.

Since that time, the idea of 'story' has caught on. In urban
schools where a miniature United Nations assembly gathers,
children are encouraged to be curious about their own story
and the story of their people. Those stories, however, are
sometimes violent. *Roots* was a grim reminder of the evils of
American slavery. Stories that are too well remembered inflame
tribal hatred in Africa, the Balkans and, indeed, around the
world.

The chaotic rootlessness of modern society as well as ethnic
strife point us to the story we have lost.[1] It is the greatest story
ever told, the story of God's saving love. That story does not
begin at Bethlehem's manger: it begins in the Garden of Eden,
when God promises that the Son of the woman will crush the

head of the serpent.[2] It continues in God's promise to Abraham, made with an oath, 'Because God wanted to make the unchanging nature of his purpose very clear to the heirs of what was promised' (Heb. 6:17). The story of the church begins with Israel, the Old Testament people of God.

As the story unfolds, God reveals more and more fully, not only what he will do for his people, but what he will be for them. God calls Abraham and promises to make of him a great nation, a blessing to all the families of the earth. He calls Israel out of slavery in Egypt to make his covenant with them at Sinai. He gives them the Promised Land, and makes David king in Jerusalem. God's judgments on Israel's sin divide the nation; both Israel and Judah are carried eastward into captivity. But God does not forsake his people.

The prophets renew God's claim on them, and predict both restoration and renewal. Their God promises to bring them back from the dead, as it were, restore them to their land, and make them a witness to the nations. To keep his promises, God himself must come: he will circumcise their hearts and renew his covenant (Is. 40:10–11; Je. 31:33–34; Ezk. 36:25–28). They will become his people indeed, and he will become their God.

Then Jesus Christ comes, not only as the promised Messiah, the anointed Son of David, but also as Immanuel, God with us. He calls his disciples and establishes his assembly. The people of God become his, heirs of his kingdom. After his resurrection, he commands his disciples to wait in Jerusalem until they receive from the Father the gift of the promised Spirit. His coming to fill the assembled disciples at Pentecost establishes the church of the New Covenant.

According to the Bible, the church is the people of God, the assembly and body of Christ, and the fellowship of the Holy Spirit. Each of these views of the church has been favoured in one of the major ecclesiastical heritages. The Reformed family of churches has emphasized the church as the people of God; the sacramental churches as the body of Christ; the Anabaptist churches as the disciples of Christ; and the Pentecostal churches as the fellowship of the Spirit.[3] No doubt we are all guilty of tunnel vision, focusing on one model. Vatican II challenged the comprehensiveness of the 'body of Christ' metaphor, and brought back the 'people of God' idiom.[4]

28

For a fresh look at the biblical doctrine of the church, a full Trinitarian approach serves best. In the history of revelation, the Old Testament people of God become the church of the Messiah, formed as the fellowship of the Spirit. The Bible does not deliver shipments of doctrine in cargo containers. Rather, the new grows out of the old, as the flower opens from the bud. The coming of the Spirit fulfils the promise to Abraham, and makes the Gentiles Abraham's seed (Gal. 3:14, 29). Only in the coming of the Spirit is the body of Christ given its full reality, just as only in Christ's redemption do sinners become the true people of God, sprinkled with the blood of the New Covenant.

Let us now consider the church as the people of God, and then in the next chapters explore how they are claimed by Christ as his Messianic assembly, and how Christ indwells his church in the fellowship of the Spirit.

> But you are a chosen people, a royal priesthood, a holy nation, a people belonging to God, that you may declare the praises of him who called you out of darkness into his wonderful light. Once you were not a people, but now you are the people of God; once you had not received mercy, but now you have received mercy (1 Pet. 2:9–10).

In these verses, the apostle Peter weaves a tapestry of Old Testament language to describe the church (Ex. 19:6; Is. 43:20–21; Ho. 1:6, 9; 2:1).[5] The relationship between God and his people was disrupted by sin, so that Israel was made *Lo-Ammi*, 'Not my people' (Ho. 1:9; Mt. 21:43); but Peter here hails the fulfilment of Hosea's promise. By God's grace, those who were 'no people', whether covenant-breaking Jews or Gentiles outside the covenant, are made the people of God and receive mercy (Ho. 1:10). Now they join in the praises of God, who called them out of darkness into his light.

God's people are his own possession, his treasure. The church is defined by belonging to God: 'I will . . . be your God, and you will be my people' (Lv. 26:12). The Bible uses many figures to describe this relation.[6] Israel is God's son, his spouse, his vine, his flock. In the New Testament, the church is

29

Christ's flock, branches of the true vine, his bride, his body, his temple, the dwelling of the Holy Spirit, the house of God.

God claimed his people in his covenant at Mount Sinai. The principal term used in the New Testament for the church, *ekklēsia*, looks back to that event.

God's assembly

The term *ekklēsia* is the Greek Old Testament translation of the Hebrew word *qāhāl*, and it describes an assembly. Matthew uses *ekklēsia* in reporting Jesus' statement to Simon Peter: 'And I tell you that you are Peter, and on this rock I will build my church [*ekklēsia*], and the gates of Hades will not overcome it' (Mt. 16:18).

Both *ekklēsia* and *qāhāl* denote an actual assembly, rather than a 'congregation' (which may or may not be 'congregated'). Is the church, then, called an assembly only because it meets together, as any group might? In that case, the term has no special significance.[7] Certainly Paul does use it to describe the actual gathering of Christians (1 Cor. 14:19, 28, 34). Luke reports its use by the city clerk at Ephesus, who reminds a mob that their grievances against Christians could be brought before a 'legal assembly' – a proper town meeting (Acts 19:39).

When Jesus speaks of the 'church', however, he uses a term rich with Old Testament meaning. Israel was God's assembly in the great day when God assembled them before him at Mount Sinai to make his covenant with them. He had brought them on 'eagles' wings' to himself (Ex. 19:4). The exodus redemption culminates at Sinai 'in the day of the assembly' (Dt. 4:10, LXX; 9:10; 10:4; 18:16). Israel was an assembly because they gathered before God, appearing in his presence (Dt. 4:10).

The later assemblies of Israel recalled that great assembly. God's trumpet blast that summoned the Sinai assembly echoed again later when the priests blew two silver trumpets to summon Israel to the door of God's house (Nu. 10:1–10). God assembled his people before him to renew his covenant (*e.g.* Jos. 24:1, 25). Three times a year Israel assembled for the feasts of the sacred calendar (Lv. 23). The prophets described the future blessing of God's presence when they announced a great festival assembly that would include the Gentiles (Is. 2:2–4; 56:6–8; Joel 2:15–17; *cf.* Ps. 87).

God's assembly includes all his 'holy ones': angelic hosts as well as earthly saints. At Mount Sinai God was present with thousands of his angels as he assembled his people at his feet (Dt. 33:2–3; Ps. 68:17).

The author of Hebrews draws the epiphany of God at Sinai to its more glorious conclusion. Though God appeared in the fire and smoke of Sinai to meet with ransomed Israel, he did not make that mountain his permanent sanctuary. Instead, he led the tribes through the desert to Mount Zion. There he fixed his dwelling, filled the temple with his glory, and called his people to his feasts. But Hebrews reminds us that even Jerusalem is not the final city. 'For here we do not have an enduring city, but we are looking for the city that is to come' (Heb. 13:14). God's people no longer gather in Jerusalem. Rather, they now worship in the city of the living God, the heavenly Jerusalem (Heb. 12:22). The earthly city was a shadow of the heavenly reality. Sinai burned with physical fire; heaven burns with the fire of God's own presence (Heb. 12:18, 29). Boldly we may approach heaven's assembly, boldly join the myriads of angels and the hosts of the redeemed. Boldly we may approach God himself, the Judge of all, for Jesus, our great High Priest, has opened the way. In the feast-day assembly of heaven, we come to Jesus, and to his sprinkled blood, the blood of the New Covenant.

To worship in that assembly is to gather in God's *ekklēsia*. We assemble here on earth (Heb. 10:25) because we assemble there, where Jesus is. Christians share in the inheritance of the saints in light (Col. 1:12); their life is already in heaven with Christ (Col. 3:1–4). Christ is the head of his body as a heavenly assembly (Col. 1:18; *cf.* Eph. 1:3; 2:5–6; Phil. 3:19–20; Gal. 4:25–26).[8] When the Corinthian Christians come together in assembly (1 Cor. 11:18; 14:26, 28), they join with 'all those everywhere who call on the name of our Lord Jesus Christ' (1 Cor. 1:2).

Not only do we come to the assembly where our risen Lord is; he comes by his Spirit to the assembly where we are. Where two or three gather in his name, there he is (Mt. 18:20; 28:20). The church is where the Lord is, not simply in his omnipresent power, but in the presence that makes the angels cry, 'Holy!', that causes the saints to sing, 'Worthy is the Lamb!', and that

humbles the sinner to confess, 'God is really among you!' (Is.
6:3; Rev. 5:12; 1 Cor. 14:25).

Because the Lord's true assembly is in heaven, it appears in
many ways on earth: in house churches, in city churches, in the
church universal.[9] Even two or three gathered in his name may
claim his power, for he is there.

God's dwelling

When God shifted his assembly from Sinai to Zion, he taught us
another principle: God came not only to meet with Israel, but to
dwell with them. Sinai was a trysting-place in the wilderness;
Jerusalem would be his dwelling-place. But already at Sinai, the
picture of God's dwelling is given. It is found in the tabernacle,
to which twelve chapters of Exodus are devoted. After God
made his covenant with Israel, Moses climbed Mount Sinai to
receive God's law, and also to receive the design of the
tabernacle, the tent where God would dwell in the centre of
the camp of Israel.

After forty days, when Moses came down the mountain, he
found Israel in full-scale rebellion against God's law, feasting
before an idol, a calf of gold. That rebellion was put down with
the death of thousands. God then proposed an alternative to the
building of the tabernacle. Because of his holiness and the
stubborn sin of the people, it was too threatening to them for
him to be present *among* them in that tent. Instead, in the form
of his angel, he would go *before* them, drive out the Canaanites
and give them the Promised Land. The change was not the
appointment of the angel in place of the Lord: the angel of the
Lord was not less dangerous than God, for the Lord's name was
in him (Ex. 23:21). The change was that God, in the form of the
angel, would go *before* them and not live among them. God
would still meet with Moses at the door of a tent set up outside
the camp, a tent where Joshua would live (Ex. 33:7–11).

Moses despaired. If the Lord did not go among them, there
was no point in going. God had promised to put his name at his
chosen place in the land, and there to live among his people.
God at a safe distance was not enough. Moses pleaded, 'Show
me your glory!' The Lord heard Moses, and gave what his mercy
had designed from the beginning. He showed Moses his glory,

and declared his name as Yahweh, full of grace and truth (Ex. 34:6; cf. Jn. 1:14). The tabernacle was built after all, and the glory of the Lord filled his dwelling.

Because Israel was indeed a stiff-necked people, and God is holy (Ex. 34:7), the design of the tabernacle provided insulation. God dwelt behind curtains, symbolically sealed off from the sinful camp. Yet the tabernacle also provided a way of approach. Sinners brought their sacrifices to its great altar; the priests entered with the blood of atonement into the holy place; the high priest, on the day of atonement, went into the innermost sanctuary, the holy of holies, to sprinkle the lid of the ark, the symbol of God's throne, with the atoning blood.

The tabernacle and the later temple declared the holiness of God and the need that his wrath against sin be assuaged through sacrifice. But the erection of God's house also declared that God had taken his people for his inheritance, that they were his and he was theirs through the provision of his grace (Ex. 34:9; Lv. 26:11–12). The presence of God separated Israel from all the other nations (Ex. 33:16). They were a kingdom of priests, a holy nation (Ex. 19:6).

God's chosen

Why did God call Israel out of Egypt to gather them in covenant assembly at Sinai? Why did he choose to dwell among them? Peter cites the Old Testament answer in his description of the New Testament church. They are God's 'chosen people', claimed as his own possession. God's choosing was not drawn by Israel's desirability:

> The LORD did not set his affection on you and choose you because you were more numerous than other peoples, for you were the fewest of all peoples. But it was because the LORD loved you and kept the oath he swore to your forefathers (Dt. 7:7–8).

What magnificent tautology! God set his affection on them because . . . he loved them! His choosing stemmed from his good pleasure, not their deserving. He would keep his own oath, made to the patriarchs whom he had also chosen.[10] God

33

expressed his own will in a choice determined by nothing outside himself.

One purpose of God's election was that his chosen ones should serve him. God called Abraham so that all the families of the earth might be blessed through him. He chose Israel to make known his salvation to all nations (Ps. 67:2). Yet God did not first *choose* Israel that he might *use* Israel. God does not choose the spiritually fit. The only fitness he requires is weakness, folly, nothingness, that no-one might glory before him (1 Cor. 1:26–31). The Lord claimed Israel, not just as his servant, but as his first-born son (Ex. 4:22), his bride (Ezk. 16:6–14), the apple of his eye (Dt. 32:10). His free love gave them their status before him.

To the grief of the prophets, God's people defied his holiness with rampant idolatry and mocked his choosing in brazen covenant-breaking. After dedicating the temple of God's presence, Solomon placed above it on the Mount of Olives a shrine for Chemosh, the god of the Moabites (1 Ki. 11:7). The Lord's judgments brought disaster as he poured out 'vengeance for the covenant' (Lv. 26:25, NASB). Assyrians swept away the northern tribes; Judah streamed into Babylonian captivity. The prophet Ezekiel saw the glory-cloud of God's presence lift from the temple and move eastward with the captives (Ezk. 11:23; *cf.* 11:16).

Was there to be no future for Israel? Ezekiel, the exiled prophet, saw a dreadful vision. After a holocaust, all that remained of God's people was a vast carpet of bones scattered on the valley floor. God asked, 'Son of man, can these bones live?' (Ezk. 37:3). Ezekiel answered, 'O Sovereign LORD, you alone know.' At God's command he then cried, 'Dry bones, hear the word of the LORD!' The Spirit of God brought life in the valley of death; God would revive and renew his people. Ezekiel was given an elaborate picture of a new temple to represent the dwelling of God among them (Ezk. 40 – 44).

God's answer through all the prophets was that his judgment was neither total nor final. It was not total, for he would spare a remnant (even of dry bones)! Prophets before the exile had stressed the smallness of the surviving remnant: one burning coal plucked from the conflagration, two legs or a piece of an ear left from a lion's kill (Am. 3:11–12). God would pick up the pieces of the scattered remnant; he would gather them from the gates of death.

If God's judgment was not total, neither was it final. He would not only spare, he would renew the surviving remnant, purifying them. The chastening of exile would bring them to confess their sin and return to the Lord (Ho. 5:15 – 6:3; Je. 3:12–14; cf. Lv. 26:40). He would give them his Spirit, exchange hearts of stone for hearts of flesh (Ezk. 11:19; 36:26–27), and make a New Covenant with them (Je. 31:31–34). In his justice the Lord cut down the cedar of Israel's pride, but from the remaining stump there would grow a shoot that would become a mighty tree, an ensign to which the nations would gather (Is. 10:33 – 11:12).

God's renewal would go far beyond restoration: with the remnant of his people he would also gather a remnant of the Gentiles. Israel had broken his covenant and forfeited any right to his promises: they could no longer claim to be his people (Ho. 1:9). Their redemption must be of God's sheer mercy, mercy that could as readily be extended to the nations. More than that, God had called Abraham with a view to blessing all the families of the earth. Since apostate Israel had not fulfilled that mission, God would accomplish it in an unexpected way. Israel's call would be fulfilled by the coming of the true Servant of the Lord. Israel had been called as God's son. God's true and only Son must appear: the Son of the woman, the Seed of Abraham, the true Isaac (Son of the promise), the Son of David, called to be God's Servant and to sit at God's right hand. He would fulfil the calling of the circumcision. In that capacity, as the minister of the circumcision, he would confirm the promises given to the fathers, that the Gentiles might glorify God for his mercy (Rom. 15:8–9).[11]

The Servant Songs of Isaiah affirm both the distinct identity of the individual Servant and his identification with the nation.[12] The individual Servant will restore the tribes of Jacob, and bring back the remnant of Israel; he will also be a light to the Gentiles (Is. 49:6). In him, God's purposes for his people would be fulfilled. 'He said to me, "You are my servant, Israel, in whom I will display my splendour"' (Is. 49:3).[13] Through his perfect obedience and redemptive suffering, the New Covenant is established.

The other side of the covenant must also be realized. Not only must the Servant come, the Lord also must come. The people's situation is so desperate that only God can deliver them. Further, the promises of God are so great that only he can make good on them. In the New Covenant God promises to circumcise the hearts of his people (Dt. 30:6; Je. 31:33–34). From the least to the greatest they will know him, and he will dwell among them. Zechariah lifts the eyes of the returned exiles beyond the feeble restoration they have seen. The day of glory will come when every pot in Jerusalem will be like a temple vessel, when the bridles of the horses will bear the inscription that was once in the turban of the high priest ('Holy to the Lord!'), and when the weakest inhabitant of Jerusalem will be like King David. In that day what will the King be like? He will be the very Angel of the Lord's Presence (Zc. 12:8).

The glory passes description, for it is God himself who will come. The shepherds of Israel have failed; God will come to be their Shepherd (Ezk. 34:15). The warriors of Israel have failed; God the divine Warrior will come, wearing the breastplate of his righteousness and the helmet of his salvation (Is. 59:16–17). The coming of the Lord and that of his Servant are drawn together: the Servant bears the names of the Lord (Is. 9:6), and the coming of the messenger (the angel) of the Lord is the coming of the Lord (Mal. 3:1–3).

When the Lord comes he will gather his people and make them his for ever (Ezk. 34:11–12, 23–24). The final festival assembly will welcome the Gentiles with the people of God (Is. 2:2–4; 25:6–8; 66:20–21; Je. 3:17). God's own presence and glory will replace the ark of the covenant (Je. 3:16). God's choosing of his people will not fail. The remnant that he spares will show his own choosing within the election of Israel. Not all who bear the name Israel are true children of Abraham (Rom. 9:6), but the Servant of the Lord is his chosen, and he will bring back the remnant of Israel and become a light to the Gentiles (Is. 49:6). God's chosen Servant, the hope of God's chosen people, will claim them for the Lord.

The story of God's people, then, takes us to Jesus Christ, in whom the old is new and the new old. We now turn to reflect on the people of God as the church of Christ.

3

THE CHURCH
OF CHRIST

How does the church of Christ relate to the Old Testament people of God? Is the church the fulfilment of Old Testament prophecy, or is it a parenthesis in God's prophetic scheme? Certainly Christ himself fulfils God's promises; this is the core of all apostolic preaching (2 Cor. 1:20). Clearly, too, the church is addressed in language that described Israel: 'But you are a chosen people, a royal priesthood, a holy nation, a people belonging to God' (1 Pet. 2:9). But how are we to understand the dramatic changes from the Old Testament to the New?

The coming of the Lord and the kingdom

The Gospels and the whole New Testament give one clear answer: the change is brought about by the coming of Jesus Christ. The heart of the prophetic message was that God will come to bring his promised deliverance and renewal. The gospel message is that the Lord himself came. In the prophets, the coming of the Lord was intimately and mysteriously linked with the coming of God's Anointed, whose name is 'Wonderful

Counsellor, Mighty God, Everlasting Father, Prince of Peace' (Is. 9:6).

John the Baptist came preaching the message of Isaiah, 'A voice of one calling in the desert, "Prepare the way for the Lord"' (Is. 40:3; Mt. 3:3). When Jesus came for baptism, John refused; he knew him to be the Lord whose coming he had announced, whose sandals he was not worthy to loose. Yet Jesus required John to baptize him to 'fulfil all righteousness'. He who is the Lord is also the Servant, identified with his people. He is both the Lord's Anointed and the Anointed Lord, the glory of his people Israel (Lk. 2:11, 26). The Gospels present him as Lord of creation, who can still the raging sea (Ps. 107:29–30), whose path is on the waters (Ps. 77:19), and whose word controls the fish of the deep. He is Master of life and death, of men and of demons; by his word he can as readily forgive sins as heal the sick (Mk. 2:8–11).

John announced that the kingdom of God was at hand. That kingdom, heralded by the prophets and in the Psalms, would come with the coming of the Lord: 'The trees of the forest . . . will sing before the LORD, for he comes, he comes to judge the earth' (Ps. 96:12–13). In the Scriptures, God's kingdom is the shadow of his presence; not so much his domain as his dominion; not his realm but his rule. God's kingdom is the working of his power to accomplish his purposes of judgment and salvation.

Jesus teaches the meaning of God's saving rule. God gives his kingdom, not to the proud Pharisee or the wealthy ruler, but to the poor and the humble, who, with little children, trust their heavenly Father. The kingdom displays God's saving will: those who think themselves first are last, and the last are first.

The kingdom came with Jesus himself. By the finger of God he cast out demons (Lk. 11:20). All will answer to him, the King, who will disown those whom he never knew, and who never knew him (Mt. 7:23; 25:41). John the Baptist, in Herod's prison, heard of the healing miracles that Jesus did as signs of kingdom power. What puzzled John was that Jesus gave such signs of blessing without bringing in the justice of the kingdom. Could it be that he was not the coming One, after all? Troubled, he sent that very question . . . to Jesus! Jesus performed more signs that clearly fulfilled prophecy,[1] and he sent John the reply: 'Blessed

38

is the man who does not fall away on account of me' (Lk. 7:23). Jesus would bring in the kingdom, not with the sword, but with the cross; he came not to bring the judgment, but to bear it. The final judgment must await his second coming.

Jesus restricted his ministry to the 'lost sheep of the house of Israel' (Mt. 15:24) that through their witness his light might shine to the Gentiles (Is. 49:6). Through him they would become a new Jerusalem, a beacon city set on a hill. As predicted, however, the leaders of the nation rejected him, the cornerstone of that city / temple. Jesus solemnly declared: 'Therefore I tell you that the kingdom of God will be taken away from you and given to a people who will produce its fruit' (Mt. 21:42–43).

Christ reveals his church: his assembly

When the crowds turned away from him because he was not a political Messiah, Jesus took his disciples off by themselves. To elicit the distinctive understanding that the apostles must have of him (Mt. 16:13–16), Jesus asked them, 'Who do people say the Son of Man is?'

The disciples assured Jesus that people still held him in high esteem. They thought of him as a prophet: Elijah, perhaps, or Jeremiah, or even John the Baptist alive from the dead. Then Jesus put the question: 'But what about you? Who do you say I am?'

Peter, the spokesman for the twelve, gave his reply: 'You are the Christ, the Son of the living God.'

Peter declares Jesus to be the Messiah, the glorious Son of Man from Daniel's vision, who will receive an eternal kingdom with the Ancient of Days (Dn. 7:13–14). But much more than that, he is the very Son of God. Jesus' response recognizes how extraordinary Peter's confession was. It could come only by revelation from the Father, who alone can reveal the Son (Mt. 11:27).

Because Peter knew on divine authority who Jesus is, Jesus acknowledged him to be a rock of foundation for the new form of the people of God. As Peter had acknowledged Christ, so Christ acknowledged Peter. Protestant exegetes have often tried to separate the confession from Peter, and to make the confession itself the rock upon which the church rests. To be sure, the name *Petros* is masculine in Greek, while the common word for 'rock' (*petra*) is feminine. This normal difference in the gender of the nouns carries no weight, however, in the face of the emphatic connection that Jesus made between the name he had given Peter and the position he assigned him.[2] Peter is Christ's 'Rock': his witness and apostle. In other contexts, of course, Christ himself is spoken of as the Rock of foundation for the church, or as the chief Cornerstone of its structure (1 Cor. 3:11; Eph. 2:20; 1 Pet. 2:4–6). Even these figures, however, do not give Christ the prominence that he has in his word to Peter. Peter is the rock, but Christ is the Builder who sets his apostle in a foundational position.

The confession cannot be separated from Peter, neither can Peter be separated from his confession. In the same chapter of Matthew's Gospel, Peter tells Jesus not to go to the cross (Mt. 16:21–22). Jesus responds with a rebuke that is as strong as was his earlier commendation. These words of Peter do not come from the Father in heaven, but from the devil. 'Get behind me, Satan!' commands Jesus. Seeking to divert Jesus from the cross, Peter becomes a *skandalon*, a stone of stumbling (16:23). In his inspired confession Peter is a stone of foundation; in his rejection of the cross, he is a stone of stumbling.[3]

Peter and his confession stand together. But if Peter cannot be separated from his confession, neither can he be separated from the eleven. In Matthew 16:18, Peter is given the authority of the keys of the kingdom. In Matthew 18:18, the disciples receive that same authority. Jesus had addressed his question in 16:15 to the disciples, and Peter's answer was given on their behalf as well as his own.

Peter is not the rock in contrast to the eleven, but in contrast to those who claim to carry the key of knowledge (Lk. 11:52), to sit in Moses' seat (Mt. 23:1–2), and to be Abraham's seed (Jn. 8:33). The authority of the latter is removed. God has hidden the mystery of the kingdom from the wise and prudent and revealed it to babies (Mt. 11:25–26). Peter, a despised Galilean fisherman, stands before the Messiah with the chosen elders of the New Covenant. The great Shepherd gathers the remnant of his people and establishes Israel anew to confess his name. Jesus undertakes God's own work to rebuild his people. God's assembly is his; he founds anew the city of God, restoring its ruins and building it again (Am. 9:11; Acts 15:17).

Paul, too, teaches that the church is built upon the foundation of the apostles and prophets (Eph. 2:20), to whom the mystery of Christ has been revealed in the gospel (Eph. 3:3–6).[4]

Christ will build his church in the power of his kingdom. He gives the keys of kingdom authority to his apostles. Jesus had already sent them out as heralds, with authority to teach, heal, and cast out demons in his name (Mt. 10:7–8). They were given kingdom authority to shake off the dust of their feet against any house or city that would not receive them (Mt. 10:14–15). That sign of judgment warned against a doom more fearful than that of Sodom and Gomorrah. The teaching authority of the keys enabled the apostles to declare on what terms the kingdom of heaven was opened or shut to men and women. The keys opened the kingdom to individuals, households or cities that received the gospel message, but closed it to those who rejected the Lord of the kingdom. Because they represented Christ (Mt. 10:40) and brought his message, what they bound or loosed on earth was already bound or loosed in heaven. Their authority did not shape the kingdom, or compose its laws. The keys of the kingdom were not blanks to be filed to their design. The authority was Christ's; they bore his words, pronounced his judgments.

Jesus declared the power of his kingdom when he said, 'The gates of Hades will not overcome it' (Mt. 16:18). In war, gates may be shut for defence or to imprison captives. They may be opened for escape or to send out an attacking army. The word translated 'overcome' can also mean 'to exceed in strength'. The figure, then, may mean that the gates of death cannot imprison the church of Christ. He will burst those gates in his resurrection triumph, and carry with him the trophies of his grace. Again, the meaning may be that the gates of Hades as the fortifications of the devil will not stand against the assault of Christ's church. More likely, however, the figure reflects Isaiah 28:15–18. There, the foundation stone of the temple is described as a sure refuge when the floods of death sweep forth from the gates of hell, carrying all before them.[5] In the final storm of rebellion and of judgment, when the waters roar

41

and the mountains are shaken into the seas, the city of God shall not be moved (Ps. 46). The house built on the rock will stand (Mt. 7:24–27).

Jesus came as Lord and as Servant to gather his remnant flock and to make them the heirs of the promised kingdom (Lk. 12:32). But his coming brings division: 'He who is not with me is against me' (Mt. 12:30). He calls as the Servant, announcing the great feast predicted in the prophets. He calls as Lord, summoning sinners. Those who reject him must hear the woe of judgment. But those who accept him are his sheep, his disciples, his 'little ones'. He will teach them the mysteries of the kingdom, open their eyes and ears to see him and hear his words (Mk. 4:11–12; Lk. 8:10). As soon as the disciples confess Jesus openly as the Messiah, his church is spoken of. Those who continue to reject Christ the Lord will forfeit their claim to be the people of God. The kingdom will be given to a nation bringing forth its fruit (Mt. 21:43). Strangers from the highways and hedges will fill the banquet seats next to Abraham, Isaac and Jacob in the kingdom, but those who have rejected the King will be cast out (Lk. 13:24–30). The kingdom has come in the person of the King; the kingdom will come again, for he is coming.

Jesus, then, summons God's assembly, gathering the scattered flock that there may be one flock and one Shepherd (Jn. 10:16). The Father has given him this flock (Jn. 10:27–29; 17:2, 6, 9), those upon whom God's favour rests, as the Christmas angels sang (Lk. 2:14). They are held in the Father's hand, and also in the grasp of the Son, where they are for ever safe (Jn. 10:29). Because Jesus is one with the Father, his people are God's chosen people, the true Israel of God.[6]

Christ's church: the Israel of God

Paul, writing to Gentile believers, eloquently summarizes the dramatic change effected by the work of Christ. Formerly the Gentiles were 'separate from Christ, excluded from citizenship in Israel and foreigners to the covenants of the promise, without hope and without God in the world' (Eph. 2:12). Separation from Christ meant exclusion from all the privileges of God's chosen people. Without Christ, heathen Gentiles were also

42

without citizenship in Israel. They had no stake in God's promises, nor were they joined to his covenant. They were without hope because they were without God.

But then comes the total change. Those who were afar off are brought near through the blood of Christ. He has made Jews and Gentiles one, reconciling them both in his one body through the cross. Both have the same access, in one Spirit, to the Father. No longer are Gentile Christians aliens from the commonwealth of Israel; they are now fellow-citizens with Jewish saints, included in God's covenant, heirs of his promises, members of the household of God (Eph. 2:19).

Gentiles become full members of God's people because they are joined to Christ, whose death is the only atoning sacrifice for Jew or Gentile. As Adam represented the old humanity, bringing death on all, so a new humanity is created in Christ (Rom. 5:12ff.). The sin of those represented by him is put to his account, and his righteousness is put to theirs. 'If you belong to Christ, then you are Abraham's seed, and heirs according to the promise' (Gal. 3:29).

In the apostolic church, the controversy over circumcision took place only because both sides thought of the church as the true Israel. Those who required Gentile Christians to be circumcised obviously thought that those converts were being added to God's people. Paul never challenged this. He never explained that Christians were joining a new entity, the church, and not Israel, and that circumcision was therefore inappropriate. On the contrary, he claimed for the church the true spiritual circumcision of Christ, gained by union with him. Apart from Christ, circumcision was only mutilation of the flesh. 'For it is we who are the circumcision, we who worship by the Spirit of God, who glory in Christ Jesus, and who put no confidence in the flesh' (Phil. 3:3).

Paul never forgot his kinsfolk, Israel after the flesh, but his hope and prayer for them was that they be grafted back into their own olive tree, the tree in which Gentile branches now bear fruit (Rom. 11:24).

Who, then, is the heir of God's promises? Christ is the Son of the woman (Gn. 3:15), the Seed of Abraham (Gn. 12:1–3), the Son of David (2 Sa. 7:12–16). He alone is the rightful heir, for he alone is without covenant-breaking sin. Those who are united to

Christ are heirs in him of all the promises of God. Christ fulfils the calling of Israel; those united to him are by that fact the new Israel of God (Gal. 3:29; 4:21; Rom. 15:8). The ethnicity of the new people is now spiritual rather than physical, making the bonds stronger and the brotherhood more intense (1 Pet. 1:22). Christians are not just born-again individuals, they are a family, 'spiritual ethnics', the new people of God in Christ. To forget this is to undercut the practice of brotherhood in all the dimensions of daily life.

Christ's church: God's dwelling with his people

In the incarnate Lord, God came to dwell among his people. The Gospel of John identifies Christ as the true tabernacle, where the glory of God is revealed (Jn. 1:14). The temple, to be sure, had its place in the history of redemption: it depicted God's dwelling on earth. Jesus called the temple his 'Father's house' and cleansed it (Jn. 2:16). But with Christ came reality, and the temple became a passing figure: 'Destroy this temple, and I will raise it again in three days' (Jn. 2:19). Jesus' enemies mocked his claim as absurd: the temple had taken forty-six years to build. But as the disciples were later to realize, Jesus spoke of the true temple, his body, and of his resurrection on the third day.

That Jesus fulfilled the symbolism of the temple is made clear in his conversation with the woman by Jacob's well in Sychar. Ignoring the barrier of hatred between Jews and Samaritans, Jesus asked her for a drink of water. He then offered her the water of the Spirit, the fountain of eternal life. When he showed knowledge of her private life, she realized that here was a Jew who was a prophet! What of the controversy between Jews and Samaritans? Was Jerusalem the place to worship God, or was Mount Gerizim, the mountain that rose just beyond them? Jesus told her plainly that the Samaritans did not know what they worshipped, while in contrast, 'we worship what we do know, for salvation is from the Jews' (Jn. 4:22). The Samaritan temple, in ruins on top of Mount Gerizim, was not God's house. But what about Jerusalem? Surely the whole Old Testament centred worship at God's temple there (Dt. 12:5, 11–14; Ps. 87:2). What did Jesus say? 'Believe me, woman, a time is coming when you will worship the Father neither on this mountain nor in Jerusalem' (Jn. 4:21). Indeed, that coming time had come, for the Father, who is Spirit, seeks true worshippers who will worship him in spirit and in truth (Jn. 4:23–24).

Is Jesus teaching that worship cannot be localized? Since God is omnipresent Spirit, he can be worshipped anywhere. But Jesus does not say that God can be worshipped *either* on Gerizim *or* in Jerusalem. He says the opposite: *neither* this mountain *nor* Jerusalem. Further, Jesus announces a great change in the coming time (literally, the 'hour'). What is the hour that is coming, and has indeed already come? It cannot be the hour of God's becoming Spirit! Jesus is not reminding the woman of a timeless truth, but announcing to her the truth of his time. In the Gospel of John, the coming hour is the hour of Christ's death and resurrection.[7] That hour changes everything. And because Jesus was already present, speaking with the woman, that hour had already come: 'I who speak to you am he' (Jn. 4:26).

The temple and all that it represented found absolute fulfilment at the hour of Christ's sufferings and death: 'Destroy this temple, and I will raise it again in three days.' Altar sacrifices had only one meaning: the Lamb of God would take away the sin of the world. God's true dwelling is not a tent of goatskins, or a temple of cedar and gold, but the flesh of Immanuel. Christ is the Sacrifice and the Priest, he is the Light of the sanctuary, and of the world. He is the Bread of life; he offers as incense his prayers and ours before the Father's throne. When he cried, 'It is finished!', the veil of the temple was torn from top to bottom, for he opened the way into the holy place through his blood (Heb.10:19–20). The function of the temple ended with his death. Jesus rose and ascended; our great High Priest entered the Holy of Holies, heaven itself, for us. Hebrews warns us there can be no going back. One final sacrifice for sin has paid the debt for ever; once at the end of the ages, Jesus put away sin by the sacrifice of himself. Jesus, the same yesterday, today and for ever, is the final Prophet, Priest and King.

What Jesus declared to the woman was not temple-less worship; it was worship at the true Temple, pitched by God not man. There, God her Father seeks her worship: not on the top of Gerizim, or at the end of the dusty trail to Jerusalem, but at the feet of Jesus. Worship is in spirit, that is, in the Spirit Jesus himself gives, the water that is not from the well. Worship is also in truth: not truth in the abstract, but truth in Jesus, the true revelation of the Father. 'I am the way and the truth and the life. No-one comes to the Father except through me' (Jn. 14:6).

God's presence makes us his people; the presence of Jesus constitutes the church as his temple, built of living stones, joined to him as God's elect Stone (1 Pet. 2:4–6). The church itself is a temple, the house of God, sanctified by the presence of the Spirit (1 Cor. 3:16).

Christ's church: the disciples of Christ

In Christ, then, God has come to claim his people and to be with them. His coming in true humanity has also opened up a new fellowship with the Lord. Moses had cried out for a closer relation with God; he would know the angel of the Lord and see the glory of the Lord (Ex. 33:12–18). When Philip asked a similar question, 'Show us the Father!', Jesus answered, 'He that has seen me has seen the Father.' John testifies that we have seen the glory of God in the incarnate Christ (Jn. 1:14, 18).

The answer to Moses' prayer came not only when glory streamed from the face of Jesus on the mountain top, but also in Peter's fishing boat, on a doorstep in Capernaum and in an upper room in Jerusalem. By word and deed Jesus revealed himself to great crowds, but particularly to his chosen disciples. The people of God became disciples of Jesus.

Disciples are learners: those to whom the Master taught the mysteries of his kingdom, which he had received from the Father. They watched his deeds closely, and witnessed his signs of the kingdom. They knew him not only from intimate association, but by revelation from the Father.

Disciples are also servants of the Master, and of others in his name. He broke the bread, gave it to them, and they carried it to the seated crowds. Though confused when he took a towel to wash their feet, they learned by his example.

Jesus, who called his disciples to be with him, also sent them as his witnesses.[8] John's Gospel speaks of witness in the legal language of the Old Testament. The God of Israel presses his law-case against the nations and their idols. Let them present their case, and bring their witnesses (Is. 41:21–22; 43:9). ' "You are my witnesses,"declares the LORD, "and my servant whom I have chosen" ' (Is. 43:10). Jesus, the faithful Witness (Rev. 3:14), vindicates God's cause, bearing witness to the truth of his Father's words and works. His disciples are called to bear witness to his witness. They attest his miracles, his death, his resurrection, and his teaching that explained how he fulfilled God's promises. They receive the Spirit, who is both attorney and witness; he will convict the world of sin, righteousness and judgment, and he will guide them into all truth (Jn. 16:8, 13). The original apostolic witness, given by the Spirit, is found in the New Testament. The Spirit continues to empower the witness of the church as it proclaims Christ according to the Scriptures (Acts 5:32).

The New Testament church establishes the Old Testament promises, even as they are carried to the heavenly glory found in Christ. That glory comes with the Holy Spirit, who is sent from Christ's throne. We must now consider the church as the fellowship of the Spirit. In doing so, we will see why Paul describes the church as the body of Christ, endued with the spiritual gifts that enrich its members (chapter 5).

4

THE FELLOWSHIP
OF THE SPIRIT

If you have visited Israel, you will have had memories as well as photographs or slides to sort through. Some may have been disappointing: gloomy memorial churches at sacred sites, vendors hawking relics made in Taiwan. Perhaps your brightest memory recalls a morning service at the Garden Tomb; however improbable as the site of the actual tomb, it has the advantage of unspoiled reality. Reality is the thrill of the whole experience: to stand where Jesus stood on the Mount of Olives, looking over Jerusalem, or to sail across the Sea of Galilee. Did being there strengthen your faith? Or did the ordinariness of reality challenge it? The real water of the lake did not look walkable!

We sometimes suppose that if we could have been there with Jesus, it would have been easy to believe in him. What an advantage the apostles had! But soon two millenniums will have passed since the morning he broiled fish for his disciples beside the lake, and the centuries rise like mist.

We can understand the fear of the disciples when Jesus told them that he must leave. Jesus reassured them, reminding them of the faith they had in God, and also in him (Jn. 14:1). He promised to come again, and told them that he would not leave them orphans, for he would come to them in the Spirit (14:16–18). Indeed, it was better for them that he went away, so that the Spirit would come (Jn. 16:7).

At Pentecost, Jesus kept his promise, which is also the promise of the Father (Acts 1:4–5). The church does not live with a fading memory of the presence of the Lord, but with the reality of his coming in the Spirit. The people of God, claimed by Christ in the blood of the New Covenant, are made the fellowship of the Spirit as they await their returning Lord.

In his Spirit, God comes to make us his and to become ours. On the one hand, God possesses his people, both individually and as a body. On the other hand, God's people possess the Lord. The Spirit seals this mutual possession. The Spirit is *God's* seal, claiming as his heritage those chosen in Christ before the foundation of the world (Eph. 1:11). The Spirit is *our* seal, too. God gives his people a claim on him as their inheritance, for the Spirit is a down-payment and a foretaste of the glory to come (Eph. 1:13b–14).

The Bible speaks of the Spirit as both Giver and Gift. As Lord, he gives gifts that empower the body of Christ, and so claims us as his possession. Yet even those rich gifts do not exhaust the fellowship of the Spirit. He also gives himself to us; we receive the Giver as Gift. For that reason, Paul can speak of our being filled with the Spirit, about our 'having' the Spirit of Christ (Rom. 8:9). If we think of the Spirit only as our possession, we risk depersonalizing him. We lose sight of his lordship if we think of the Spirit merely as spiritual voltage into which we can plug. On the other hand, if we forget that we possess him, we lose sight of the mystery of his power in our lives and service.

Pentecost put the capstone on God's covenant with his people in two ways. First, God claimed his people by coming to dwell in his temple of living stones. Secondly, the disciples were endued with the Spirit as the gift sent by the Father and the Son. God restored and renewed his people in a New Covenant (Ezk. 36:25ff., 37). Moses had longed for God to put his Spirit on all his people (Nu. 11:29); at Pentecost Peter preached the fulfilment of that desire and of the prophetic promise (Joel 2:28–29; Acts 2:16).

The bombs of Hiroshima haunt us with the spectre of desecrating power. But the power released at the resurrection

50

was a life-giving power, that mushroomed out all over the world. Peter declared: 'God has made this Jesus, whom you crucified, both Lord and Christ' (Acts 2:36). The risen, triumphant and glorified Jesus gave the Spirit in full measure from the throne of heaven. As Servant, Jesus was anointed of the Spirit (Is. 11:2; 42:1; 61:1; Mk. 1:10–11); as Lord, he gave the Spirit (Jn. 4:10, 14; 7:37–39). He sealed the authority of his resurrection when he breathed his Spirit upon them (Jn. 20:22), but they must wait for the promise of the Father (Lk. 24:49; Acts 1:4–5, 8), which was also his own promise to baptize them with the Spirit (Mt. 3:11; Acts 1:5; 11:16).

The coming of the Spirit of the Father and the Son

For the Spirit to come, Christ had to be glorified (Jn. 7:39; *cf.* 16:7), but the Spirit did not supplant the Son. The Spirit does not carry us beyond Christ, but to Christ (Eph. 4:4, 13; Jn. 16:14–15). In the mystery of the Trinity, the Lord who sends the Spirit as 'another Advocate' also comes in the Spirit (Jn. 14:16, 18). The Spirit of Christ the Son is the Spirit of sonship who reveals the Father, enabling us to cry 'Abba', the very word that was on the lips of Jesus (Rom. 8:14–15; Gal. 4:5–7).

In the Spirit the Father and the Son take possession of the church. Nothing from God's past revelation is lost. Through the Spirit the church is united to Christ in the fellowship of his sufferings, and of his glory. The presence of the Spirit is therefore both promise and realization (2 Cor. 1:22; Eph. 1:14), for in the Spirit of glory we now begin to taste the goodness of the Lord, the delight of eternity.

The Spirit comes to realize God's promises. He makes the church the people of God as the prophets predicted, giving them new hearts in the New Covenant (Ezk. 36:25–28). He joins them to Jesus Christ, for no-one can say 'Jesus is Lord!' apart from the Spirit (1 Cor. 12:3). The church is therefore the people of God and the assembly of Christ because it is the fellowship of the Spirit. The Spirit fulfils; he does not obliterate membership in God's people or discipleship in following Christ.

The Pentecost event dramatized the gift of the Spirit and the enduement of the disciples. The flame divided to rest on each

51

one, and the gift of tongues enabled them to share in inspired praise. Yet the rushing wind and the flame were also signs of the divine presence. The disciples were not only given power; they were filled with the Holy Spirit. Baptism by the Spirit in fire rather than water showed that their cleansing and renewal came from God's holy throne.

At Pentecost the Lord came to take possession of his people, filling his spiritual house with his presence. The phenomena of Pentecost recalled the wind and fire of Sinai, as well as the cloud of glory that filled the tabernacle. As the prophets had promised, the praises of the Lord sounded from Jerusalem, calling the nations to worship (Is. 2:2–4; 25:6–8; 66:19–21; Ps. 96:7–9; Zc. 14:16). The disciples marvelled at the presence of the Lord; as they praised him, God gave them speech in the languages of the nations. Peter, taught by Jesus and filled with the Spirit, could proclaim the fulfilment, not simply of one prophecy, but of God's whole plan (Acts 3:18–21).

The Spirit came upon the Christian community, assembled in Jerusalem. The event was public, for it signalled a new epoch in the history of redemption. The Spirit's baptism at Pentecost was not the Lord's response to concurrent acts of personal commitment on the part of 120 disciples. Neither was the Spirit given merely to empower them for witness on this one occasion. Rather, as the Spirit came upon Christ at his baptism, so Christ baptized the church with his Spirit at Pentecost.[1] The two baptisms are not identical: only Jesus, the God-man, possesses the Spirit beyond measure. Neither is the church a continuation of the incarnation. The Spirit is the gift of the risen Christ; the church, therefore, cannot be called Christ's resurrection body. Christ did not die to be raised in the church. But while the Spirit does not incarnate the Son in the church, the Spirit does bring him to the church in a union that only the Spirit can accomplish.

The abiding presence of the Spirit determines the characteristics of the church. Because the church is the temple of the Holy Spirit, it is holy (1 Cor. 6:19–20; 2 Cor. 6:16–7:1). The ceremonial purity of Old Testament symbolism finds its ethical realization in the church. Yet the holiness of the church is imperfect, and the temple of the Spirit is incomplete. The Spirit who resides in the church must be at work there, building his own temple of living stones (1 Pet. 2:5; Eph. 2:21).

Further, the abiding presence of the Spirit joins the church together into one. There is but one holy temple of the Lord, one body of Christ where the Spirit dwells. The Spirit binds the church together in the unity of a common life. In Paul's letters, this unity is applied especially to the joining together of Jews and Gentiles (Eph. 2:11–22). In the power of the Spirit, the church went from Jerusalem to Judea, Samaria and the ends of the earth. Gentiles presented their bodies as living sacrifices, performing the spiritual service of the New Covenant (Rom. 12:1–2; 15:16). The temple of God was no longer local, on a Judean hillside, but universal, wherever the saints gathered to join in heaven's praise.

At the same time, the presence of the Spirit of Christ, though a foretaste of glory, also joins the church to Christ in his suffering, and shows us the glory of the cross. The Spirit who groans in yearning for the glory to come joins us to Christ in our present suffering. The Spirit girds the church militant for struggle even as he carries us forward to the sure hope of Christ's return.

The reality of the coming of the Spirit at Pentecost moves us to ask two questions. First, did the church begin at Pentecost? Second, does the Spirit who dwells in the church also work outside the church?

Did the church begin at Pentecost?

This first question finds an answer in the history of redemption. Pentecost did not create the people of God, but renewed them. Jews praised God in Gentile languages: the sign of the inclusion of the nations that accompanied the promised renewal of Israel in Christ (Is. 49:6). God's rebellious people had been disinherited, declared to be no people (Ho. 1:9). Yet God, in his mercy, had still promised healing and restoration (Ho. 14:4–5). The prophets promised that from a spared remnant the Lord would raise up a believing Israel, who would walk in the steps of Abraham, circumcised not in their flesh, but in their hearts (Ezk. 36:26). In Christ, the true Israel, God's chosen and faithful Servant (Is. 49:3; Rom. 15:8), God's people are transformed (Is. 49:6), and there is hope for the Gentiles (Eph. 2:12, 20). As we saw in the last chapter, those who are united to Christ are united to Israel. They are Abraham's seed (Gal. 3:29), members of the commonwealth of Israel, fellow-citizens with the saints, God's covenant people (Eph. 2:11–19). If the natural branches of God's olive tree have been pruned for unbelief, wild branches (Gentiles) may be grafted in by faith in Christ (Rom. 11:17–24).

But if one enters the people of God only by being united to Christ, what of the Old Testament saints? The New Testament gives a clear answer. Old Testament believers looked forward to Christ. They trusted the promises of God, spoken by prophets who themselves sought to understand more about the 'who' and the 'when' of God's coming salvation (1 Pet. 1:11).[2] The Spirit who inspires the prophets is the Spirit of Christ. The Old Testament tells the story of those who believed God's promises. Hebrews reminds us that Moses accounted 'disgrace for the sake of Christ as of greater value than the treasures of Egypt' (Heb. 11:26). Such a statement is not an anachronism. Moses received God's promise that another Prophet would be raised up, a Prophet like him but greater (Dt. 18:18).

The relation of Old Testament saints to the Lord required the presence of the Holy Spirit before Pentecost. There were, to be sure, episodes of the Spirit's presence as God empowered or overcame individuals: the Spirit came upon the elders under Moses, upon Samson, even upon King Saul. The prophets, too, were possessed of the Spirit to utter oracles of God. But the work of the Spirit is not limited to such visitations. God's Spirit instructed Israel in the desert (Ne. 9:20) and was grieved by Israel's behaviour, for it was he who had led them and cared for them in the wilderness (Is. 63:10–11; Acts 7:51). God's covenant at Sinai promised his abiding presence with his people, a promise he kept through the abiding of the Spirit (Hg. 2:5).

Can we account for both continuity and discontinuity between the Old and New Testament people of God? Not if we ignore either, or suppress evidence on either side. Abraham, Isaac and Jacob will sit down with Peter, James and John in the feast of the kingdom (Lk. 13:28–30). The new Jerusalem of John's vision has the names of the apostles on its foundations, and the names of the twelve tribes of Israel on its gates (Rev. 21:12–14). Yet the change brought about at Pentecost was so startling that the New Testament writers could look at the whole Old Testament as preparation. Although the saints of the Old

Covenant waited in faith for the promise, they did not receive it. 'God had planned something better for us so that only together with us would they be made perfect' (Heb. 11:40).[3]

That verse gives balance to our thinking. The key is God's one plan, a plan that unfolds so that his later and better covenant does not invalidate the earlier, or exclude its participants. Rather, the greater blessings given to us are the very blessings they sought, and that they will receive together with us. The two great administrations of God's one plan are distinguished in time and form, but not in God's purpose, or in the nature of his salvation, then, now, and for ever. We best understand the relation between them as we trace the Word of the Spirit, who shows us the treasures of Christ in the new and the old (Mt. 13:52). The shadows of the Old Covenant are not deceptive wraiths; they are 'fore-shadows' that enable us to understand better that which comes in Christ.

Is the Spirit confined to the church?

The second question concerns the limits of the Spirit's work. If the Spirit dwells in the church, is he confined to the church?

Hans Küng has reminded Roman Catholic theologians that the church does not already exist as an organized, hierarchical institution that the Spirit enters and empowers.[4] Rather, the church is created by the Spirit, the author of life, who grants the gift of faith.[5] Yet, as Küng also says, the Spirit is free to bind himself to the word and sacrament.[6] Does the Spirit, then, bind himself to the church, where the means of grace are offered and dispensed? Küng answers that the Spirit's binding of himself to the word and sacrament puts an obligation on us, not on him. He demands of us our unconditional faith. 'Neither word or sacrament work automatically; where there is no faith, they are not operative.'[7] At this point, Küng has called into question the ex opere operato view of the sacraments, so central for the sacramental theology of the Roman Catholic Church.[8] Certainly to tie saving grace to the sacramental administration of an organized and authorized priesthood is to create a dispensary in which grace becomes a commodity, rather than the sovereign working of the Lord.

On the other hand, as Regin Prenter has pointed out, there is an opposite tendency that can end in the same error. Protestant 'spiritualism' avoids institutional management of grace, but it may repeat the error of putting the Spirit under human control: the control in this case being that of the individual rather than the church. Both liberal rationalism and fundamentalist emotionalism subject the Spirit to the individual. The rationalist bolts a grille on his window to bar supernatural intrusions of the Spirit. In his private world he demands his freedom of choice. The emotionalist uses the chemistry of his feelings to summon, measure and monitor the Spirit.

Hans Küng carries the freedom of the Spirit much further. He declares that the Spirit cannot be restricted to the clergy, to Rome, to the Catholic Church, or even to Christianity. He asks, 'Might *Christians* not be more cautious, more open and just in their judgments and attitudes towards the great non-Christian religions of the world if they were completely convinced of the fact that the Holy Spirit, who is revealed in and through the Church, is the free Spirit of the Lord of the whole world, who is at work where he wills?'[9]

As we saw in chapter 1, this apparently modest suggestion has been carried further by Vatican II and now has the support of radical theologians prepared to deny the uniqueness of Christianity. Is the Spirit to be free, not only of the church, but of Christ?

To be sure, the Holy Spirit of God cannot be boxed in by the constraints of human institutions. He is the Creator Spirit, sovereign and omnipotent, who governs all things. The Spirit is not confined to the church as his only field of operation. The Spirit restrains human iniquity; God does not always or at once give up sinners to the evil of their own hearts (Rom. 1:24; Mt. 5:45; *cf.* Jn. 16:8–11). The Spirit reveals in nature the invisible qualities of God, so that none can plead ignorance (Rom. 1:19–20). But God also carries out his purposes of grace through the Spirit. The Spirit's faithfulness to his own saving work is not a limitation of his freedom but the exercise of it. The zeal, the jealousy of God, that burned against Israel's idols still flames against any substitute for his beloved Son in the worship of his creatures. The Holy Spirit binds the Trinity in the infinite, mutual love of the Father and the Son. He ministers the salvation of Christ, and leads the apostles to declare that there is no other saving name but the name of Jesus (Acts 4:12).

Since salvation is only in Christ, there is a sense in which there is no salvation outside the church of Christ, for those whom the Spirit unites to Christ, he unites to all others who are in Christ. When he makes God our Father, he makes us brothers and sisters in the family of God. All who know God's salvation know it as members of the body of Christ. Since the Spirit dwells in the church and fills the church with gifts for witness, nurture and worship, the church may well be called the mother of the faithful. John Calvin says of the visible church:

> We may learn even from the title of *mother*, how useful and even necessary it is for us to know her; since there is no other way of entrance into life, unless we are conceived by her, born of her, nourished at her breast, and continually preserved under her care and government till we are divested of this mortal flesh, and 'become like the angels'.[10]

Calvin explains that 'It is God who inspires us with faith, but it is through the instrumentality of the gospel, according to the declaration of Paul, that "faith cometh by hearing".'[11]

The call of Jesus joins us in his community, the community of his Spirit, where we serve one another in the path of discipleship.[12] The church is God's household (1 Tim. 3:15). From the church the gospel goes forth, and those who are added to the Lord are added to the company of his people (Acts 2:41, 47; 5:14; 11:24). They are not added to the Lord because they are added to the church.[13] The body of the individual believer and the body of the church are alike the temple of the Holy Spirit (1 Cor. 6:19; 3:16).

Paul emphasizes both individual union with Christ and community in the body of Christ. 'So it is with Christ. For we were all baptized by one Spirit into one body – whether Jews or Greeks, slave or free – and we were all given the one Spirit to drink' (1 Cor. 12:12–13). Paul says, 'So it is with Christ', because the body to which we are joined by the baptism of the Spirit is first the body of Christ on the cross, and thereby his body the church. The Spirit joins us to Christ, and therefore to those who are Christ's.

The Spirit cannot be confined to the church any more than

the kingdom of God can be identified with the church. The power of the Spirit creates the church, but the Spirit's work is defined by his own purposes of salvation, revealed in Scripture and accomplished in Jesus Christ. Those whom he joins to Christ he joins to the body of Christ, a communion gathered by the Word and marked by the sacraments.

The church, according to Scripture, is not a religious club, a voluntary association of like-minded Christians who cultivate friendship and engage in joint projects. It is rather the institution of Christ and of the Spirit, formed by his power and governed by his Word.

The presence of the Spirit

Two attributes define the Spirit's purposes as he founds the church: he is the Spirit of truth, and he is the Spirit of life.

First, as the Spirit of truth, he confirms the witness of the Old Testament to Christ. Peter declares that the fountain of Old Testament prophecy was the Spirit of Christ (1 Pet. 1:10–12). The Spirit reveals the truth as it is in Christ to his apostles (1 Cor. 2:10–16; Eph. 2:20; 3:3–5; Heb. 1:1; 2:3–4), reminding them of Jesus' words and deeds (Jn. 14:17, 25–26; 15:26; 16:12–14).

The Spirit who inspired the Scriptures illumines the minds of believers to understand them. Since the Bible comes from the Spirit, humankind cannot control its interpretation (2 Pet. 1:20–21). Apart from the Spirit, the truth of God seems foolish, but one who has the Spirit will judge all things in the light of the whole counsel of God (1 Cor. 2:14–15; 1 Jn. 2:27).

During the Reformation in England, advocates of the authority of the Roman Catholic Church argued for the necessity of an infallible Pope by appealing to the need for a judge in a lawcourt. To settle a controversy, they said, codified laws were insufficient. A judge must interpret the law and render a verdict. In religious controversy, the Bible (and tradition) provides the law, but a judge must give the sentence.[14] The Protestant Reformers answered that argument in the language of the Westminster Confession:

> The supreme Judge, by which all controversies of religion are to be determined, and all decrees of

councils, opinions of ancient writers, doctrines of men, and private spirits, are to be examined, and in whose sentence we are to rest, can be no other but the Holy Spirit speaking in the scripture.[15]

The Westminster divines did not turn from a Pope to a council for authoritative interpretation of Scripture. Though they held church government to be representative rather than monarchical, they had a deeper concern. Popes, councils and all other human authority must be put in the same place: under Scripture.

The Spirit uses the Word as his sword to convict and sanctify believers (Eph. 6:17; Heb. 4:12). In the Word the Spirit speaks, giving his verdict as Judge on the issues of life. For that reason, the Word is 'most necessary', as the Westminster Confession says. Paul assures Timothy that the God-breathed Word equips him as a 'man of God' to teach, rebuke, correct and train in right-eousness (2 Tim. 3:15–17). The Spirit who gave the Scriptures gives understanding in them and fills us with saving wisdom to perceive the will of God in our lives (Eph. 5:15–18; Col. 1:9).

As the book of Acts shows, the Spirit of truth also directs the witness of the church to the world (Acts 5:32). So closely is the growth of the church connected with the witness of the Word, that Luke can say the *Word* increased (Acts 6:7; 12:24; 19:20).

Secondly, the Spirit who possesses the church is also the Creator Spirit, the Author of life. The biblical terms for 'spirit' are the words for 'breath' (Heb. *rûaḥ*; Gk. *pneuma*). The Spirit of God is the life-breath, as it were, of the Creator. Nature springs to life as the Spirit/breath of God sweeps over it (Ps. 104:29–30). God is the living God, in contrast to dead idols or doomed demons (1 Cor. 8:4; 10:20). Adam, created as a person in God's image, is distinct from the animal creation.

The life that the Spirit gives is not raw energy, not even divine energy. We share God's life, born of the Spirit to be children of God as we partake in the resurrection life of Jesus. Images of the Spirit (breath, cloud, fire, wind, water) will be completely misunderstood if we forget that they express God's revelation of himself. The living God is not an abstract life principle, nor is he a cosmic soul embodied in matter. He is not less personal than we are, but infinitely more so. Jesus, alive after death, breathed on his disciples and said, 'Receive the Holy Spirit' (Jn. 20:22). The life that Jesus gave them was his, not an impersonal energy. He did not merge with them, but sent them in his name (20:21). The more abundant life that he promised is a life of personal fellowship, life that tastes the glory of his presence (Rom. 8; 1 Cor. 2:10–15; Gal. 5:22–25; 1 Pet. 4:14).

The presence of the Spirit is now, as at Pentecost, a community blessing. Christ has removed the outward constraints of the Old Covenant; his Spirit provides a unity that could never be achieved through external structures. The new wine of the Spirit bursts the old wineskins. The prophets promised that God would circumcise the hearts of his people, and dwell among them. The Spirit keeps that promise. Painful divisions that have shattered the unity of Christ's church cannot shred the consciousness that Christians have of their shared life in Christ. The first disciples shared their capital goods as well as their prayers in the fellowship of the Spirit (Acts 2:42). Sharing the life of the Spirit drew them to share their living (Rom. 15:26; 2 Cor. 8:4; Heb. 13:16). To speak of the sharing of the Spirit is to recognize that the Spirit who possesses us also is possessed by us.

We turn now to consider our sharing the gifts of the Spirit in the body of Christ.

5

THE GIFT
OF THE SPIRIT

American state schools struggle to define the outcomes they
seek in education. Kentucky's Department of Education defined
one such outcome: 'Students demonstrate positive strategies for
achieving mental and emotional wellness.'[1] They are to 'establish goals for improving and maintaining self-esteem; plan,
implement, and record accomplishments'. We may grant that
students who don't have a problem with self-esteem probably
should have, but we may wonder about their recording those
self-esteem accomplishments in a diary.

The American cultivation of self-esteem has its foolishness,
but the problem of low self-esteem is real enough, and not only
among abused children in inner-city schools.

The Spirit of God has a programme for providing the only
mental and emotional wellness that can endure the day of
judgment. He gives the peace *with* God that comes with the
collapse of a sinner's self-esteem at the foot of the cross, and he
gives the peace *of* God, in which the Spirit assures us that we are
children of God in Christ.

To cherish that work of the Spirit, we need to think of the Gift
before the gifts. Like the Levites of old, we have the Lord

himself as our inheritance (Nu. 18:20; Dt. 10:9). The psalmist embraced that promise: God himself is his portion, his joy (Ps. 16:5–11). To possess, in the Spirit, the Lord himself is the seal and down-payment of glory (2 Cor. 1:22; 5:5; *cf.* Col. 1:27).

The sealing of God's Spirit, however, does not remove us to glory. Here in this disordered world we remain as God's family and as his servants. God's Spirit of sonship assures us that we are family; the gifts of God's Spirit equip us as servants. We cannot despise what we are in Christ, but we can boast in him only, and we can rejoice in serving him.

There might seem to be a paradox here. On the one hand, the Spirit is the wind and fire of God's triumphant power, the breath of resurrection life; yet, on the other hand, the Spirit of glory does not transport us straight away to glory. Instead, the gifts of the Spirit equip us to serve the Lord, and to do so in circumstances that may be humiliating.

How can the power of heaven's glory equip slaves to wash feet or scrub floors?

In his first letter, Peter answers that question. First, he claims for the church all the glory of God's calling: 'a chosen people, a royal priesthood, a holy nation, a people belonging to God' (1 Pet. 2:9). You are blessed, he says, 'for the Spirit of glory and of God rests on you' (4:14). But how do we taste that glorious blessing? By suffering in fellowship with Christ, bearing insults for his name (4:13–14). Christ's Spirit leads the church down the path the Saviour took, the path to Golgotha. 'To this you were called, because Christ suffered for you, leaving you an example, that you should follow in his steps' (2:21).

In the gospel of the cross, grace and glory are joined together. Paul learned that Christ's power was perfected in weakness. Peter calls on the church to gird on humility like an apron, just as Christ set aside his robe, tied a towel around his waist and washed the disciples' feet (1 Pet. 5:5). Jesus took the towel, knowing who he was, from where he had come, and where he was going (Jn. 13:3). Secure in that knowledge, he was untouched by the defensiveness of insecure pride. So, too, the knowledge of glory equips us to serve: first as sons in the Son, then as servants in the Servant. With the cry 'Abba, Father' on our lips, we can take the towel as Jesus did.

God's grace first saves us and then equips us for service. We enter the kingdom only as children, completely dependent on our heavenly Father. We serve as we use the gifts of the Spirit. Our ministry is therefore humble service, not selfish manipulation. All Christians are to gird themselves with humility to serve one another (1 Pet. 5:5). Peter is not denying a difference in roles between those who exercise governing oversight and the members of the church who must recognize their authority. Yet those who join in governing are not to be little Caesars, lording it over the church; they are shepherds, called to serve the flock.

The Spirit of sonship

The Holy Spirit, as the Spirit of sonship, joins us to Christ. Because we are united to him, we are all sons of God, for in Christ there is no male or female (Gal. 3:28).

Our union with Christ is, first of all, representative. Paul's image of the church as the body of Christ begins with Christ's physical body hanging on the cross. This is clear from the way he speaks of how Jews and Gentiles have been made one body in Christ. The enmity was abolished in Christ's flesh, for the far-off Gentiles were joined to the nearby Jews by the blood of Christ's sacrifice (Eph. 2:13–18). They were made 'one new man' in Christ. Paul says that they were both reconciled 'to God in one body through the cross' (Eph. 2:16, NKJV).

What is the 'one body' in that phrase? Does it describe the church, the 'new man' in Christ? Or does it describe the body of Christ that bled on the cross? The context supports both interpretations, and that is the point: when Paul thinks of the church as Christ's body, he thinks first of the body of Christ on the cross. It is because we were united to him, to his body, as he paid the price of sin, that we are now one body.

When the church at Corinth was beginning to divide over which leader to follow, Paul cried out, 'Is Christ divided? Was Paul crucified for you?' (1 Cor. 1:13). The union of the church with Christ is representative: as Adam represented all humankind in him, so Christ represents all who are united to him (Rom. 5:15–19). When Christ died, we died; when he rose, we rose. Therefore Paul urges those who have died with Christ to put to death sin in themselves, and those who have risen with Christ to seek the things that are above (Col. 3:1–5).

Secondly, our union with Christ is vital. We are joined to him as branches to the vine. When, after the resurrection, Jesus breathed his Spirit into his disciples (Jn. 20:22), he anticipated in the upper room what he would confirm at Pentecost. The Holy Spirit, the Spirit of Christ, joins us to him.

Paul's figure of the body of Christ starts with his body given on the cross and received in the sign and seal of the sacrament (1 Cor. 10:16–17). He extends it, however, to describe the 'one new man' in Christ. The relation of Christ the Head to the body compares to the union of man and wife as 'one body' in marriage (1 Cor. 11:3; Eph. 5:28–32). In 1 Corinthians 12, the 'head' is not identified with Christ in distinction from the trunk and limbs as members of the body, for the 'head' is seen as a 'member' (12:21), along with eyes, ears and nose. Paul never thought of Christ as a head in need of a body.[2] The church as the 'one new man' in Christ is not identical with Christ, but is, through the Spirit, in vital union with Christ.

Union with Christ, both representative and vital, is sealed by the presence and work of Christ's Spirit in his people. By the fruits of his grace (Gal. 5:22–23), the Spirit of Christ draws us to God the Father and binds us together as children of God. The love of God, poured out in our hearts by the Spirit, finds expression in burning love for one another (Rom. 5:5; 1 Jn. 3). So, too, peace is the fruit of the Spirit, and the peace of our reconciliation to God brings peace with one another. These graces that we share unite us with other believers; Christian joy and hope are contagious.

We may distinguish the varied graces, or fruit of the Spirit, tokens of our sonship, from the gifts of the Spirit that equip us for service. The graces of the Spirit, on the one hand, make us like Christ and like one another as we grow in faith, hope and love. The gifts of the Spirit, on the other hand, distinguish us from one another, qualifying us for distinct ministries in the service of Christ. Since the use of our individual gifts marks out our calling in Christ's service, we are eager to identify them. Yet our interest in gifts contrasts with the old Puritan emphasis on fruit. The Puritans focused on the *goal* served by the ministry of gifts: holiness, the fruit of the Spirit.

Holiness is the goal of the growth of the church as the body of Christ (Eph. 4:15). We are to grow together to the full maturity of Christ. We know that, when the Lord comes, we shall be made like him (1 Jn. 3:2). For that reason, perhaps, evangelical Christians have discounted the importance of the transformation that the Lord seeks now, before his coming. Paul laboured night and day to present the church as a pure virgin to Christ (2 Cor. 11:2). He did not limit his work to saving souls, in the relaxed confidence that the Lord would finish their sanctification when the trumpet sounds. Rather, his prayer and labour for the Thessalonians were that they might be 'blameless and holy in the presence of our God and Father when our Lord Jesus comes with all his holy ones' (1 Thes. 3:13).

No-one laboured more intensively than Paul to evangelize and plant churches, yet his descriptions of church growth focus, not on numerical growth, but on growth in holiness, looking toward the day of the Lord.[3]

The Spirit of stewardship

The church, then, grows to be more like Christ through the transforming work of the Spirit of sonship. The Spirit who assures us of our communion with the Lord is also the Spirit of stewardship who equips us to serve him. We are stewards of the gifts that he gives. The church's service has three goals: to serve God in worship; to serve one another in nurture; and to serve the world in mission. We will consider each of these goals later on, for many of the issues facing the contemporary church have to do with how we should worship, what Christian growth means, and what is the mission of the church today (see chapters 9 to 11).

As we serve in Christ's church, our individual gifts determine our specific calling. When the apostle Paul says, 'For by the grace given me I say . . .' (Rom. 12:3), he means, 'I say as an apostle, in virtue of my calling . . .' His distinctive gifts qualify him as the apostle to the Gentiles (Rom. 15:15–16).

The possession of gifts for service in Christ's church constitutes a call for their use. We are not to wrap our gifts in a napkin and bury them (Lk. 19:20). Stewards (servant managers) must be trustworthy. We use our gifts in order to serve God, not in order to advance ourselves, attract the admiration of others, or even find satisfaction and fulfilment. We cannot demand that the Lord provide precisely the socket into which our gifts may best be plugged. Our first goal is to get the job done, and only secondarily to find the best use of our gifts. To be sure, the Lord who calls us will provide opportunities for the use of the gifts he has given. Paul sought open doors of gospel witness and urged Christians to do the same, 'buying up' the opportunities that God provided (Eph. 5:16). But Paul did not disdain tent-making when that served Christ's mission.

In advancing the work of the Spirit, we cannot sharply separate natural gifts from spiritual gifts. Both come from the Creator Spirit. There is a difference between those abilities that have been ours from childhood and new gifts that surprise us in service. Yet even our spiritual gifts are often renewed and heightened forms of natural gifts. When Augustine's preaching takes us to the manger of the infant Lord, his unction carries him beyond his eloquence in Latin rhetoric; the Spirit has touched both his nature and his nurture. Martyn Lloyd-Jones once observed that it is not difficult for a preacher to distinguish between mere pulpit eloquence and spiritual unction. The first will lift him up; the second will humble him in awe.

As Christians we cannot activate a spiritual gift by flipping some inner switch of awareness. We seek God's glory, not our own, trusting the Spirit to enable us in speech and action. Since all is of him, there is nothing the Spirit cannot use. Desire to please the Lord clarifies our purpose. We discover the gifts he supplies and earnestly pray for greater ones, not to enhance our role but to get the job done – to reach a neighbour, teach a child, feed the hungry, counsel the confused, correct the erring, save a marriage, to endure and even befriend a boss.

The priorities of the kingdom determine our use of the gifts of the Spirit. The Spirit is with us because we are in the last days (Acts 2:17; 3:24; 1 Pet. 1:10–12). Christ has conquered Satan; he sends the Spirit from his throne to finish on earth what he has completed in heaven. Along with the taste of heaven, the Spirit brings the power of Christ's resurrection so that we can resist the devil, endure suffering, and wait for the coming of the Lord.

The gifts are not designed to provide relaxation and bliss. Such blessings are reserved for the world to come. True, there is breadth to our stewardship, for we must do everything to the glory of God (Col. 3:17). We gain exhilarating freedom in our daily employment, knowing that Christ makes everything new. Our Lord, the second Adam, has fulfilled Adam's charge,[4] freeing us to serve him in cultural tasks. The sweep of our calling, however, must not divert us from the emergency situation in which the Spirit has come. The Spirit now gives us a sword, the Word of God, and equips us with armour that will protect us in battle against the powers of darkness (Eph. 6:10–18). The Great Commission is not a theme float for mission in a long parade of cultural triumphs. It is the marching orders of the Lord for his church. The Lord of the harvest calls us to call to him to thrust forth labourers into his harvest. He must send, but he moves us to pray and leads us to go. The church's primary task is to make disciples. To this task the gifts of the Spirit are directed.

The Spirit's wisdom enables us to discern the times (2 Cor. 6:2), to look for the coming of the Lord, and to gather and prepare his own to meet him (1 Thes. 1:10; 3:13; 4:13–18; Tit. 2:13; Col. 1:28–29; 4:12). Wisdom seizes opportunities even in evil days (Eph. 5:15). The church in the Spirit cannot settle for business as usual, but looks for breakthroughs, God-given moments to be seized in faith. Some opportunities are vast and evident: the astonishing changes in Eastern Europe, for example. Others are vast but not so evident: the eroding of confidence in the mind of modernity. Other opportunities are personal and immediate: daily occasions to confess Christ's name and witness to his grace.

To recognize the moments and seasons brought by the Spirit requires alertness and realism – the opposite of drunken stupor and hallucination. For this reason the apostles call on us to be spiritually sober (1 Thes. 5:6, 8; 1 Pet. 1:13; 4:7; 5:8; Rom. 12:3; Eph. 5:18).

It is in Christ's spiritual kingdom that our gifts function. When that is forgotten, the gifts of the kingdom are ignored or abused. The Roman governor Pilate asked Jesus if he were the king of the Jews. He must have put the question scornfully, perhaps almost with pity. What had this so-called king done, so to anger his subjects that they would deliver him to the hated Romans? In his answer Jesus declares the nature of his kingdom, of his people, and of his church. 'My kingdom is not of this world. If it were, my servants would fight to prevent my arrest by the Jews. But now my kingdom is from another place' (Jn. 18:36).

Christ's kingdom is from heaven. It is not to be established by battles on earth. Muhammad launched his *jihad* with the sword; Jesus refused to take the sword or to allow his disciples to do so in his name. He refused even the sword of angels, for he could have summoned twelve legions of mighty ones (Mt. 26:53). Yet in withholding the sword Jesus did not withhold power. Even a cynical world that measures might by the megaton sees the convictions in people's minds break down walls of oppression. The collapse of Soviet Communism demonstrated that once more. Yet the wind of the Spirit is not the power of ideology, but the deeper power of the Creator who makes all things new.

The apostle Paul's enemies accused him of weakness, instability and vacillation. He was not a true apostle, they said, but an unauthorized, unqualified interloper who was understandably afraid to demand pay for his activities. Paul replied that his ministry was not in his skills as an orator, his techniques as a manager, or his pedigree as a Pharisee. He was weak in a way they could not understand. They missed the point. Measured by their standards, Paul was overqualified: a rigorously trained rabbi who had been commissioned by the risen Lord. But measured by his own standards, Paul counted as rubbish all that they valued. He knew his own weakness, but gloried in it, for he had learned to depend on the power of the Spirit (2 Cor. 10:3–5).

In the Spirit, Paul wore the armour of God, equipped to stand against the devil and all the powers of darkness (Eph. 6:11–17). In defence he was invincible, in attack irresistible, wielding weapons mighty beyond all superlatives. No tower of pride could withstand the assault of the Spirit. God's prophets were set over kingdoms (Je. 1:10; 18:7), pronouncing doom over Tyre and Babylon. Tolkien's description of the thundering crash of the tower of Barad-dûr in the climax of his trilogy *The Lord of the Rings* touched many a reader of fantasy fiction with an uneasy realization: there is abroad in the world a greater power than that of the ultimate evil empire. History does move toward God's consummation, and his Spirit controls the outcome.

Ministry in Christ's church must be governed by the wisdom of the Spirit, wisdom sought in prayer and soaked in Scripture, wisdom that seeks God's glory, wisdom that rejoices in weakness.

The rapid growth of some American churches has carried a deadly danger: not that the church may be overwhelmed by new converts, but that the church will be secularized by fascination with the methods of growth. Jesus did promise an abundant harvest; small may be beautiful, but smallness does not guarantee spirituality. Many church leaders, however, will learn to their sorrow that neither does size impress the Holy Spirit. The great resource in the building of Christ's church is the gift of his Spirit. The great question before the church is, 'How can we best seek the Spirit's blessing in receiving and using his gifts?' The answer to that central question is never a matter of technique, but always of faith and prayer. Unless the church seeks holiness, unless it heeds the revealed will of God and treasures Calvary above all else, greater size will only erect towers for sounding brass and clashing cymbals.

The filling of the Spirit

'Be getting filled with the Spirit', Paul tells the Ephesians (Eph. 5:18).[5] He constantly calls believers to the combined soberness and exuberance that mark the presence and work of the Spirit.

As John Stott has pointed out, the New Testament contains no command for Christians to be baptized with the Spirit, for the baptism of the Spirit is the initial blessing of the Spirit's cleansing and renewing; it is the reality of which water baptism is the sign.[6] As Paul tells the Romans, all Christians have the Spirit, or they would not be Christians at all (Rom. 8:9). At Pentecost, all the disciples were baptized with the Spirit. This baptism and filling marked the gift of the Spirit from Christ's throne of glory. It brought the fulfilment of the promise of the Father, and the sealing of the New Covenant. It was not an episode in the spiritual development of the disciples for us to imitate; it was the beginning of a new epoch in the history of redemption.

We cannot so press the figure of 'filling' that we begin to think of the Spirit as a liquid or a force instead of a person. We must not suppose that the disciples were filled at Pentecost, but then were a little depleted by Acts 4 and so needed topping up.

What the filling of the Spirit describes is the gift of power and blessing that accompanies the renewal of God's own presence. The fact that the Lord is with his child at one moment in no way lessens the new sense in which he may be with him or her in the next. Filling, we should remember, is applied not only to the Spirit. Christ, who fills all things with his power and control, also fills his church in a personal sense by his presence, so that the church is his body, the fullness of him who fills all in all (Eph. 1:23). The church, in becoming mature, attains to 'the whole measure of the fulness of Christ' (Eph. 4:10, 13). Paul prays that the church may know the love of Christ in order that they 'may be filled to the measure of all the fulness of God' (Eph. 3:19). If we separate the filling of the Spirit from the filling of Christ and the filling of God, we will surely think impersonally of the Spirit. This comes about because the Spirit reveals the Father and the Son, more than himself. To be filled with the Spirit is to be filled with Christ, to know the Saviour and his love. To be filled with the Spirit is to know the love of God as the Spirit pours it out in our hearts (Rom. 5:5). To be filled with the Spirit is to know the intimate communion with God that enables us to cry, 'Abba, Father' (Rom. 8:15–16).

The biblical doctrine of the church begins with the saving work of God the Father, Son and Holy Spirit. On that understanding, we may now consider the characteristics of the church, its service to God and humankind, and how its structure relates to the orders of this world. For these much debated issues, the teaching of Scripture provides a compass in the sea-changes of our time.

6

'I BELIEVE ...
THE HOLY
CATHOLIC CHURCH'

Is the church to be *believed*? The Apostles' Creed does not confess that we believe *in* the church in the same way that we believe in God the Father, Jesus Christ and the Holy Spirit. Yet we do *believe* the holy catholic church; the church itself is a matter of Christian faith.

Why is this so? Because, as we have seen, the church is God's creation, not simply a human institution. It is different, even strange. The favourite fantasy of science fiction is true of the church: its members are aliens, even though they lack pointed ears. Their astral home is not another planet, but God's own heaven. It is not surprising that sociologists find the church rather puzzling. Even Christians have extraordinary difficulty in describing the church. Luther claimed that a girl of seven knows what the church is, but that he had to pen thousands of words in order to explain what she understood. The church is different because it is the born-again family of God, the assembly and body of Christ, the dwelling of the Spirit.

How may we describe the church? One approach is to use biblical figures. The church is the body of Christ, the household of God, the temple of the Spirit. Paul Minear found no fewer than ninety-six figures and analogies that are applied to the church in the New Testament.[1] Some figures have become master metaphors, shaping the understanding of the church. The figure of the body of Christ has been used to advance a sacramentalist view of the church: that the church itself has become a sacrament, in continuation of the incarnation. Using the same image, liberals who deny the physical resurrection of Christ have claimed that Jesus rose from the dead only metaphorically, *i.e.* that he rose in his body, the church. Even a scriptural figure may therefore mislead us, if taken out of context. No one image summarizes all the others, nor does it incorporate all the non-figurative statements of the Bible.[2]

The Nicene Creed defines the attributes of the church as 'one, holy, catholic and apostolic'. The Westminster Confession uses the contrast between visible and invisible. Other such distinctions have been made: local and universal; militant and triumphant; organization and organism. When the Reformers, accused of schism, faced the crucial question of the *marks* of the church, they spoke of the Word and the sacraments (administered with discipline) as marking the true church of Christ.

To avoid bewilderment among these many perspectives on the church, we need to focus on the apostolic gospel by which the New Testament church was founded. The saving truth of the gospel is to be believed, and proclaimed to the nations. The gospel is also to be lived, for holiness, no less than truth, marks the Spirit's work. Further, this believing, proclaiming and living take place within a community. Those who are in Christ are joined to one another in an organism. There is a holy, spiritual order to God's community. It is not formed like other organizations, but it is a colony of heaven, a pilgrim people, travelling toward the day of Christ's return.

Viewing the church in terms of the gospel helps us to see how the various descriptions fit together. The church is *apostolic*, because it is founded on the apostolic gospel and called to fulfil the apostolic mission. The *holiness* of the church means that life, as well as truth, marks Christ's church; the behaviour of Christians in the world must be remarkable enough to cause grudging admiration, astonished curiosity or threatening hostility (1 Pet. 2:12; 3:16; Jn. 15:18). The *unity* of the church requires a new community, joined in a common faith and life. The *catholic* character of the church flows from the fact that the church is a colony of heaven; it cannot conform to the social castes and sectarian goals that divide a fallen world, for it is the beginning of the new humanity in Christ.

The heavenly definition of the church explains the contrasts of its existence in time (*militant / triumphant*) and space (*local / universal*), as well as the perspectives of earth and heaven (*visible / invisible*). The distinction between the church as *organization* and *organism* describes how the church is to live in both the ardour and the order of the Spirit.

The apostolic church

The marks of the church, as developed during the Protestant Reformation, centred on the church as *apostolic*. The sure sign of Christ's true church is the preaching of the apostolic gospel. Jesus chose the twelve to be his apostles (Lk. 6:13; Mt. 10:2; Mk. 3:16).[3] They were called to be with him, so that they could be his witnesses, attesting his words and deeds.[4] They were also sent in his name, first to the towns of Galilee, then from Jerusalem and Judea to Samaria and the ends of the earth (Mt. 10:5; 28:19–20). Those who received Christ's apostles received him; those who rejected them rejected him as well (Mt. 10:40; *cf.* Jn. 20:21–23).

Jesus made the confessing Peter a rock of foundation in his church. He was given, along with the other disciples, the authority of the keys of the kingdom of heaven. The broad description of the power of the keys in Matthew 16 is applied to practice in Matthew 18. Anyone who will not submit to the discipline of the church is to be 'bound' – declared to be as a Gentile and a publican, outside the company of the kingdom. Jesus extends the power of the keys to later situations in the church, where two or three are gathered to judge an offence committed by a brother (Mt. 18:19). The use of the keys is not to be limited to the twelve, but is an authority possessed by his church.[5] Yet Peter and the eleven bear the keys with distinctive authority. The foundation of God's house does not run on indefinitely, like a roadbed, but is laid once for all. Jesus Christ gives this authority to those who are his original witnesses, and sends them in his name to declare his terms for entering the kingdom. The calling of the apostles resembles to a degree the

73

function of the *šālîah* in Jewish law.[6] A *šālîah* was commissioned to represent his sponsor in a specific matter. The apostles represent Christ, and they act in his name. Those who receive them receive Christ, and those who reject their message will be doomed in the day of judgment (Mt. 10:40). Yet the apostles are not given power of attorney to negotiate the terms of the gospel. It is *Christ's* word that they carry; the message and the authority are his. Indeed, the strongest affirmation of their authority is also its severest limitation. Those who receive them receive Christ, just as those who receive Christ receive the Father (Mt. 10:40). Jesus did not bring his own message, but the words that he received from the Father (Jn. 7:16; 8:26, 38). That message, and no other, is what the apostles must proclaim.

The church is apostolic because it is built upon the apostolic foundation. Changing the expression, but not the sense, Paul spoke of laying one foundation, Jesus Christ. Other teachers might build on that foundation with marble and wrought gold, or only with plasterboard, but they can lay no other foundation (1 Cor. 3:1). The apostle's task was to build on the foundation laid by Jesus himself.

The function of the apostles was unique and unrepeatable; they received the revelation that is the meaning and the message of the church. Paul grounds his authority on that revelation (Eph. 2:20; 3:2–7). In the Spirit the apostles were chosen (Acts 1:2); through the Spirit they remembered Christ's words and deeds (Jn. 14:26; Acts 10:41); through the Spirit, too, they received the complete revelation of the risen Christ (Jn. 15:26–27; 16:13–15).

The founding authority of the apostles was sealed by the mighty works they performed in the name of Jesus. Jesus restored a girl to life with the words, '*Talitha koum!*' ('Little girl . . . get up!' Mk. 5:41); Peter, after prayer to the Lord, commanded a deceased widow, '*Tabitha koum!*' ('Tabitha, get up!' Acts 9:40). The signs, wonders and mighty works that accompanied Paul's ministry at Corinth were signs of his apostleship (2 Cor. 12:12). He had to remind the church at Corinth, proud of their charismatic gifts, that it was through his ministry that they had received those gifts. It was 'by signs, wonders and various miracles, and gifts of the Holy Spirit distributed according to his will' (Heb. 2:4) that God authenticated the apostolic witness to the words of the Lord.

The church carries the apostolic gospel down through the centuries and around the globe. What it bears is neither a memory of the gospel enshrined in tradition, nor a new gospel, appropriate to a later age, but the apostolic gospel, recorded in the inspired words of the New Testament. Paul delivered to the Corinthian church what he had received: 'that Christ died for our sins according to the Scriptures, that he was buried, that he was raised on the third day according to the Scriptures' (1 Cor. 15:1–4). Paul reminds the Corinthians of his message, taking care to record for them the gospel that he preached. 'His concern is that the church retain the tradition in the *words in which he had proclaimed it*, and for that reason he repeats those words in writing.'[7]

Paul teaches that the New Testament apostles and prophets are the foundation of the church because they have received by revelation the mystery of the gospel. What was not made known in other generations has now been 'revealed by the Spirit to God's holy apostles and prophets' (Eph. 3:5). Writing in this confidence, Paul expects his letters to be read in the churches along with the writings of the Old Testament prophets, whose words they confirmed (Col. 4:16; 1 Thes. 5:27; *cf.* Rev. 1:3).[8] The commandment of the apostles is on a level with the canonical authority of the Old Testament prophets; Paul's writings can be classified with the other (Old Testament) Scriptures (2 Pet. 3:2).[9] The church is not the source of the divine revelation given through the apostles (Gal. 1:1, 6–9). Rather, New Testament revelation is part of Christ's work through his Spirit; it is the apostolic foundation on which Christ builds his church. The gospel witness that Christ gives through his apostles is not repeated, nor is their written testimony to be amended. The finality of the book of Revelation applies equally to all the apostolic scriptures (Rev. 22:18–19).

The recognition of apostolic authority gave coherence to the witness of the early church. The church fathers appealed to the unity of the apostolic teaching in contrast to the many varieties of Gnosticism. In the New Testament itself, the similarity between Peter's and Paul's writings is striking. Although Peter knew Jesus intimately, he presents not his personal reflections but the apostolic tradition. He tells of the sufferings of Christ and the glory to follow (1 Pet. 1:11; Lk. 24:44–49; Acts 17:2–3).

To compromise the authority of Scripture is to destroy the apostolic foundation of the church. When the integrity of Scripture is surrendered, and the New Testament is thought to contain many contradictory theologies, then Christianity must be defined instead by church history.[10] The compromise comes by adding to Scripture as well as by subtracting from it. Hans Küng observed a major difference between the Reformers and Roman Catholic theology: where the Reformers demanded 'either . . . or', Catholic theology offered 'both . . . and'.[11] For Luther, salvation is by faith alone, through grace alone, on the authority of Scripture alone. At each crucial point, the Council of Trent added an 'and': faith *and* works, grace *and* merit, Scripture *and* tradition.

But did not an apostolic tradition precede New Testament Scripture? Does not the church inherit both?

To certify the legitimacy of orthodox teaching, the early church fathers appealed to the close links between bishops and apostles. In the second century, as the church struggled with Gnostic heresy, there was a strong incentive to appeal to oral testimony. The Gnostics twisted the Scriptures to their own purposes, and generated their own bogus 'Gospels' and 'Acts', for which they claimed apostolic authority. The orthodox fathers therefore found supporting testimony for their cause in the continuity of apostolic teaching at the local level. The argument seemed particularly persuasive in the second century, when the long life of a bishop like Polycarp in Smyrna (d. 165 AD) brought the apostolic days almost into living memory. Even then, however, Irenaeus had to list as many as twelve bishops in Rome in order to link Eleutherus, the incumbent, with the apostles.[12] Clearly, the longer the succession list of bishops, the more tenuous the claim to untainted apostolic tradition, unless some other guarantee could be found. Irenaeus found it in the grace of ordination, the gift of certain truth granted to presbyters and bishops.[13] Later, when heretical bishops appeared, the claim of guaranteed authority was narrowed to the bishop of Rome. The doctrine of apostolic succession in the Pope gave tradition an authoritative source, but misconceived the calling of the apostles. No later bishop of the church could meet the requirements the apostles laid down in the choice of Matthias (Acts 1:21–22). No Pope could claim to have seen the risen Lord. Hans Küng observes: 'As direct witnesses and messengers of the risen Lord, the apostles can have no successors . . . Apostleship in the sense of the original and fundamental ministry of the first witnesses and messengers died out with the death of the last apostle.'[14] Paul speaks of himself as the last apostle, not in the sense of confessed unworthiness, but as the apostle to the Gentiles, bringing the whole history of redemption to its predicted climax by summoning the nations to the Lord.[15] The inspired apostolic testimony given in the New Testament Scripture is both sufficient and final.

The apostles were sent to carry the gospel as well as to teach it. Paul, deeply aware of his calling as the apostle to the Gentiles, was a foundation-laying missionary. He travelled to the western limit of the Roman empire to lay a foundation for later builders (1 Cor. 3:10; Rom. 15:20–21). Other missionaries were called evangelists, and sometimes apostles, as being those 'sent' with the gospel; but these did not share the apostolic authority of Paul and the twelve.[16]

In Acts, Luke features the foundational role of the apostles. He highlights the choice of Matthias to complete the number of the twelve (Acts 1:26), and he traces the leading role of the apostles as the church was established (e.g. Acts 2:42). Yet he also uses the term to describe missionaries (Acts 14:14). Paul, too, uses 'apostle' not only in the restricted sense (Gal. 1:1, 17; Rom. 1:1; 11:13; 1 Cor. 15:9; Eph. 2:20; 3:5; 1 Tim. 2:7),[17] but also more generally to identify fellow-missionaries (Rom. 16:7) and emissaries of the churches (2 Cor. 8:23; Phil. 2:25). They are his fellow-workers, watering where he has planted, building where he, a master-builder, has laid the foundation (1 Cor. 3:5–15).[18]

The church is apostolic because it is founded on apostolic teaching, and also because of its charge to carry out the Great Commission. The gospel is a deposit of truth, but not a deposit to be wrapped up for safe-keeping. Though the Reformation grasped Paul's theology anew, some set aside his missionary vision, convinced that the apostle had finished the job. In the eighteenth century, William Carey's colleagues disputed his missionary call to India. Had not the apostles reached the whole world (Rom. 10:18; 1 Cor. 4:9; Col. 1:6)? Carey reminded his opponents of Jesus' promise to be with the church to the end of

77

the age (Mt. 28:20). The Lord evidently expected the mission of the church to continue.[19]

An opposite misinterpretation of the apostolate claims that the church does not have a mission, but *exists* in mission. Emphasis on the mission of the church cannot be faulted; the difficulty is the denial of the church's existence as the chosen people of God, separate from the world. There is irony in the symbol of the ecumenical movement – a graphic icon of Noah's ark bearing the cross. It would be hard to find a more powerful image of the separation of the saved from the lost. Yet the ecumenical movement rejected precisely this separation by affirming, in its theology of the 'servant church', that the whole world is saved; the only difference between the church and the world is that the church is aware of the world's salvation.[20] Leaders scorned evangelical theology as presenting a lifeboat of the lucky few floating in a flood of drowning sinners.[21] There can be no 'apostolate' of the church without the apostolic gospel, a gospel in which the wrath of God is revealed, as well as his saving righteousness in Jesus Christ (Rom. 1:18–32).

The unity of the church

What unity does Christ require of his church?

We clasp hands in a circle and sing, 'Blest be the tie that binds', but what does that tie look like? It is invisible, of course, and we may like it that way. The more invisible the better. If it were not for that invisible tie, we might feel that we had to do something about our divisions. As it is, we can be almost proud of them. Do they not show a healthy variety of Christian expression? Since nothing can destroy the spiritual unity of Christ's true church, our disunity cannot be very serious, we may say; at any rate, disunity is better than an institutional super-church. We don't want the tie to bind in the form of ecclesiastical handcuffs.

There are, however, hand-clasps as well as handcuffs. If Christ has not 'handed over'[22] his church to an enthroned successor to Peter, or to a beatified bureaucracy, has he left her with no word about her corporate life in the world?

Evangelicals can no longer avoid this question. We are driven to consider not only what the Lord calls us to *do* together, but also what he calls us to *be* together.

Jesus Christ builds *one church* on the foundation of his apostolic witnesses. The unity of the new people of God is part of the good news proclaimed by Paul to the Gentiles. Israel's Messiah, the Saviour of the world, by his cross broke down the wall of separation between Jew and Gentile. Gentiles, far from the God of Israel, were brought near through faith in Christ. The apostle Paul was ready to give his life in to order establish the unity that Christ accomplished in his body (Eph. 2:11–22).[23] He claimed for Gentile believers the true circumcision of Christ (Phil. 3:3).

It is union with God that creates the unity of God's people. Paul's plea is urgent:

> Make every effort to keep the unity of the Spirit through the bond of peace. There is one body and one Spirit – just as you were called to one hope when you were called – one Lord, one faith, one baptism; one God and Father of all, who is over all and through all and in all (Eph. 4:3–5).

The term that Paul uses here is stronger than is suggested by the translation 'make every effort'. It actually means our total dedication to the unity of God himself. We are to be one because we serve one God. If we served many gods – Isis, Apollo, Dionysos, Demeter – then we might form different cults, for there were 'gods many and lords many'. But we serve the one true God, who is also the heavenly Father of his one family (Eph. 3:14). The love that responds to his love will draw us to one another as surely as it draws us to him from whom it comes. If anyone claims to love God and does not love his brother, he is a liar and self-deceived (1 Jn. 4:20). No-one dare approach God in worship who will not be reconciled to his brother; let him first leave his gift at the altar and seek out his brother (Mt. 5:24).

As the church is one with the Father, so it is one in the Lord Jesus, the one Shepherd who gathers one flock (Jn. 10:16; Eph. 4:5). This is what Paul pleads when he confronts the beginning of denominationalism at Corinth. Some claimed to be 'of Paul', some 'of Apollos', some 'of Cephas', and some (disdainful of the others) 'of Christ'. No-one prized more highly than Paul his own calling and the revelation given to him. He even spoke of 'my gospel'. But he does not commend his own followers as we might imagine, or say, 'You do well to follow me, for I alone have the full gospel for the Gentiles.' Instead, he reproaches those who used his name: 'Is Christ divided? Was Paul crucified for you? Were you baptized into the name of Paul?' (1 Cor. 1:13). For Paul, the body of Christ is not merely a symbol of the church. Representative union with Christ is the salvation of the church. Paul says, 'But now he has reconciled you by Christ's physical body through death' (Col. 1:22). The church is joined to the one body of Christ given on the cross. If some Corinthians were to be 'of Paul', then Paul's body would have had to have been given for them.

Baptism is a mark of union with Christ. It is a name-giving ceremony, with a sign of cleansing, and the name that is given is the name of Christ. We are not of Paul, Apollos, Peter, Luther, Calvin, or Wesley: we are Christians, bearing the name of the Lord Christ. To be sure, Paul recognizes divisions that separate Christians from heretics, but not those that separate Christians from one another (1 Cor. 11:18–19).

The Lord's Supper, no less than baptism, proclaims the unity of Christ's church. We are one body as we share in the one bread (1 Cor. 10:17). The sacrament is eloquent with the symbolism of our union with Christ in his death on the cross.

The vital union of Christians with Christ also demands our unity. Jesus prayed that all believers 'may be one, Father, just as you are in me and I am in you. May they also be in us so that the world may believe that you have sent me' (Jn. 17:21). Jesus asks that the unity of believers, not just with one another, but with him and with the Father, will convince the world.

To the one Father and the one Lord, Paul adds the one Spirit (Eph. 4:4). The church is to keep the unity of the Spirit, for it is by the Spirit that the church is united to Christ and to the Father. There is one great misunderstanding that can nullify all that we may learn about the unity of the church in the Father and the Son. It is the 'spiritualizing', or even the 'vaporizing', of the Holy Spirit. We may think of the bond of the Spirit as insubstantial. We piously agree to any form of unity in Christ, provided it be strictly 'spiritual', but this is sheer worldliness.

The Creator Spirit is the One who forms both the first creation and the second. Christ's resurrection is in the power of the Spirit; the spiritual body of our resurrection hope has reality that makes our present flesh seem heavy clay indeed. The work of the Spirit is to give reality, to actualize. The Spirit is the down-payment, the reality of the final redemption given in advance (Eph. 1:11, 13–14). The fellowship of the Spirit is more than a sense of camaraderie. It is a sharing together in the presence of the Spirit, and of his gifts. Those who share the Spirit are of one accord, united in the love of Christ (Phil. 2:1–2). Fellowship in compassion includes fellowship in material blessings: those who share a common life will share daily bread and clothing. *Koinōnia* in the New Testament often means sharing of this kind (Acts 2:42; Rom. 15:26; 2 Cor. 8:4; Heb. 13:16). The unity of the Spirit must be as tangible as a hand-clasp or a cup of water.

The gifts of the Spirit do differ, but they never divide, for they enable the church to function as an organism, the body of Christ. The Spirit's 'dividing' of gifts (*diairesis*, 1 Cor. 12:4, 11) is the opposite of fleshly 'divisions' (*hairesis*, 1 Cor. 11:19). The eye needs the foot; the ear needs the hand. Organic unity requires diversity of function (1 Cor. 12). Christians who are 'noses' may be tempted to fraternize in order to sniff out worldliness in other members of the congregation. But Christians often most need those who differ from them the most with regard to spiritual gifts. Seeking the unity of the Spirit means appreciating the diversity of the Spirit's gifts and learning from one another – growing together to the full maturity of Christ.

Beside the gifts by which we differ, there are those graces or fruit that make us like one another, as we are made like Christ. These fruits of the Spirit preserve unity: lowliness, meekness, longsuffering, forbearance, and above all, love (Gal. 5:22; Eph. 4:2; 1 Cor. 13).

The sectarian spirit that Paul decried at Corinth lacked that love, and that same spirit has shattered the unity of Christ's body throughout the history of the church. In denominational communions, Christians exercise a measure of fellowship toward one another that is denied to Christians in other denominations. Efforts to overcome division by launching a new, undivided church have only repeated the mistake of the 'Christ' party at Corinth – and created yet another denomination. Nor can division be denied by tracing one line of legitimate succession that can expose and unchurch the members of every schism. A group of congregations may err by severing fellowship with a particular denomination, but that error does not prevent the schismatic group from evidencing, either at once or eventually, the marks of the true church. This is all the more clear if faults on both sides have lead to the division. In every situation, however, the imperative to seek healing remains, and must begin with repentance and renewal in faith and love.

Just as the apostolic doctrine of the church must be evident in its teaching, so, too, the unity of the church must be evident in its fellowship. While no church is perfect in its teaching, we must distinguish between churches that are defective in doctrine and those that are apostate, having renounced the apostolic 'pattern of sound teaching' (2 Tim. 1:13–14). This distinction is no less urgent with respect to the unity of the church. During the Reformation, the Reformers had to face the fact that they were no longer in fellowship with the Pope at Rome. Were they therefore outside of the fellowship of Christ's church? To answer this question, they analysed the marks of the true church (which we will consider in chapter 8).

The church that is to be one in the Spirit, united to Jesus Christ, and one in the faith, holding to the purity of the apostolic gospel, must also be God's holy people on earth, growing in likeness to Christ, and transcending worldly divisions as the beginning of a new humanity in Christ. We turn now to consider the holiness and catholicity of the church.

7

HOLINESS AND CATHOLICITY

'To the church of God in Corinth, to those sanctified in Christ Jesus and called to be holy . . .'(1 Cor. 1:2). Paul's salutation makes us uncomfortable: 'called to be holy ones', literally, 'saints'. In our world, saints populate stained glass windows, medals and automobile dashboards. A politician will sometimes assure us: 'I'm no saint.' He makes this modest disclaimer to divert attention from his past and assure us that he is human.

Under the scorn that dismisses saintliness lies a guilty avoidance of what it means to be human. As rebels, we prefer to think that a saint is abnormal – to be admired, perhaps, as a Mother Teresa, but not a real human being.

But to be holy is to be genuinely human, for holiness is godliness, and life without God is life without meaning. J. I. Packer has likened the English Puritans to the giant redwoods of California, overtopping the trees of the forest, resistant to storm and fire. So the Puritans, he says, were spiritual giants, leading unfrilled lives in mature holiness and seasoned fortitude.[1] It is not enough, however, for us to leave off caricaturing Puritans and admire them. We must learn from them: holiness is the calling of all God's people. The church is a *forest* of redwoods.

The holiness of the church

The apostle Peter writes to Gentile churches:

> Do not conform to the evil desires you had when you lived in ignorance. But just as he who called you is holy, so be holy in all you do; for it is written: 'Be holy, because I am holy' (1 Pet. 1:14–16).

Peter's quotation from Leviticus formulates the relation between God and his people (Lv. 11:44–45; 19:2; 20:7). To begin with, the Lord God is the Holy One. His holiness describes his transcendance, the gulf that separates the Creator from his creation. In his presence the seraphim can only cry,

> 'Holy, holy, holy is the LORD Almighty;
>   the whole earth is full of his glory' (Is. 6:3).

Isaiah, however, cannot cry 'Holy!' with the seraphs; he must cry, 'Woe to me!' He is a man of unclean lips, and his eyes have seen the King (Is. 6:5). For sinful human beings God's holiness burns with the fire of his righteousness. When, at the word of Jesus, fish filled Peter's nets to bursting, he fell down and cried, 'Go away from me, Lord; I am a sinful man!' (Lk. 5:8). Seeing the power of Jesus, Peter recognized the Holy One, and in a rush of awareness knew that he was a doomed sinner, in a boat with the Lord himself.

How, then, can God say to his people, 'Be holy, because I am holy'? Surely we cannot share God's exalted separation from all creation. Neither can we meet his standard of perfect righteousness. A call to *his* holiness brings despair to our hearts. But we must taste that despair, as Isaiah did, before we will bear the touch of a coal from the altar on our unclean lips.

The Bible gives us God's own plan for claiming a holy people. Because they belong to the separated One, his people are separate: a redeemed people, cleansed of sin and drawn closer than the angels to the love of the righteous Father. In the Old Testament, an elaborate structure of ceremonial and civil law marks out the distinctiveness of the people God calls to be holy. Sin is imaged as filth, and as ceremonial 'uncleanness'. It is a contagion, linked with diet, blood, bodily excretions and death. The radical revelation of the Old Covenant is that the Holy One, who dwells on high, and whose eyes are too pure to look upon evil, nevertheless comes to dwell among his people. Because God walks in the camp of Israel as he once walked in the Garden of Eden, the camp must cover excrement, exclude 'unclean' animals, and observe rituals of purification.

Ceremonial cleanness symbolizes the holiness that God's presence demands. Israel is 'a kingdom of priests and a holy nation', because it is God's 'treasured possession' (Ex. 19:6). The 'cleanness' metaphor not only dramatizes the difference between the holy and the unholy; it shows that God can provide cleansing through sacrifice. The rationale is clear: blood cleanses because it is the seal of a 'perfect' life that has been forfeited for that of the defiled sinner.

The symbolism of ceremonial holiness points beyond itself to the moral sphere. 'Corrupt are they and not his children, a generation warped and twisted to their shame' (Dt. 32:5, NIV margin). The prophets condemn the people's sanctimonious observance of ritual cleanness alongside their practice of oppression and adultery (Is. 1:11–17; Am. 5:21–24).

God's does not discard ceremonial regulations, however. What they symbolize is fulfilled in the sacrificial death of the Suffering Servant. Jesus came not to destroy the law, but to fulfil it. Paul applies the 'cleanness' requirement to the church, since it is the people among whom God dwells (2 Cor. 6:16–7:1). He quotes passages addressed to Israel: that God will be their God, and they his people, and that he will live with them and walk among them (Lv. 26:12; Je. 32:38; Ezk. 37:27); that they are called to come out and to be separate, touching no unclean thing, in order to be received by the Lord as his children (Is. 52:11; Ezk. 20:34, 41). Paul describes these passages as promises, and concludes: 'Let us purify ourselves from everything that contaminates body and spirit, perfecting holiness out of reverence for God' (2 Cor. 7:1).

The cleanness, the holiness, of the people of God must mark them as his. Now that the outward regulations have dropped away, the inner meaning applies with full force. Paul therefore contrasts Moses' description of Israel with his own description of the church: children of God without fault, blameless and pure (Phil. 2:15; cf. Dt. 32:5).

How can Paul so describe the New Testament church? He addresses the Corinthian church as those called to be saints (1 Cor. 1:2), indeed, as made up of saints (2 Cor. 1:1). Yet Paul must deal with their pride, strife and gross sexual immorality, not to speak of abuses in worship and misuse of spiritual gifts. Are these Corinthians really saints?

Hans Küng lists three solutions to this problem.[2] The first is the effort to purify the church by excluding a category of sinners, so that the church is composed of saints only – as defined by one party, at least. Gnostics excluded the orthodox who did not possess their secret knowledge; the Novatians and the Donatists rejected those who had yielded to Roman persecutions. Augustine complained that Donatist holiness was sadly lacking in love.

In his second solution, Küng describes the Roman Catholic distinction between the church and its members. The church is described as holy, even when its members are sinners. As Yves Congar has expressed it: 'There is no more sin in the Church than in Christ, of Whom she is the body; and she is His mystical personality.'[3] This position makes the church, as distinct from its members, irreformable.[4] As Congar's words show, the body-of-Christ figure serves as the basis for identifying the church with Christ. When Vatican II added a description of the church as the people of God, it also acknowledged the sin to which the church in its pilgrimage is still liable. The Pope, however, intervened to qualify 'sin' by adding the decisive words, 'in its members'.[5] Küng responds, 'There is no such thing as a Church without members . . . It is human beings, not God, not the Lord, not the Spirit, who make up the Church.'[6] As we shall see in considering the catholicity of the church later in this chapter, Roman Catholic dogma here faces a critical issue.[7]

Küng mentions, thirdly, the effort to set the division within individual church members by distinguishing between the 'holy' and the sinful parts of the Christian. The Christian, he says, does not have a 'better half' that might pray for his 'worse half'. 'It is as a wretched sinner that he is a member of the Church.'[8]

How, then, may the church be not only called to holiness, but also declared to be holy, a company of 'holy ones' – the very term that is also used in the Bible for the angels as 'sons of God' (Eph. 1:1; Col. 1:2; Dt. 33:2)?

Paul gives the answer in the phrasing of his salutation. The Corinthian Christians are 'those sanctified in Christ Jesus and called to be holy' (1 Cor. 1:2). United to Christ, they have been justified, declared righteous before God, since Christ's perfect righteousness has been put to their account, just as their sins were put to Christ's account (Phil. 3:9; 1 Pet. 2:24). In Christ they have also been sanctified, for they are no longer separated from God, without Christ and without hope (Eph. 2:11–22). They have been brought near as members of God's covenant and fellow-citizens with the Old Testament saints (Eph. 2:19; 'saints', not just 'people' as in the NIV). Once they were not a people, but now they are God's chosen people, a royal priesthood, a holy nation (1 Pet. 2:9–10). They are no less than God's own family, his sons and daughters in his one and only Son (Eph. 3:14–15; 1 Pet. 1:3; 1 Jn. 3:1).

There is a notable difference between God's initial saving deed when he pardons our sins and receives us as righteous in his sight, and the ongoing work of his grace that continues until the day when he will complete it in glory. Both flow from his grace, but saving faith receives Christ's righteousness; the walk of faith follows him in righteous living. Classical Reformed theology distinguishes between God's *act* of justification (and adoption) and his continuing *work* of sanctification.[9] The Bible, however, does not restrict the language of holiness to God's ongoing work.[10] Paul writes, 'But you were washed, you were sanctified, you were justified . . .' (1 Cor. 6:11; *cf.* 2 Thes. 2:13; Eph. 4:24). When God makes us his own through the work of the Spirit in our hearts, he sets us apart, for he claims us as his holy children. The righteousness he gives us is Christ's righteousness, but the union with Christ that makes Christ's righteousness ours also makes us holy in God's sight.

Paul, then, in his address to the Corinthians, speaks both of our initial sanctification in Christ and our calling to holy living (1 Cor. 1:2). The distinction is central for the teaching of the New Testament about the Christian life. First comes the statement of what God has done for us in Christ; then comes the command to live accordingly. If we have died with Christ, then let us put to death sin in our members. If we rose with Christ, then let us walk in newness of life (Col. 3:1–5).

This perspective in the New Testament explains both the status of the church as God's holy people and the calling of the church to realize holiness in the fear of the Lord. The church is a holy nation, not just ideally, but actually, because it is composed of people who are united to Jesus Christ in God's electing love and by his effective calling. Though Paul knows there may be hypocrites in the Corinthian church, he addresses it in terms of its status before God. Corinthian believers are sanctified in Christ, even though their calling to holiness is far from realized, and the Lord knows those who are his.

The holiness of the *congregation* before God has often been lost from view behind the screens of holy places filled with holy things served by holy people. Christ's astonishing answer to the Samaritan woman (Jn. 4:21)[11] shows that the image of God's temple was fulfilled in his body (Jn. 2:21). The only place of worship was at his feet, through his gift of the Spirit. They who are united to him are living stones, built as his spiritual house, a holy priesthood, offering neither bulls, lambs nor incense, but the spiritual sacrifices of their lips and their lives (1 Pet. 2:4–5; Heb. 13:15–16).

The apostolic gospel affirms the holiness of the church in Christ, and therefore calls for holiness of life. Paul tells the Thessalonian church that their sanctification is the will of God (1 Thes. 4:3), and urges them to continue to please God more and more in the way they live (4:1). He prays that God will strengthen them so that they will be blameless and holy at the coming of Christ (3:13). Even though he knows that the process of sanctification will be completed in that day (4:17), Paul never supposes that progress now is unnecessary. To the contrary, he prays and labours to prepare the bride of Christ to meet the Lord (Col. 1:28–29; 2 Cor. 11:2; Eph. 5:25–32).

The bride must respond to the purpose of Christ's love. Those who are travelling to meet the Lord yearn for his 'Well done!' Their progress now will measure their joy then. Jesus promised a greater sphere of service in glory for his most faithful stewards.

The Puritan John Owen wrote: 'Holiness is nothing but the implanting, writing and realising of the gospel in our souls.'[12] What Christ seeks in his church is what the gospel promises and provides. The quest for gospel holiness cannot mean acquiring confident expertise in the practice of the virtues. When Benjamin Franklin proposed to reform his life by shedding one vice at a time, he prepared an unintentional caricature of a Puritan spiritual journal. The life of holiness is the life of faith in which the believer, with a deepening knowledge of his own sin and helplessness apart from Christ, increasingly casts himself upon the Lord, and seeks the power of the Spirit and the wisdom and comfort of the Bible to battle against the world, the flesh and the devil. It is not a lonely or cheerless struggle, for Christ gives the Spirit to the members of his body to help one another. Even suffering can be borne with joy, for the Christian walks in the steps of Jesus Christ who takes us by the hand. Maturing in holiness means maturing in love, love that knows God's love poured out in our hearts, and answers with love that tastes the goodness of the Lord.

Growth in true holiness is always growth together; it takes place through the nurture, the work and worship of the church. Simeon the Stylite, the renowned Syrian monk who for thirty-six years sought holiness on top of a pillar, still needed the ministry of less lofty church members to service the basket tied to his rope.[13] Not only anchorites, however, seek holiness in isolation. How many Christians see fellow-believers as obstacles rather than aids to spiritual growth? Of course, personal piety closes the door to pray in secret; but the church together seeks maturity, 'attaining to the whole measure of the fullness of Christ'. Together we grow up into him who is the Head, that is, Christ (Eph. 4:13, 15). In the book of Acts, Christians are called the people of the Way (Acts 9:2; 18:25; 22:4; 24:14). Like Israel in the wilderness, they travel together, following Christ along the way of the cross that leads to the Father's house. Together they find Jesus himself to be the Way, the Truth and the Life.

The Puritans sought holiness through a diligent use of the outward 'means of grace': the Word, the sacraments, and prayer. These ordinances of Christ are given to the church: it is not simply the reading, but especially the preaching of God's Word that is an effective means 'of convincing and converting sinners, and of building them up in holiness and comfort, through faith, unto salvation'.[14] The sacraments of baptism and the Lord's Supper are celebrated in the community of the church; the

Lord's Prayer is a 'we' prayer, given by Christ to his disciples as a model for their praying together.

The Spirit makes these outward means of grace effective. He is not bound by water, wine or bread, but he does honour his own promises and uses the Word and the sacraments to sanctify us. No such divine blessing is promised on imaginatively induced mental images!

The gifts of others encourage us when we despair, minister to us in sickness, and remind us of the faithful promises of God. They also warn and rebuke us, even declaring God's condemnation of our sin. Discipline is essential to the pursuit of holiness. God himself chastises us as children, and he uses fellow-Christians to hold us responsible to our common Master. Discipline, as we shall see, is not first an exercise of negative judgment, a matter of church courts and censures. It begins with the care of friends with whom we strive to follow Christ, and to whom we are, in a measure, accountable. We now sometimes use 'disciple' as a transitive verb, which is how the Greek word is used in the Great Commission.[15] But Christians are Christ's disciples, not ours. We serve others as we minister the truth and love of Christ.

In all the nurture of his church, Christ uses his Word and Spirit. Peter reminds Christians that they have been 'born again, not of perishable seed, but of imperishable, through the living and enduring word of God' that was preached to them (1 Pet. 1:23, 25). The Word of God by which they came to Christ is the Word by which they grow; they must crave it as newborn infants crave milk (1 Pet. 1:22; 2:2). The Puritan piety that Packer describes was nurtured on the pure milk of Scripture, used not as a thesaurus of inspirational texts, but as God's revealed will in order to direct us in what we are to believe and how we are to live.

The catholicity of the church

Protestants have often been puzzled by the words in the Apostles' Creed that confess belief in a 'holy *catholic* church'. That the church is to hold to the apostolic gospel; that it is to be one in Christ; that it is called to holiness: all these things are clearly taught in the New Testament. But where does the New

Testament teach the 'catholicity' of the church? Are the debates about this notion mostly due to the fact that the New Testament says nothing about it?

The Greek term *katholikos* means that which is universal or general, having to do with the whole; it is not used in the New Testament to describe the church.[16] The early church fathers used it to express an important New Testament teaching: that the church as a whole is more than the local church. Ignatius of Antioch, who died about 110 AD, wrote in his letter to the church in Smyrna: 'Wherever the bishop shall appear, there let the people be; even as where Christ Jesus may be, there is the catholic church.'[17]

As the church struggled against false teaching, the term 'catholic' came to be used to describe the orthodox church as distinct from the Gnostic, Montanist and Arian heresies. Hans Küng points out, 'The great turning point came with Constantine, or more precisely with Theodosius, for under the religious edict of 380 the "*ecclesia catholica*" became the only lawful national religion . . . Paganism and heresy became political crimes, "catholicity"became orthodoxy, defended by law.'[18]

Catholicity took yet another meaning when the Novatians and later the Donatists held to orthodox theology, but separated from the church. To refute the Donatist claim to be the true church, Augustine appealed to the geographical spread of the catholic church. The Donatists might unchurch those from whom they separated in North Africa, but what of the church of Antioch in Syria? Could they really claim to be the church catholic, the church universal, when they were to be found only in one geographical area?

At the time of the Reformation, Augustine's argument was used again against the Reformers. The Protestant Reformation was limited to Europe, and particularly to northern Europe. How could the Reformers claim to represent the church catholic when only the Roman Catholic Church was spread around the world? To spatial extension, the apologists of the Counter-Reformation also added numerical preponderance; the Catholic church was the true church for it enclosed the largest number of members.

The Reformers replied by pointing to another dimension of

catholicity: its extension in time. Their movement did not yet have the extension in space of the Roman communion, but it could claim continuity with the early catholic church, a continuity that had been severed by the false teachings and corrupt practices of Rome. For Luther and Calvin, the preaching of the apostolic gospel defined the true church. Apart from gospel orthodoxy, Rome's claim to catholicity was meaningless.

With the rise of nationalism in Europe another facet of catholicity gained attention. Describing the catholicity of the church under the gospel, the Westminster Confession notes that it is 'not confined to one nation, as before under the law . . .'[19] The international and cross-cultural extension of the church has given urgency to our understanding of catholicity. The history of Christian missions illustrates the conflict between colonialist exploitation of non-European peoples and continuing missionary advocacy of their place in Christ's universal church. When Spanish *conquistadores* in the New World exploited and enslaved the Indian people, Bartolomé de Las Casas, a Dominican missionary, denounced their atrocities, and laboured for the conversion and welfare of the Indians. He secured from the Emperor Charles V the 'New Laws' of 1542, favouring the rights of the Indians, but this legislation could not be enforced against the colonists.[20] De Las Casas himself failed when he sought to block the enslavement of Indians by substituting the importation of black slaves from Africa.[21]

Commitment to mission has driven Christ's church to deal with the issues of globalization. As the church catholic, it is called to set before the world a new humanity that joins together in loving fellowship the races and peoples of planet Earth.

Do the dimensions of catholicity derive from a central meaning, or are they only the different ways that the abstract idea of 'totality' can be applied to the church?

Hans Küng provides a definition: 'The catholicity of the Church, therefore, consists in a notion of entirety, based on identity and resulting in universality.'[22] If that summary seems condensed, it is. Küng chooses the word 'entirety' to describe a totality that is more than quantitative or external. He rejects the catholicity of space, time and numbers developed by the Roman Catholic polemicists of the Counter-Reformation. An ecclesiastical imperial structure that is more widely spread than any other may yet be unfaithful to the nature of the church, and therefore no longer catholic. Maximal membership may be gained at the price of spiritual devaluation. A church may claim to be the oldest, and boast in its tradition, but become no more than a monument to tradition. Küng also declares that catholicity is not primarily a sociological concept.[23] There is no point in embracing the widest varieties of culture if the church becomes the instrument of a culture, race or class, or if it sinks into an amalgam with paganism.

The wholeness of the church, its entirety, Küng points out, must be grounded in its identity. Otherwise, the dimensions of catholicity lose their meaning. Faithfulness to its identity, however, does not mean that the church is to be self-absorbed, for its missionary calling has reference to the whole world. Its identity results in universality through its mission.

Küng is right in finding the catholicity of the church to be grounded in its identity, and not simply in geography, numbers, or sociological statistics. The identity of the church catholic must be found in another relation: its relation to the triune God.

Avery Dulles makes this the first dimension of catholicity, calling it the dimension of *height*.[24] The source of 'catholicity from above', he says, is the divine fullness, and specifically the fullness of Jesus Christ. He finds three aspects of the 'catholicity of Christ'. The first is in the incarnation, as 'a mystery of divine plenitude'. In the Word made flesh, God's fullness (*plērōma*) dwells with us in bodily form (Col. 2:9). Christ is 'full of grace and truth', and we have all received of his fullness (Jn. 1:14, 16). Dulles then distinguishes a second aspect: Christ's fullness as the head of creation: '. . . all things were created by him and for him. He is before all things, and in him all things hold together' (Col. 1:16–17). Christ 'fills everything in every way' (Eph. 1:23).[25] The third aspect of Christ's catholicity appears in these same texts: his headship over the church. 'Unlike *plērōma* (fullness), which can embrace the whole universe in its relation to Christ, *sōma* (body) includes only the Church.'[26]

Reflecting on these passages of Scripture, J. A. Heyns concludes: 'Were we, in fact, to sum up in one phrase the Church's catholicity viewed from this angle, it would be: *Christ always all in all*. Understood in this way, catholicity is an *exclusive* concept.'[27] The exclusiveness of Christ is, in fact, the point that

Paul makes in the letters he writes from prison. Because all the fullness of the Deity is in Christ, we are not to turn from him: 'See to it that no-one takes you captive through hollow and deceptive philosophy, which depends on human tradition and the basic principles of this world rather than on Christ' (Col. 2:8).

Sad to say, the meaning of Christ's cosmic power and glory has sometimes been inverted. The 'cosmic Christ' has been presented, not as the Creator and Lord of all, but as incarnate in the cosmic process. The New Testament does not universalize Christ by identifying him with the cosmos or the structures of the world. He fills all things as Lord: *i.e.* he controls all things, and is everywhere present in his deity to sustain and direct the course of his creation. This is the sense in which God says through Jeremiah, 'Do not I fill heaven and earth?' (Je. 23:24).

To be clear about the relation of the church to the world, we must be clear about the relation of Christ to the world. In this respect, the Roman Catholic understanding of catholicity claims careful attention. Though Küng and Dulles distance themselves from earlier Roman polemics against Protestantism, they fault Reformation theology for positions they regard as extreme. The Catholic method, they say, is 'both . . . and', not 'either . . . or'. According to Dulles, the incarnation exhibits the catholic mediating principle of 'reconciled opposites'.[28] Man is a microcosm of the universe in the hierarchy of his being, and 'The Word of God, in assuming a full human existence, entered into a kind of union with the cosmos'.[29]

According to Pierre Teilhard de Chardin, Christ has not only a divine and human but also a cosmic nature, co-extensive with the material universe.[30] Evolution not only came to a peak in Christ, but continues to unfold toward the future Christ. Dulles finds Teilhard de Chardin's views 'intriguing but idiosyncratic',[31] yet observes that the 'pan-Christic' universalism of Teilhard de Chardin and Maurice Blondel has, in some respects, become official Catholic teaching in the documents of Vatican II.[32] Pope John Paul II made more emphatic the universal language of Vatican II by affirming that 'man – every man without exception whatever – has been redeemed by Christ . . . because with man – with each man without any exception whatever – Christ is in a way united, even when man is unaware

94

of it'.[33] Such a statement certainly subordinates redemption to
an incarnational union, although it does not express the cosmic
identification taught by Teilhard de Chardin. To suggest that
Christ is incarnate in the cosmos is to introduce the very
confusion that the Chalcedonian creed condemned. The divine
nature of the Son of God is joined to his human nature in the
unity of his Person, but a non-personal union of the divine
nature with cosmic dust or cosmic process is pantheism, not
incarnational theology.

Central to the incarnational theology of the Roman Catholic
Church is the Eucharist, viewed as the real presence of the body
of Christ offered as a bloodless sacrifice.[34] The sacrament also
defines the church.[35] When it partakes of the body of Christ, the
church is itself sacramental, continuing the incarnation. Christ
the Head is in glory, but the church, his body, is on earth.[36]
Vittorio Subilia shows how this understanding determines
Catholic dogma regarding the church and its teaching. He
argues that the Gnostic myth of the cosmic Man influenced the
way Paul's teaching about Christ as the Head in Colossians and
Ephesians was later understood. This error transfers to the
church the authority of Christ and is the 'problem of Catholicism'.[37]

Dulles limits the sense in which incarnation can apply to the
church. Members of the church are pre-existing persons, given
new life by the Spirit. They are not instances of the divine Word
assuming human nature.[38] The Spirit does not become
incarnate in us, but mediates Christ's presence to us.

In spite of this, Dulles insists on the sacramental meaning of
the church as he describes 'catholicity from below'.[39] Between
Roman Catholic theology and that of the Reformers he finds a
fundamental difference concerning nature, and specifically
human nature. The theology of the Reformers, he says, lacked
the catholicity-in-depth recognized by the Roman Catholic
Church. He alleges that the Reformed doctrine of justification
by faith exhibits the Manichaean heresy by viewing nature itself
as evil. Although he ignores the distinction the Reformers made
between justification and sanctification, he accurately represents the Reformed doctrine of justification: sinners are dead in
trespasses and sin, unable to do anything pleasing to God.
Justifying righteousness must, therefore, be God's gift: 'By faith,

God imputes to us the merits of Christ as if they were our own.'[40] He contrasts that with the Catholic view: nature, including human nature, is fundamentally good, and remains so, even though wounded by sin. The sinner, using his free will, need not sin, and 'consents and disposes himself' with the help of grace, for the further divine gift of new life in Christ.[41] Catholicity, so defined, is inclusive by adding works to grace for justification (as the Council of Trent did in condemning the Reformation).

The Catholic view of the universality of Christ's salvation provides possibility, not actuality. That possibility may be carried in two directions. It is either a treasury of grace dispensed by the church, or it has some saving significance for every human being. The first option was taken in post-Reformation Roman Catholic theology. The second is now emerging as Catholic thinkers find elements of grace in non-Christian religions, and make salvation possible outside the institutional church and even outside the response of saving faith.

The Roman Catholic concept of catholicity, framed in inclusive categories, does not flow directly from the transcendental fullness of Christ. Christ's fullness, as Paul's exposition of it shows in the letter to the Colossians, does not point the church toward inclusivism, but toward uniqueness. Christ's universal rule as Creator and his sovereignty as Saviour mean that he, and no other, is the Lord of salvation. His Word, given in the Spirit, as he promised, to the apostles whom he chose, is not to be moderated by human traditions. Catholicity does not tone down apostolicity. The Fourth World Conference on Faith and Order held in Montreal in 1963 defined catholicity in terms of theological pluralism. It was alleged that there is an 'endless pluralism in the Spirit's activity and in the conscious responses which have been made to that activity'.[42] Under the impact of the radical New Testament criticism of Rudolf Bultmann and Ernst Käsemann, it was held that because there are many theologies in the New Testament there must be room for many in the church. 'We are convinced that whenever awareness of this "catholicity" of the whole Bible is deficient, the conception of catholicity in the Church will be similarly deficient.'[43]

As John Hick and others have pointed out in *The Myth of Christian Uniqueness*, a simple extension of this reasoning takes pluralism beyond the concessions of the World Council of

Churches and of Vatican II to a total relativism that denies the uniquenes of Jesus Christ.

Catholicity is not a wide gate opening to a broad road, but that narrow gate to which the Lord of the church calls us. Catholicity means that the church is Christ's. We cannot exclude those whom he welcomes, or welcome those whom he excludes. No attribute has a more evident application to the church today. Sectarianism denies catholicity, for by its refusal to recognize other communions as true churches of Christ, it denies the fellowship that Christ requires. Protestants may point to the sectarianism of Vatican II, as it declares of the one, holy, catholic and apostolic church: 'This Church, constituted and organized as a society in this present world, subsists in the Catholic Church, which is governed by the successor of Peter and by the bishops in communion with him.'[44] Yet within Protestantism, denominational sectarianism seldom takes seriously the bonds of catholicity. In practice, many an independent Bible church or mission hall has its pope. True catholicism involves sincere and humble efforts to reason with the Roman Catholic Church where its leadership offers opportunity. Love cannot ignore the seriousness of error, but neither can it forget the power of the truth.

Racism also denies catholicity. Not long ago, white American churches stationed 'color guards' to bar black worshippers, directing them to a suitable congregation on the other side of the tracks. The church has often been put to shame by its failure to practise true catholicity and to condemn racial prejudices.

Catholicity is sometimes denied in more plausible ways. Advocates of the church growth movement have observed that churches grow faster if they restrict their evangelistic efforts to a homogeneous population. The seventeenth-century Jesuit missionary to India, Robert De Nobili, had great success by observing Hindu caste distinctions, and limiting his ministry to upper-caste Hindus.[45] It is not just in India, or in tribal societies, where caste distinctions are evident. Churches that begin with a strategy of evangelistic approach to a targeted population may end as a sect, defined not by the gospel but by society. Church growth has been successful under South African *apartheid*, but at a price.

Catholicity may be denied by defining a church's goals

specifically, as though a church might restrict itself to an emphasis on worship, or evangelism, or nurture. Much as such emphasis might be needed for a time, to correct an imbalance in the church's life and ministry, no church of Jesus Christ can be defined in terms of a specialty. Every true church of Christ is a manifestation of the new people of God, composed of citizens of heaven, not of devout people forming their élite club.

Catholicity must be precious to Christians, for it means submission to the Lord of the church. He alone can build it, and he chooses for his living stones not many wise, powerful, or wealthy. It is composed of losers – those who have lost everything for Christ's sake, but have found everything in him.

8

THE MARKS
OF THE CHURCH

The express train that flies up the eastern coast of England and Scotland to Edinburgh rolls by wide pastures of grazing sheep and wider vistas of cold sea. Villages flash by, sometimes guarded by a castle on the hill above. A spire marks every town or village, recalling an earlier time, when each town had a church – only one.

It did not remain so. Through this same country, armies marched in the Civil War. King and Parliament struggled over the government of the nation and the form of the church. In the end, a single form of religion for Great Britain was not to be achieved. Today we can no longer designate the church by the name of the town. Letters cannot be addressed, as the apostle Paul addressed them, to 'the church of God in Corinth'.

Church attendance has shrivelled, but church groups have proliferated. Some have separated from older church bodies, while others are newly organized congregations. Many cults claim the name of Christ. If the church is a religious country club, this merely reflects the comfortable pluralism of our democratic way of life. Let the minority who feel that religion is important join with like-minded co-dependants and call the organization whatever they please – within the range of decency.

For believers, however, the church is more than a voluntary club. It belongs to Christ, and he has warned us against false shepherds, whether they come from within or without. Some have formed organizations that consciously perverted Christian teaching and never were true churches of Christ. On the other hand, some churches were once Christian, but have departed from the faith. In the United States, the Unitarian Church has denied the deity of Christ. Although the Mormon church sprang from Christian roots, its founder Joseph Smith claimed divine revelation for new doctrines that superseded the New Testament.

More confusing are the churches whose basic beliefs are in flux. The headquarters of denominational churches have disseminated all manner of heresy, often to the distress and chagrin of congregations within their ecclesiastical fellowship. The glorified Christ said to the church at Sardis: 'I know your deeds; you have a reputation of being alive, but you are dead. Wake up! Strengthen what remains and is about to die . . .' (Rev. 3:1b–2a). The Sardis church was on the verge of spiritual extinction, but Christ still addressed it; it might yet recover. When does an apostatizing church become apostate?

How shall we understand the spreading parachurch organizations? Some are designed to supplement and assist the churches, while others appear to be churches in all but name.

In this welter of missions, house churches, fellowships, crusades and denominations, are there any criteria that will help us to distinguish true from false churches? Would such marks also help relate other Christian groups to what we may properly call 'the church'?

Like the catholicity issue, this is not a new question. In the third century, the Novatians separated from the church, judging it apostate because it readmitted penitents who, under persecution, had offered incense to Caesar. Only fellow-separatists would they regard as members of the true church. Augustine confronted the Donatist schism, in which separatists again claimed to be the true church, and viewed the Catholic church as apostate.

The Protestant Reformation made the issue crucial once

more. Polemicists of the Counter-Reformation regarded the attributes of the church as perfectly visible marks by which the true church could be recognized. How could Protestants maintain the unity of the church apart from the Pope who, as the Vicar of Christ, bound together the body of Christ? Did not the Apostolic See guarantee the apostolicity of the church in its uninterrupted succession from Peter? As for the holiness of the church, was it not established and maintained by the infusion of sacramental grace in the Mass, administered by the priestly hierarchy? Finally, how could the Reformers claim to be the universal church of Christ when their movement was not world-wide, but confined to the countries of northern Europe?

In response, the Reformers continued to affirm the attributes of the church from the Nicene Creed. They protested, however, against the external and institutional way in which the Roman Catholic apologists interpreted them.[1] As we have seen, they pressed for a biblical and spiritual understanding of the church's attributes. Above all, the Reformers emphasized the meaning of apostolicity. To be apostolic, the church must be built upon the doctrine of the apostles (1 Cor. 3:10–11; Eph. 2:20; 3:4–5). Not the pretended *chair* of Peter, but the *teaching* of Peter was the real mark of apostolicity.

The Reformation made the gospel, not ecclesiastical organ-ization, the test of the true church. Yet the Reformers, particularly in the Calvinistic churches, sought biblical standards for the organization of the church.

Three marks were defined in distinguishing a true church of Christ: true preaching of the Word; proper observance of the sacraments; and faithful exercise of church discipline.

John Calvin defined only the first two marks in his *Institutes*, but included discipline in the proper observance of the sacraments. He recognized that no church could perfectly match the Lord's pattern in Scripture, but his aim was to describe practical standards, standards necessarily more object-ive and stringent for the organized church than for individual believers. The ministry of the Word and sacraments is, he says, 'a perpetual mark and characteristic of the Church':

> That is to say, that wherever *that* exists entire and
> uncorrupted, no errors and irregularities of conduct

form a sufficient reason for refusing the name of a Church.[2]

Calvin allowed for errors in preaching, so long as the 'grand doctrine of religion is not injured' and the basic articles of faith are not suppressed. Irregularities in the administration of the sacraments do not destroy the church, provided the 'legitimate institution of their Author' is not abolished or subverted.

> But as soon as falsehood has made a breach in the fundamentals of religion, and the system of necessary doctrine is subverted, and the use of the sacraments fails, the certain consequence is the ruin of the church, as there is an end to a man's life when his throat is cut, or his heart is mortally wounded.[3]

Calvin compared the Roman Catholic marks of the church to the externalism condemned by the Old Testament prophets. The people supposed that God could never desert his temple (Je. 7:4), or reject his priesthood, but his judgment fell on those who rejected his Word. Priestly succession did not make Caiaphas a true heir of the promises when he betrayed Christ; no more does it authenticate a ministry that has forsaken the gospel for a religion of good works.[4]

The New Testament grounds the church in God's revealed truth. The apostles established the church by preaching the Scriptures and their fulfilment. The fellowship of the church in the book of Acts exists among those who continue in the apostolic teaching (Acts 2:42). The growth of the church is described by Luke as the growth of the Word (Acts 6:7; 12:24; 19:20). The ministries by which the church is built up are ministries of the Word (Eph. 4:11). The apostolicity of the church, therefore, means that the church is built on the foundation of the apostolic gospel. All other attributes of the church derive from this.

Seen as a doctrinaire commitment to formulas from the past, orthodoxy is scorned now in the religious world as well as in the secular mind. It is seen as chained to archaic ideologies insensitive to human need, and enforced in history by horrendous intolerance and oppression. Roman Catholic orthodoxy in Spain conducted the Inquisition; Reformation orthodoxy in Geneva burned Servetus. Competing orthodoxies in Europe devastated the continent for decades. In an age of rights, orthodoxy appears to violate all freedom of choice – which is much the way the serpent presented it to Eve: 'Did God really say . . .?' (Gn. 3:1).

Dreadful harm has indeed been done by those who have taken the sword in Christ's name, against his specific command. Yet the holocaust in Nazi Germany and Stalin's purges in the Soviet Union warn us of the even deadlier danger that lurks in the renunciation of a divine standard for thought and life. Without truth there can be no liberty, as the mind of modernity is belatedly beginning to discover. Roberto Unger has shown the bankruptcy of the liberal ideal of liberty: it cannot provide neutral and impersonal grounds for curbs on the liberty to do what you want.[5] Before the twentieth century began, Friedrich Nietzsche saw that abandoning Christian morality removes the framework of Western culture.

The teaching of Jesus delivers us from the tyranny of arbitrary law: 'My yoke is easy and my burden is light' (Mt. 11:30). Christ calls us to take the yoke of wisdom which is the liberating truth of the gospel, the knowledge of the Father that is given by the Son. 'If you hold to my teaching, you are really my disciples. Then you will know the truth, and the truth will set you free' (Jn. 8:31–32).

If Christian orthodoxy turns the joy of the gospel into sour legalism, then it is not really orthodox, nor is it the apostolic proclamation. The great mark of the church is in the message it proclaims: the gospel of salvation from sin and eternal death through the cross and the resurrection of Jesus Christ, who alone is the Way, the Truth, and the Life.

A preacher proclaiming the gospel in a market-place does not fulfil the New Testament description of the church, however. As Calvin affirms, the gospel must be heard and heeded as well as proclaimed. There must be a community of believers showing the root of faith in the fruit of love. Jesus promised to build his assembly, his community, giving new form to the people of God (Mt. 16:18). He said that his name must be confessed before men, and he made baptism the sign of discipleship (Mt. 28:19).

Those who say that church membership is not necessary, or

even that it is unbiblical, fail to grasp what the New Testament teaches about the church and the administration of the sacraments. Jesus accompanied his promise to build his church with the gift of the keys of the kingdom. Those who do not heed the final discipline of the church are to be regarded as Gentiles and publicans, that is, as outside the membership of the community (Mt. 18:17).

The lists of names in the book of Numbers give evidence of God's concern to define membership in his people; God's book of life is the archetype of the earthly register of his people (Ex. 32:32–33; Mal. 3:16). A prophetic psalm foresees the recording of Gentile names on the rolls of Zion (Ps. 87:4–6). The names of Euodia, Syntyche and Clement, recognized members of Christ's body at Philippi, are in the book of life, according to Paul (Phil. 4:2–3). Matthias, chosen in the place of Judas, is numbered with the eleven apostles; those who were added to the church were numbered with the disciples, so that total numbers could be set down (Acts 1:26; 2:41; 4:4). Significantly, the first total of three thousand is given in connection with baptism (Acts 2:41).

Baptism is recognized as the mark of membership in Christ's community by those outside it. Some Muslim communities tolerate conversion to Christian beliefs as long as baptism does not mark adherence to the Christian church. The Reformers, therefore, made the sacraments as well as the preached Word a mark of the church.

The question is not where *our* names are written, but where *his* name is written. In baptism we are numbered among the children of God, receiving the name of our Father, written, as it were, on our foreheads (Mt. 28:19; Rev. 14:1). To be sure, the washing of God's regenerating grace is accomplished by the water of the Spirit, not that of the font, but the outward sign functions precisely because it is outward; it is the Lord's visible seal of his invisible grace.

Some sects regard themselves as too spiritual to obey the Lord's command to baptize or to remember the Lord's death at his table. An advertisement in an American TV magazine asks, 'If Christian Scientists don't break bread or drink wine, how do they hold communion?'[6] The answer given is that 'their idea of communion isn't ritual. It's spiritual.' Two brief sentences curtly dismiss Christ's atonement, denying the gospel to which the sacraments bear witness: 'Nothing can draw God closer to man'; and the ancient formula of self-salvation remains: 'But by discovering the true meaning of Jesus' words and works, man can – and will – draw himself closer to God.' Jesus shows us how to do it, but we (with help from Mary Baker Eddy, the movement's founder) can find our own salvation. The advertisement ends with a taunt that reveals the real reason for the Christian Science rejection of communion: 'You may find communion a lot easier to swallow.'

If the church is identified by the Word and the sacraments, church discipline uses the keys of the kingdom to maintain that identity. Baptism administered apart from any creditable profession of faith on the part of those claiming God's promise ceases to function as a mark of the church. In the setting of a national church, it may become no more than a mark of national citizenship. So, too, the Lord's Supper may be so profaned by careless disorder as to lose its meaning in identifying those who partake of the one bread as one body.

Where do we draw the line in applying the marks of the church? Formulated church orders offer practical help, but they cannot be a substitute for wisdom and love – both love that is willing to overlook faults where there is zeal for the Lord, and also love for the Lord that recognizes his zeal for his house (Jn. 2:17).

The erosion of credal commitment has created a major issue for identifying the church. The Enlightenment view of the Bible surrendered its authority and undercut credal subscription. Liberal or 'modernistic' leadership radically altered the programmes and witness of many denominations. In some cases the credal standards of the denomination have remained unchanged, though considered a dead letter. Increasingly, though, the creeds have been amended. An escape from the authority of written Scripture was crafted in the Confession of 1967, adopted by the United Presbyterian Church, USA. The Confession altered the doctrine of Scripture found in the Westminster Confession of Faith, substituting the Barthian position that the Bible contains prophetic and apostolic witness to revelation, but is not to be identified with revelation.[7] The new Confession was included in a *Book of Confessions*, containing the Westminster Confession and other historic creeds. Under the revised constitution, officers of the church vowed to be guided by these confessions, but were no longer required to subscribe to any. The result of the change was that a minister denying the deity of Christ was confirmed by the same denomination that had earlier removed J. Gresham Machen from its ministry for refusing to resign from the Independent Board for Presbyterian Foreign Missions, an agency erected to send out only confessionally orthodox missionaries.[8]

Do such actions make a denomination apostate, no longer a true church of Jesus Christ? Certainly the official change of creed regarding the authority of Scripture put a knife to the throat of the church, to use Calvin's figure.[9] Since apostatizing is a process, individuals and congregations must judge as to its degree in relation to counter-measures for reform. Synods or assemblies may reverse decisions at later gatherings. And how do we discern apostasy in a congregation, as over against a denomination? Does denominational apostasy remove legitimacy from a gospel-preaching congregation? Denominational councils may be moving rapidly in a direction that would remove the church from its apostolic foundation, while particular congregations still resist efforts to deny to the Lord of the church the authority of his Word. No doubt the 'frog in the kettle' parable comes to mind. Unless local congregations and individual believers put loyalty to the Word of the Lord above loyalty to a denomination, the great mark of the church has already been denied. The issue is likely to be centred on the refusal of a local congregation to submit to unbiblical directives, or to condone heresy by silence and inaction. Contemporary churches need to hear again what the Spirit says to the churches in the book of Revelation.

We must still keep the marks of the church in view when we consider fellowships that do not call themselves churches. Many of these exist because of the denominational dividedness of the church. Mission agencies functioning in the Third World and on university campuses link members of many denominations. Publishers of Sunday School materials and of Christian books have created their own constituencies as they serve the educational ministry of the church. Indeed, even the preparation of candidates for the ministry of the Word has been undertaken by institutions that are not under denominational control. Churches worship with hymnals, song books and overhead transparencies from a wide variety of sources. Friction is inevitable, since such activities are also conducted by denominations. To whom, for example, does the overseas missionary look for direction? Is he first responsible to his mission board, to the church or churches that sent him, to the organization of his missionary colleagues, or to the national church on the field?

The church, shattered by denominational division, dare not label parachurch organizations illegitimate. In part, they are simply activities of church members. In an undivided church, there would be 'lay' organizations, under the broad oversight of the government of the church, but not the immediate responsibility of church officers. In part, they represent shared ministries across denominational barriers. That such ministries may be regarded as irregular in denominational polity may reveal more about sectarian assumptions in the polity than about violations of New Testament order.

Dangerous irregularities arise for both denominational churches and parachurch groups when they ignore their limitations. The limitation of the denomination (more serious than supposed) is that it does not give full expression to the body of Christ, and needs, therefore, the wider relations that parachurch groups help to supply. The limitation of the parachurch group is that it lacks some of the marks of the church. It needs denominations because it does not provide the ordered structure of office, worship, sacrament and discipline that a denominational church offers. Because such groups are not churches, they do not dismiss members to churches or receive them from churches, and rightly find no difficulty in recruiting members of denominational churches.

Some parachurch groups are moving toward denominational status. They baptize and celebrate the Lord's Supper, conduct regular worship services and set apart their own staff for ministry. The Christian and Missionary Alliance, for example, is a denominational church that was initially founded in the USA as a parachurch. The difficulty in such a transition is, first, whether a new denomination can be justified, and, second, the fact that the privileges of the church may be claimed even though the biblical requirements for the responsibilities of the

107

church have not been met. An example would be the kind of celebration of the Lord's Supper that is sometimes conducted during conferences and conventions. Gatherings of thousands of people may be offered the elements without the oversight that Christ has appointed for the church. To be sure, such celebrations are accompanied by the preaching of the Word, and mark for many a sweet foretaste of the final gathering of the people of God. If an adequate warning is given to those who might partake unworthily, some measure of discipline is exercised. Yet the service assumes that the conference organizers, who have no personal knowledge of most of those who attend, may welcome them and others to the table of the Lord apart from the order and shepherding of the church.

Perspectives on the church: visible and invisible

To define the marks of the church, we must assume that the church has a visible form, that it is organized on earth as an observable society. But is the church heavenly or earthly, visible or invisible?

The Bible certainly speaks of the church in heavenly terms. Chosen to holiness in Christ before the foundation of the world (Eph. 1:4–5), it is not to be likened to the kingdoms of this world (Eph. 1:23; 5:23, 32; Col. 1:18; Jn 18:36). It is the dwelling of God, built of living stones on Christ as the chief cornerstone (Eph. 2:20; 1 Pet. 2:5). Only the Lord knows infallibly those who are his, and they are joined to him by the secret working of his Holy Spirit (2 Tim. 2:19; Jn. 3:8).

The Reformers disputed the external description given by Roman Catholic apologists. It is *spiritually* that the church is one, holy, catholic and apostolic. Cardinal Bellarmine took no account of New Testament language when he said that the church was just as visible as the republic of Venice.[10] As Hans Küng points out, a church so completely visible would not be an object of faith ('I believe . . . the holy catholic church').

Yet the church is identifiable in the world. It has members and officers; its sacraments are outward signs of its faith and hope. It does, however, include hypocrites: in the New Testament as in the Old there are those of Israel who are not Israel (Rom. 2:28; 9:6). The wicked must be put away (1 Cor.

5:13); in a great house there are vessels of dishonour (2 Tim. 2:20). There are those, writes John, who went out from us because they were not of us (1 Jn. 2:19).

We can deny neither the visible nor the invisible aspects of the church. Limiting the church to its visible aspect erases the reality of God's election. Since the Lord knows his own sheep, given him by the Father, we may say that the church invisible is the church as God sees it. We hear words and observe actions; we can be deceived by hypocrisy, or fail to recognize true faith. God alone knows every heart.

A simple diagram of two overlapping circles may illustrate this. One circle describes the 'invisible' church, *i.e.* all the saints known to God, past, present and future. The other circle describes the 'visible' church, *i.e.* as it appears to us. There is a significant overlap. Many of the Lord's people are well known to others of the Lord's people (though Elijah felt that he alone was left, whereas in fact God had 7,000 others who had not bowed the knee to Baal, 1 Ki. 19:18). In the circle that describes the 'visible'church, however, but not included in the overlap, are all

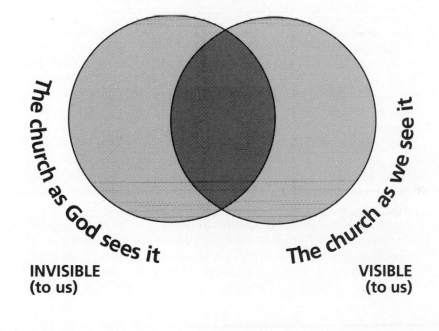

The church as God sees it

The church as we see it

INVISIBLE (to us)

VISIBLE (to us)

those professing Christians to whom the Lord will say at last, 'I never knew you.'

The Westminster Confession defines the church as visible and invisible, recognizing the two aspects, but speaking of them as distinct. The invisible church 'consists of the whole number of the elect, that have been, are, or shall be gathered into one, under Christ the Head thereof' (XXV.I). The visible church 'consists of all those throughout the world who profess the true religion; and of their children' (XXV.II). The sharp differentiation indicates that we can deal only with the church visible. By recognizing that, we will avoid the mistake of demanding dramatic conversion accounts from believers to prove their regeneration. Yet we must also recognize that it is God's knowledge that finally determines church membership. The hypocrite who reveals his fraud can take no refuge in his outward membership, much as its privileges may increase his judgment.

Evangelicals have often excused a deep neglect of the order of the church by emphasizing its invisibility. If only the church invisible matters, there need be little concern about the unity, holiness, catholicity, or even apostolicity of the church. Loss of concern for the church visible has also opened the way for reinventing the church. Assuming that the New Testament has little to say about church form, leaders trained in management have set about organizing it according to the latest theories of social science.

All this has been less disastrous than might be supposed. In spite of neglect of the church, the fruit of the Spirit among Christians has found expression in genuine care for one another. Parachurch groups have often accomplished what the Lord designed the church to do, providing nurture and encouraging evangelism. The Navigators, for example, were first organized to bring fellowship to sailors in the American Navy who were cut off from regular church attendance. The movement developed programmes of Scripture memorization, Bible study and personal discipleship that have since been carried over into many churches. In publishing this book on the doctrine of the church, Inter-Varsity Press demonstrates a concern for Christ's church that goes well beyond its ministry to Christians on campus. Christians active in the Universities and Colleges Christian Fellowship (UCCF) in Britain and in the

InterVarsity Christian Fellowship (IVCF) in the United States have experienced spiritual culture shock when they have graduated and taken their places in local congregations. They have missed the support and accountability of small groups in prayer and Bible study, the concerted efforts at evangelism, and the joy of singing psalms of praise together. The shock is less today, however, in part because former campus leaders have brought renewal to the churches.

The Bible does not give a detailed blueprint for all church order, but provides principles that find expression in the varied cultures of the globe. In applying those principles, studies of human behaviour are useful. Knowledge of small-group dynamics may help a leader draw out a person who fears to participate, or warn of the dangers of the premium put on consensus.[11] Yet the behavioural sciences cannot be the starting-point for the spiritual order of the church, for those sciences will not support the servant-leader's self-sacrifice that derives from the theology of the cross, or the appeal to the authority of the Word of God that marks all church order.

Perspectives on the church: local and universal

Just as the church is both visible and invisible, so is the visible church both local and universal. The invisible aspect of the church determines its earthly form. As the author of Hebrews tells us, in worship we gather with the festival assembly of the saints and the angels where Jesus is in glory (Heb. 12:22–24). Many or few, we gather here because we all gather there.

The church has long disagreed over whether the universal church or the local church is primary. The Roman Catholic Church has strongly advocated the primacy of the church universal.[12] In this view, local parishes are not so much churches as parts of the church proper. In contrast, congregationalism holds that it is the local church that deserves the name; associations of churches are not the church as such.

Both sides appeal to the New Testament. We read of house churches in the greetings at the beginnings of Paul's letters. All the churches of the Gentiles are grateful to Priscilla and Aquila, and Paul greets them, along with the church in their house (Rom. 16:3–5). In 1 Corinthians 16:19, Aquila and Priscilla are

111

in Ephesus, and the church in their house is sending greetings, along with 'the churches of Asia'. We read of a church in Laodicea in the house of Nympha (Col. 4:15), and in Colosse at the house of Philemon (Phm. 2). Paul mentions the house church in the same breath with the churches of the Gentiles, or of Asia. House churches are found in places where city churches are addressed (Rome, Laodicea, Colosse). Similarly, the 'church in Jerusalem' is spoken of (Acts 8:1), while the phrase 'from house to house' (Acts 5:42) refers to the teaching of the apostles in house-church fellowships.[13] The account of Peter's mission to the house of Cornelius indicates how a house church might be established among the Gentiles (note Acts 10:24, 27).

Further, the term 'church' may be applied not only to house and city fellowships, where the members could meet together, but also to the church in a province (Acts 9:31; 15:3). At the same time, Paul speaks, as we have just seen, of the churches (plural) among the Gentiles.

Finally, 'church' in the singular is used of the church universal (1 Cor. 10:32; 12:28; 15:9; Gal. 1:13; Eph. 1:22; 3:10, 21; 5:23–32; Col. 1:18, 24).

How can one term be used with such flexibility? Simply because it is not the geographical size or location that defines it. Even those committed to the local-church definition must ask which is the local church in the New Testament. Is it the house church, or is it the city church?

We do better to conclude that the church can be expressed at more than one level: in smaller or in larger fellowships, or even in gatherings like that in Jerusalem (Acts 15), representing the whole church, in order to deal with issues that concern all.

Perspectives on the church: institute or organism?

'Where is the church on Monday?' asks an author who raises the perennial issue of the relation of the organized church to the organic life of the body of Christ.[14] Does the Lord's assembly exist only when it is assembled? Or is it found only where its officers and staff are at work: in the church building, perhaps, where the pastor and staff are reviewing the Sunday services, or in a hospital room where a chaplain is visiting a patient

112

recovering from surgery? Does the church remain invisible except when members and officers meet in Christ's name?

Clearly the church visible does not vanish when no meeting is in progress, or when the staff attend to no 'official' duties. The church is present wherever its members are. One great gain of the Protestant Reformation was its recognition of the place of the 'laity' in the church. Rejecting the Roman Catholic view of a separate priesthood endowed with sacramental grace, the Reformers taught that all believers have priestly access to the heavenly sanctuary and to every saving grace, needing no other Mediator but Jesus Christ.

Vatican II gave eloquent exposition to the 'apostolate of the laity'.[15] 'Participators in the function of Christ, priest, prophet and king, the laity have an active part of their own in the life and action of the Church.'[16] This description seems to affirm the priesthood of all believers and to declare their prophetic and kingly offices as well. The patronizing tone of the sentence is not accidental, however. The thoughtful and extensive description of the functions of the laity is accompanied by unreduced claims for the 'apostolate of the hierarchy'. Lay people may participate in Christ's offices, but not in the bishop's. Only because the bishop is invested with 'the fullness of the sacrament of Orders' can he offer the eucharistic sacrifice, or ensure that it is offered, and it is from the Eucharist that the church derives its life.[17] The bishops have no authority unless united with the Roman Pontiff, and he, 'by reason of his office as Vicar of Christ, namely, and as pastor of the entire church, has full, supreme and universal power over the whole Church, a power which he can always exercise unhindered.'[18] For Vatican II, it remains true that in authority the Pope plus the hierarchy equals the Pope minus the hierarchy.

Partly through reaction to the hierarchical claims of the Roman Catholic Church, some evangelical churches have sought to remove all office from the church. Such a position is justified if 'office' means 'Orders', i.e. investment with sacramental gifts that other church members do not possess. This is not the New Testament teaching. Those who exercise special office in the church are those who possess gifts for teaching, ruling or showing mercy to a greater degree than others. The church needs to acknowledge such gifts. 'Office' in the biblical sense is a function that requires community recognition to be

113

exercised effectively. Later on, in chapter 14, we will discuss gifts and office, but the distinction between 'officers' and 'members' will help us to understand where the church is on a Monday.

The church is found where the saints are found, and where they are fulfilling their calling from Christ. The bane of clericalism has been the definition of the church, theoretically or practically, in terms of the clergy, or of the 'religious'. Even the term 'vocation' was once co-opted by this approach, as though only priests, monks or nuns were called by the Lord.

The right response to this error is to turn it on its head. Christ himself came not to be ministered to, but to minister and to give his life for many. Those who would be first in the service of Christ must have the same mind. As the Lord wore a towel, so all who would be leaders in the church must understand leadership as service.

The work of church officers, therefore, should not be modelled on the military or on big business. Officers are coaches, who train, assist and encourage the saints who carry out the calling of the church in the world.

That principle rights our present situation in two ways. On the one hand, it puts the calling of believers in its place. They are not at the fringes of the work of the church; they *are* the church, filled with the Spirit, doing its work in the world. As they better understand their kingdom calling, they will know that they are lights and leaven in the world, and that they bear spiritual weapons. Though heavenly citizenship does not bar them from belonging to earthly kingdoms, it commits them to discharge their duties and seize their opportunities as servants of Christ. As they take their calling seriously, they are likely to create more, not fewer, 'parachurch' groups. All Christians, whether homemakers, educators, statesmen, lawyers, doctors, nurses, merchants, artisans, labourers, counsellors or social workers, need to explore together the demands of their work. In every calling, the application of biblical principles can best be worked out by those who are daily confronted with its problems and opportunities.

On the other hand, when biblical humility turns the tables on clericalism, it does not create a new arrogance, a laicism that will tell those with gifts for teaching and for managing, 'We have no need of you!' Rather, as church members begin to take seriously their individual and corporate calling in the world, they will feel more keenly the need of the instruction and spiritual direction for which Christ has appointed under-shepherds.

The tension that is sometimes felt between the office of all believers and the special offices in the church is not a tension between worldly institutionalism and spirituality. As we have seen, the Spirit is the Author of order as well as ardour. If he brought order out of chaos in the work of creation, he will not reduce order to chaos in the new creation. When the apostle Paul calls for order rather than disorder or frenzy in the worship of the church, he is not quenching the Spirit, but seeking what the Spirit alone can give.

9

THE SERVICE
OF WORSHIP

The Lord does not ask for references commending us for his service. He calls us – not because he needs us, but because we need him. Yet we cannot know him without also serving him.

The church is called to serve God in three ways: to serve him directly in *worship*; to serve the saints in *nurture*; and to serve the world in *witness*.

For centuries, nothing was more fixed in Christendom than the form of worship. Priests recited the Latin Mass to uncomprehending parishioners assembled to receive the body of Christ. Today, nothing seems fixed: the varied styles of Christian worship reflect the patchwork of world cultures and the kaleidoscopic tastes of current entertainment. The church of your choice is the church that styles its worship to your beat. Evangelism drives change, wishing to make services 'seeker friendly', yet it can clash with the desire to make worship more participative, and strangers may demur at the hand-clapping exuberance of incantational choruses.

Before we divide the church over, for instance, obtaining a new chancel screen for the overhead projector, we need to reflect on what makes worship pleasing – pleasing to the Lord.

God's glory attracts worship

In worship, even now while here on earth we join the saints and angels in the festival of glory (Heb. 12:22–29). Because we gather with Jesus there, we are exhorted to gather with him here (Heb. 10:19, 25). God's assembly stands in his presence; to be the assembly, *i.e.* to be the church, is to worship God together. To say that God made us in his image is to say that God made us for himself, and that he made us to worship him. Worship is not an imaginative capacity, capable of projecting a satisfactory vanishing-point for religious emotion. Neither worship nor religion can be defined apart from God, for worship is the response of the creature to the revealed glory of the Creator. When the total abandonment and devotion of worship are directed to any lesser god, its very nature is perverted. This perversion initiates the downward spiral of idolatry that the apostle Paul traces (Rom. 1:18–32). Worship becomes depraved, not first in cult prostitution, or in rituals of blood lust, but at the point where human creatures refuse to acknowledge the only One worthy of utter, absolute, irrevocable devotion (Rom. 1:21–23).

The transcendent glory of God draws worship.[1] The heavens declare the glory of God (Ps. 19:1); our minds reel before the vastness of the universe. A 'major' earthquake that fills us with terror is less than infinitesimal when compared with the force that flings galaxies across light years of space, or holds them together in the wrinkles of background radiation. One short thunderstorm, a tiny moment in the atmospheric history of our small planet, can leave us breathless (Ps. 18:7–15). But God is exalted above *all* his creation; no cosmic process can disclose the immensity of his being or the infinite simplicity of his wisdom. The prophet Elijah was filled with terror when the hurricane flung rocks down from the mountains, and when the ground shook and fire fell, but God revealed himself in a gentle whisper; his mere word would accomplish the mystery of his design (1 Ki. 19:15–18).

God was present in that whisper to Elijah. He was present when he proclaimed his name to Moses: Yahweh, the faithful God, full of grace and truth (Ex. 34:6). If every word from God requires the response of worship, how much more must his *name*! The names given to God are symbols for worship: he is the Almighty, the High God, the God of Bethel, the Lord who sees (and provides), the Banner lifted over Israel. But above all, he is Yahweh, the God of the covenant, present to judge, but also to save his people.

Isaiah saw the Lord in the temple, enthroned among the flaming angels. With wings shielding their faces, they cried, 'Holy, holy, holy is the LORD Almighty . . .' Their cry was not the repetition of an assigned heavenly liturgy, but the ever-fresh response of these holy beings to wave after wave of divine glory sweeping over them. But Isaiah must groan, 'Woe to me!' God's holiness overwhelms a sinner with the condemnation of divine righteousness. It is well for Isaiah that he stands in the temple where God's altar is; he needs its cleansing fire.

The glory of the Creator appears especially in his saving deeds. The people of Israel sang the praises of the Lord on the shores of the sea where he delivered them from Pharaoh's pursuing chariots. The grand theme of the Old Testament is the final vindication of God's glory in the salvation of his people. Although they have wandered from him, and have suffered exile, he will save a remnant, then bring a renewal that will surpass all imagination, for he himself will come to save them. The Old Testament anticipates the worship of the day when every pot in Jerusalem will be as a holy temple vessel, and when King David will be the Lord himself, ruling among them (Zc. 12:8; 14:20–21). In that day, the Lord will deliver his people not only from their enemies, but from their sins (Mi. 7:18–20).

These promises are realized in the New Testament. Jesus comes, announced by John the Baptist, attested by his miracles, and revealed in the wonder of his teaching, the sternness of his rebuke and the tenderness of his compassion. As he drew near to the cross, his prayer was, 'Father, glorify your name!' (Jn. 12:28). John tells us that the name of God declared to Moses was revealed in Jesus Christ: he is the Word become flesh, full of grace and truth (Ex. 34:6; Jn. 1:14, 17). When Philip asked, much as Moses had, 'Show us the Father!', Jesus replied that he who had seen him had seen the Father (Jn. 14:8). Thomas fell down before the risen Jesus to cry, 'My Lord and my God!' (Jn. 20:28).

The overwhelming glory of God, revealed in the gospel, is the

119

glory of his grace. It is not just the transcendent power, wisdom and righteousness of God that demand our worship, but, above all, his love and mercy. The adoring church hymns praises that even the angels cannot sing, for only the church has known the divine love that bore the doom of lost sinners and gave them sonship with the Beloved. The height of redemption towers over its depth:

> And we, who with unveiled faces all reflect the Lord's glory, are being transformed into his likeness with ever-increasing glory, which comes from the Lord, who is the Spirit (2 Cor. 3:18).

The glory of the Lord that draws our praise becomes a blessing that increasingly transforms our existence, and that will finally make us like Christ.

God's will directs worship

God's glory *draws* our worship, and God's will *directs* our worship. God is a jealous God, *i.e.* he has burning zeal for the holiness of his name. He will not share worship with another:

> Do not worship any other god, for the LORD, whose name is Jealous, is a jealous God (Ex. 34:14).

God forbids the use of idols in worship (Dt. 4:23–24) not only because idolaters usually worship other gods, but also because God wants Israel to understand the form of worship that pleases him. God warns his people that when they have settled in the land, they must not enquire about the worship of the heathen gods, saying,

> 'How do these nations serve their gods? We will do the same.' You must not worship the LORD your God in their way, because in worshipping their gods, they do all kinds of detestable things the LORD hates. They even burn their sons and daughters in the fire as sacrifices to their gods. See that you do all I command you; do not add to it or take away from it (Dt. 12:30–32).

The Lord's warning is not limited to such practices as human sacrifice. Worship is made a special case; Israel is to worship God as he has commanded and in no other way. Israel is not forbidden to acquire farming or construction methods from the Canaanites; Solomon used builders and craftsmen from Tyre to construct the temple, following a design given by God. The Lord did not require distinctive houses or pottery. The praises of Israel could be sung to the music of the ancient Near East and in the poetic forms of its culture. Outward marks distinguished Israel as God's peculiar people, *e.g.* circumcision and the blue tassels worn on their shawls, but the distinctiveness of the law of God and the worship of God made Israel a light to the nations.

The Reformers, working to restore biblical worship, faced many of the same questions that we face today. Are there biblical norms for worship? Do the varying cultures of the world shape the way its peoples offer worship that is acceptable to God? Do God's instructions to Israel apply to worship in the New Covenant? The New Testament contains no book of Leviticus, nor any *Manual of Discipline* like that of the Dead Sea community. Does the freedom of the New Covenant therefore mean that the church's worship needs no scriptural authorization? Surely we must avoid anything that God has forbidden, but does that mean that everything else is permissible?

The Westminster Confession of Faith affirms that in worship, as in doctrine, the church cannot go beyond God's revealed will. No preacher, church or Pope can require Christians to believe what the Bible does not teach, or to practise in worship what God has not required.

> God alone is Lord of the conscience, and hath left it free from the doctrines and commandments of men, which are, in any thing, contrary to His Word; or beside it, if matters of faith, or worship.[2]

In the next chapter of the Confession the principle is applied specifically to worship:

> But the acceptable way of worshipping the true God is instituted by Himself, and so limited by His own revealed will, that He may not be worshipped accord-

121

ing to the imaginations and devices of men, or the suggestions of Satan, under any visible representation, or any other way not prescribed in the holy Scripture.[3]

This distinctive principle for the divine regulation of worship has been either rejected or forgotten by most churches today. James I. Packer, in rejecting it, parts company with the Puritan divines whom he understands and expounds so well:

The idea that direct biblical warrant, in the form of precept or precedent, is required to sanction every item included in the public worship of God was in fact a Puritan innovation, which crystallised out in the course of the prolonged debates that followed the Elizabethan settlement.[4]

The Puritan reformation did require divine warrant for every element of worship, and at times applied the principle in a legalistic way, but it was not a Puritan innovation. Calvin says of worship: 'First, whatever is not commanded, we are not free to choose.'[5] In the *Institutes*, he develops the argument concerning liberty of conscience to which the Westminster Confession later appeals. Calvin denies that the church has power to make ordinances for worship beyond what God has commanded. The church has authority to order worship (1 Cor. 14:40), but not to introduce new elements beyond those that God has provided. Appealing to Colossians 2:16–23, Calvin says of the apostle Paul:

But at the end of the chapter he condemns with greater confidence all self-made religion, that is, all feigned worship, which men have devised for themselves or received from others, and all precepts they of themselves dare promulgate concerning the worship of God.[6]

For Calvin and for the Westminster divines, liberty of conscience was the issue. Any communal activity requires direction, and corporate public worship is no exception.[7] The church, in its rightful sphere of authority, may order worship. But ordering worship activities that the Lord approves is not the same as adding those that he has not approved, especially since participation in public worship is not optional. The Reformers believed that the corporate exercise of devotion demanded conscious participation on the part of every worshipper.

Few consciences today would be violated by anything that happens in a church service. People think of the church as offering religious platform presentations: a pageant of some sort, or a speaker offering professional opinions on such things as stress reduction and family values. Participative services may be viewed as spiritual talent shows, or as large-group therapy. Sadly, churches have contributed to such misunderstanding by losing the awe as well as the joy of meeting God in worship. In the New Covenant we must not forget the lessons of the Old. God invites worship on his terms, not ours. The Reformers often reminded the church of the words that God spoke after judging Aaron's sons, the priests Nadab and Abihu, who had broken the law by burning incense with fire that had not been taken from God's altar (Lv. 10:1–7; *cf.* 16:12):

> Among those who approach me I will show myself holy;
> in the sight of all the people I will be honoured (Lv. 10:3).

Or, as the author to Hebrews tells us: 'Worship God acceptably with reverence and awe, for our "God is a consuming fire"' (Heb. 12:28–29).

Ordered freedom in worship

New Covenant worship is not free from awe in the presence of the Holy One, but is free from the rituals of the Old Testament temple with its holy place, its sacred seasons and its ceremonies. We saw that Jesus, in his conversation with the Samaritan woman at Jacob's well, announced the coming of the hour when worship at the temple in Jerusalem would lose its divine mandate.[8] Jesus is Immanuel, God with us; the destruction of the temple of his body was the ultimate act of desecration. Yet his atonement, accomplished on the cross, fulfilled the temple symbolism of entrance into the presence of God through

123

sacrifice. At his death, the veil of the temple was torn from top to bottom; the symbol gave place to the reality.

God's presence was no longer localized at the temple in Jerusalem, but in Christ himself. Worship must now be in the Spirit whom he gives and in the Truth that he is. Worshippers do not look to a place on earth, because they look to where Jesus is, at the right hand of the Father. This shift of venue to the heavenly sanctuary demands a shift from the ceremonial, the typical, the symbolic, to the spiritual reality of our coming to Jesus and his coming to us. This is the message of the letter to the Hebrews. The simplicity of the sacraments that Jesus gave to his church warns against our elaborating a form of worship that turns back to holy places, holy actions and the ritualizing of our meeting with the Lord. The heart of spiritual worship is hearing what the Lord says to us, responding to him in prayer and praise, and encouraging one another in his fellowship. Ironically, congregations that reject the required rituals of high-church worship sometimes incorporate into worship drama and dance devoid of the depth of the religious symbolism that is cherished in traditional rites.

Does Puritan simplicity, then, require a worship service that is reduced to dreary singing, a lengthy pulpit prayer and an academic discourse? Of course not, although a service so described might still bring glory to God's name and blessing to his people. Those psalms and hymns that are set to quaint tunes are rich with scriptural truth; pulpit prayers may storm the gates of heaven; and a preacher like Jonathan Edwards, while not really academic, was surely more weighty than brief.

How can the church find the freedom of spiritual worship and also escape both the laws of custom and the mandates of ritual?

The elements of worship described in the New Testament provide the key. They are not presented as a little black book of prescribed practices, but as dimensions of fellowship with the living God and his people. To appreciate the liberty of spiritual worship, we must make some distinctions.

The first distinction is between the *activity* of worship and the *attitude* of worship that undergirds our lives as Christians.

The story goes that certain Franciscan monks felt that their weariness during the 2 a.m. offices of Matins and Lauds would

124

be relieved if they could smoke. They addressed a petition in faultless Latin to the Roman Curia seeking permission, but were not surprised when, in due time, the petition was denied. When they later attended a gathering of religious orders with some Jesuits, they were astonished at Matins to see the Jesuits, to the man, light up! They protested, of course, pointing out that they knew that smoking was not permitted, because their petition had been denied by the Holy Father. 'Oh, but we, too, sought permission, and our request was granted,' said the Jesuits.

The Franciscans had trouble with this, and expressed themselves somewhat indiscreetly. 'Hold on,' said a Jesuit. 'What did you ask the Curia?'

'We asked if we could smoke while praying, of course!'

'Ah,' came the Jesuit reply, 'we asked if we could pray while smoking!'

The story, doubtless apocryphal, makes the point well. If we are to do all to the glory of God, and pray without ceasing, we must certainly keep tuned to God in the midst of all the experiences of our lives. Does this, then, remove all constraints from worship? Does the sanctification of all of life remove the necessity, and perhaps even the propriety, of special activities of worship?

These questions are most readily answered with respect to public worship. The apostle Paul instructs the Corinthians in the special nature of the Lord's Supper. He reminds them that they had houses in which to eat and drink, and that those who were treating the Supper as a common meal were despising the church of God (1 Cor. 11:22). If all of life is sacramental, the distinctiveness of the sacraments is lost. But the sacraments *are* distinctive, and so is the corporate worship of God, of which they are a part.

Perhaps we can best recognize the distinctiveness of the elements the Lord has appointed for worship by reflecting on one that he has not appointed: the act of sexual union. The marriage bed is honoured in God's Word; the union of man and wife is made a symbol of the union of Christ and the church. The Word of God blesses sexual union; indeed, it forbids continued abstinence on the part of married couples. Can this human activity, so absorbing for the whole person, so profound in its emotional roots, be made an element in corporate worship? It is quite feasible to do so; other religions have incorporated into worship sacred prostitution or the joint celebration of conjugal union. Something of the sort has been done in certain Christian communes; where in the Bible is it forbidden?

The simple answer to any proposal to use sex as an element of public worship is that God has not told us to do so. Further, it does indicate that there is a difference between what we may do to the glory of God and what we do in the special activity of worship. In the same passage where Paul warns against undue sexual abstinence, he also acknowledges the value of periods of abstinence in order to take time for prayer: 'Do not deprive each other except by mutual consent and for a time, so that you may devote yourselves to prayer' (1 Cor. 7:5).

In private, as in public, a worship activity such as prayer is distinguished from the regular activities of life. Though we do all to the glory of God, not all that we do is the special activity of worship. Our worship in the church together requires more order than does private worship. Yet both in public and in private, the same distinction applies between what we may do to God's glory and what we may do as an act of worship.

A second helpful distinction for understanding the freedom of worship that pleases God is the difference between the *elements* of worship and accompanying *circumstances*.

The New Testament gives us principles, not an order of service or detailed directions for conducting worship. Among those principles, however, is the command that 'everything should be done in a fitting and orderly way' (1 Cor. 14:40). Paul gave that direction to a church that had allowed worship to become chaotic and disorderly. He had given some specific instructions (for example, that two prophets are not to speak at once) but his general command indicates that they are free to arrange the circumstances of worship in a respectable and orderly way. (The term 'respect' appears also in 1 Thes. 4:12, where he asks that Christians live respectably toward outsiders.)

Calvin and the Westminster Confession carefully defined this area where the church need not look for specific direction in Scripture. In the words of the Confession:

> There are some circumstances concerning the worship
> of God, and government of the Church, common to

> human actions and societies, which are to be ordered
> by the light of nature, and Christian prudence,
> according to the general rules of the Word, which are
> always to be observed. [9]

'Common to human actions and societies' implies the many things that must be done in order to arrange and order divine worship that form no part of worship itself, but that reflect the culture in which the worship takes place.

The extent of this exception has not always been recognized. Many have forbidden the use of musical instruments to accompany singing, since instrumental music was not commanded for worship after the Old Testament period. But to accompany singing with instruments is surely common in our culture, and instrumental music is a circumstance, not an element in our worship of God. It helps to order our singing together.

Much controversy now surrounds the use of drama and dance in worship. The distinction between element and circumstance is helpful here. What is perceived as a circumstance will vary with cultures. There are no doubt cultures in which a leader conducting worship at a funeral might have to pause to allow for traditional expressions of grief. To do so would recognize a common circumstance; it would not introduce collective wailing to be required as an element of worship. The same principle applies to both drama and dance. The preaching of George Whitefield was dramatically delivered.[10] There is, however, a clear difference between suggesting actions and emotions in a manner appropriate to public discourse, and acting out roles in a performance. A preacher may ignore this distinction and attempt to turn the pulpit into a stage, but to do so substitutes entertainment for proclamation.

In New Testament times, drama was staged in the major centres of the Hellenistic world and was immensely popular. The apostles, however, delivered the urgent gospel messsage in direct teaching and preaching, not through the indirect communication of dramatic performance. We recognize the need for direct communication in situations of supreme seriousness. An American president would not air a dramatic skit to appeal for national support in a declaration of war.

Cultural circumstances do determine where the lines are drawn. There are cultures in which any story-telling involves more enactment than would be the case in our own. In such cultures, a greater measure of drama in preaching would be taken for granted as a circumstance rather than as an element in worship.

May dance also function as a circumstance, rather than an element of worship? We cannot fault an individual worshipper who beats on his breast as the publican did in the temple. So long as good order is maintained in congregational worship, there should be no objection to the spontaneous movements of individuals in their natural responses of grief or praise. Like the running and leaping of the healed lame man in the temple, there may be impulsive pirouettes of joy on the part of worshippers. Again, the customs of a culture help determine the bounds of good order. There are certainly cultures where joyful singing is normally accompanied by rhythmic or ecstatic bodily movements.

Yet the introduction into worship of dance as a performance or a symbolic ritual goes beyond any circumstance of worship. It has been made an element of worship in which all worshippers must be expected to participate, at least in spirit. The issue then becomes whether dance is an element of worship that the Lord asks of his New Covenant people. Those who affirm the place of dance in worship usually appeal to two verses in the Psalms, and to David's dancing before the ark as he brought it into Jerusalem (2 Sa. 6; 1 Ch. 15:25–28).

> Let Israel rejoice in their Maker;
>   let the people of Zion be glad in their King.
> Let them praise his name with dancing
>   and make music to him with tambourine and harp.
>   (Ps. 149:2–3)

Psalm 150 calls on everything that has breath to praise the Lord, in his sanctuary and in the heavens, praising him with trumpet, harp, lyre, tambourine, dancing, strings, flute and cymbals.

David's dancing was accompanied by musical instruments; perhaps he was playing one as he danced. Others joined with him in dancing. David's example is in accord with the language of Psalms 149 and 150. The link with the music of triumphant praise is clear, as is the context of theocratic war. The psalmist calls for Israel to exult in dancing, having the praise of God in their mouths and a two-edged sword in their hands (Ps. 149:6–7).

Although dancing is nowhere mentioned in connection with New Testament worship, are we to conclude that the Psalms and David's example establish it as an element of worship pleasing to God? David's dancing was connected with the carrying of the ark of God's presence into Jerusalem. The occasion was unique; if it were celebrated in later processionals, they too would have been centred on the rituals of the temple, and of the ceremonial law.[11]

Set in its cultural context, David's dancing appears to be a circumstance, rather than an element, in worship. In any case, the outward elaboration of the ceremonial law provided for ritual actions that now have a spiritual fulfilment for those whose worship takes them to the Holy Place of heaven. The reality of entering into the presence of the Lord in New Testament worship contrasts with every effort to incorporate entertaining performances in the public worship of God.

The elements of worship

The elements of the worship that the Lord asks of us are simple, but they are neither sterile nor dull.

Preaching the Word

The church is founded upon the Word of Christ given through the apostles, and the spread of the church is the spread of the Word. Just as the reading and preaching of the Bible mark the existence of the church, so they also mould its worship. We are seeing the power of Scripture anew as the Bible becomes available in communist countries where it once was banned. Even this recovery, however, can scarcely compare with the explosion of Bible preaching, translation and printing that propelled the Reformation. Luther, Zwingli, Calvin, Knox – all were biblical preachers.

There had been eloquent preaching in the late Middle Ages, especially in the monastic orders; the manuals of the latter have influenced the teaching of preaching to this day. Tetzel hawked indulgences with eloquence, but Luther countered him with gospel truth:

> 'Let the prophet who has a dream tell his dream, but let the one who has my word speak it faithfully. For what has straw to do with grain?' declares the LORD. 'Is not my word like fire,' declares the LORD, 'and like a hammer that breaks a rock in pieces?' (Je. 23:28–29).

The power of the preached Word transformed Europe, and it has now reached every nation on earth. Preaching lies at the core of worship. It is designed to present Jesus Christ as Saviour and Lord by telling the truth about his person and work. The response of worship must begin where it began for Isaiah in the temple – in an encounter with the glory of the Lord. Preaching that never evokes the response 'Woe to me!' is unlikely to bring about repentance and faith.

Public worship addresses God in the presence of his people; it also addresses God's people in the presence of God. Preaching is not prayer; it is not directed to God, but to God's people and to any who will hear the message. We have all heard prayers turn into sermons, as though the Lord needed instruction. Easier to understand is the preacher who interrupts his sermon to pray for grace, or to praise God for the light of his Word. Both preacher and congregation, however, must be clear as to who is addressing whom. Preaching is part of worship, not because of a sprinkling of prayers, or by the use of a special 'holy' language, but because both preacher and people know that the Lord is present among them, and addresses them through his Word.

Because the church is the Lord's assembly, and because the hearing of the Word of God forms and directs the life of the assembly, there can be no spiritual renewal of the church that does not restore the place and power of preaching. Paul's last charge to Timothy remains the Lord's word to the church in the twenty-first century:

> In the presence of God and of Christ Jesus . . . I give you this charge: Preach the Word; be prepared in season and out of season; correct, rebuke and

encourage – with great patience and careful instruction . . . (2 Tim. 4:1–4).

Prayer in worship

Prayer was so central in the worship of the synagogue that its
location was called 'the place of prayer' (Acts 16:13). In the shift
from the synagogue to the church (Acts 18:7, 11; 19:8–10), the
church meeting was also a gathering for prayer. Churches today
have increased participation in prayer during public worship.
Free prayer finds a place in some church worship where once
only prescribed forms of prayer were permitted; in evangelical
churches, prayer in public worship is seldom limited to clergy.

For the revision of the Roman liturgy at Vatican II, the
Constitution on the Sacred Liturgy advocated 'full, conscious, and
active participation' of all the faithful in liturgical celebrations.
But this goal was tempered by a limitation:

> In liturgical celebrations each person, minister, or
> layman who has an office to perform, should carry out
> only those parts which pertain to his office by the
> nature of the rite and the norms of the liturgy.[12]

Subsequent regulation permitted the participation of lay
persons as part of the 'Prayer of the Faithful' in the Liturgy of
the Eucharist.[13] The rubric for this prayer is offered by the priest
on behalf of the people, but specially composed 'intentions'
relating to local situations may be read by lay people. In the
Roman liturgy, the laity still participate in prayer principally by
mentally following the priest, and by reciting the hundreds of
prayers assigned to the congregation in the Masses for each day
of the year (the introit, gradual, tract, offertory, and communion prayers).

Evangelical practice has long been divided between that of
the Lutheran and Calvinist churches on the one hand, and of
the heirs of the Anabaptist reformation and of Pietist movements on the other. Luther, in his 'Deutsche Messe', put the
Mass into German and revised it drastically, but he still followed
a fixed pattern for the service, and continued the recitation of
prayers by the clergy.[14] Calvin at Geneva patterned the service
on that used in Strasbourg; again the prayers were repeated by

the ministers on behalf of the people. Participation by the people in these services was extraordinary.[15] The people heard the service in their own language, and learned to sing in that tongue the metrical psalms and hymns of the Reformation. There was, however, neither set nor spontaneous prayer by individual laity in public worship. Forms of prayer in the Lutheran and Reformed services used the rich heritage of the Catholic church with increased dependence on Scripture. To follow such prayers in understandable language was a glorious experience for those who had come to know the doctrines of God's grace.

In the medieval church, secular clergy and men and women in religious orders observed daily hours of prayer. Referring to the hours of prayer in the Old Testament and in Judaism, the church had always sought to practise times of daily devotion.[16] These had been formalized in the Quire Offices, carried over into Lutheranism and the Church of England as morning and evening services. In Geneva, there were morning services of Scripture exposition and prayer, but daily morning and evening worship was shifted to times of family prayer. The establishment of family prayers became a mark of the Reformed churches, and an anchor for the devotion of the New Covenant.

In this practice of family prayer, the Reformed churches resembled developments in the more radical wing of the Reformation, and in later Pietist circles. Anabaptist efforts to begin anew in worship rather than to reform the worship of the medieval church freed them to seek more participative forms of worship. Persecuted Anabaptist groups were forced to meet in small groups; others, like the Hutterites, formed communes to live together. Similarly, in Pietist groups, dissent from state church liturgies resulted in the development of smaller groups more akin to the house churches of the New Testament. In many different times and places, reaction against the clerical domination of worship led to free participation in prayer and praise on the part of laymen. The Plymouth Brethren movement later rejected all special offices. In their services for 'the breaking of bread', members with gifts for praying and exhorting shared leadership roles.

The greatest recent influence on the participation of church members in public prayer has been the spread of the

Pentecostal and charismatic movements. The claim to Spirit-given prayer, particularly in tongues, affirms for the church today the same experience as in apostolic times, and has therefore opened the way for any man or woman with charismatic gifts to pray publicly in worship, subject to the controls that Paul enunciated for the church at Corinth. Such participation is now also encouraged for others without a claim to utterance in the Spirit, and has influenced evangelical practice generally. Whether in formal or informal gatherings, fervent corporate prayer is the life-breath of Christ's church. 'Concerts of prayer' for spiritual awakening and world evangelization seek for renewal that only the Lord can give.[17] Prayer binds worship with nurture and witness, for we grow together as we pray with and for one another, and the mission of the church begins at Christ's throne, for the Lord sends out his labourers as his people pray.

Song in worship

The singing of God's people is another element that marked Old Testament worship and is explicitly continued in the New.

Music, it may well be pointed out, is not in itself an element of worship, but a way of praying, praising, proclaiming or exhorting.[18] Indeed, it is not so much song as poetry that sets apart worship in this form. We think of the Psalms as being the response of God's people to his revelation; Psalm 119, for example, celebrates the wonder of the law of God. In the book of Deuteronomy, however, God himself gives to Moses the song that Israel is to sing to him:

> 'Now write down for yourselves this song and teach it
> to the Israelites and have them sing it, so that it may be
> a witness for me against them' (Dt. 31:19).

Poetic response to God's saving works and words is also God-given, and it becomes, together with the law, part of God's witness to his people. The Psalms record a wide variety of poetry, presumably set to music for temple choirs or the people. Some are songs of individuals, especially psalms by and for the king. David, the sweet psalmist of Israel, identifies himself with his people in his complaints, his petitions and his praises. They, in

133

turn, identify themselves with him in his sufferings and triumphs. A single psalm of lament, like Psalm 22, may contain cries of abandonment, descriptive lamentation, confessions of trust, prayers for deliverance, vows of praise and doxologies calling for universal adoration. There are also 'we' psalms, where the people of God collectively engage in the same forms of lamentation, confession, petition and praise. The 'wisdom' psalms of instruction are sometimes arranged in acrostic form, presenting alphabets of memorable teaching and praise. There are royal psalms, acclaiming God's anointed, even celebrating the royal marriage. There are psalms of refuge, where the psalmist takes refuge from the false accuser in God's presence and pleads his innocence of the charges levelled against him (Pss. 7; 11; 71).

Poetry abounds throughout the Bible, both in God's solemn blessings and covenants, and in the prophetic promises both of blessing and of the righteous wrath of God that is to be poured out. These elements, picked up in the Psalms, form part of the songs in which God's people respond to him, encourage one another in his presence, and bear witness before the nations. In the praises of the Psalms, the nations are summoned to join in the adoration of God's glory and mercy. Psalm 96 exhorts God's people to 'Declare his glory among the nations, his marvellous deeds among all peoples' (96:3). Biblical evangelism is doxological, for we declare the praises of him who called us out of darkness into his marvellous light (1 Pet. 2:9).

Song is not only memorable but moving, expressing emotional depth as well as reflective breadth. In a passage that inspires devotion, God describes his joy over his people as that of a bridegroom singing over his bride (Zp. 3:17).

In the New Testament, Jesus Christ comes as the Son of David, the sweet singer of Israel, to reveal God's love. In the upper room, Jesus sang with his disciples before he went out to the Garden of Gethsemane. On the cross, he uttered the opening cry of Psalm 22, 'My God, my God, why have you forsaken me?' Hebrews attributes to Christ a later verse from that same psalm: 'I will declare your name to my brothers; in the presence of the congregation I will sing your praises' (Heb. 2:12; Ps. 22:22).

Jesus, who voiced the opening plea of dereliction, also utters the cry of triumph in the same psalm, and now sings in the midst of the congregation as he pays his vow of praise. Our triumphant King is a singing Saviour. He sings with us here on earth, and we with him in the assembly of heaven. Jesus is the heavenly Choirmaster, the Lord's Anointed (2 Sa. 23:1).

The apostle Paul presents Jesus as singing the missionary hymn to the Gentiles. He says that Jesus became a minister of the circumcision (in the sense that he was circumcised and fulfilled the ministry of Israel) so that the truth of God's promises might be confirmed, and so that, as God had promised, the Gentiles might glorify God for his mercy. Supporting his statement, Paul applies to Christ the words of Psalm 18:49: 'Therefore I will praise you among the Gentiles; I will sing hymns to your name' (Rom. 15:9).[19]

As Paul discharged his ministry among the Gentiles, he set them singing the praises of God, and thought of Jesus as leading their songs of joy.

Forms of poetry and of music vary both across cultures and across time. Hebrew poetry, because it is formed more on the play of sense than of sound, survives translation well, and the Psalms continue to influence the songs of the church. In fact, the variety of the Psalms encourages variety in song beyond what is usually found in our churches. When Paul instructs the church in praise, he tells them to teach and admonish one another as they sing songs with gratitude to God (Col. 3:16). In song we address God, but we also address one another, and our songs go out to the world. In a secularized world, 'Amazing Grace!' still bears witness; the Billy Graham evangelistic team has wisely used 'How Great Thou Art!', a hymn of adoration, as keynote for the music of their campaigns.

Paul exhorts the saints to teach and admonish one another in the wisdom that is found in the richly indwelling Word of Christ and the filling of the Spirit (Col. 3:16; Eph. 5:18–19), and maybe surprising is the fact that Paul instructs them to do so in singing. The advantage of song is that it implies a gathering as the *ekklēsia* of God, that it links encouragement and praise as the Old Testament psalms do, and that it enables us to concert our words to admonish and instruct one another. A theological student who was leading a song service once had his peers sing while standing in pairs facing each other. He may have rather misunderstood how mutual encouragement operates, but he did grasp the importance of the apostle's words.

Those who insist that the church should sing biblical psalms exclusively need to consider more carefully the apostle's words in Colossians 3:16 and Ephesians 5:18–20. It is the wisdom that is the enduement of the Spirit-filled church, taught by the Word of Christ, that enables them to admonish and teach one another; they do so in psalms, hymns and spiritual songs. Paul's expression shows that he is thinking of the wisdom that composes psalms, and therefore not of the psalms of David. Nor do his words refer to inspired compositions exclusively. The context of his use of spiritual wisdom in Colossians 1:9, his prayers for wisdom, and his charge to walk in wisdom show that he thinks of the wisdom of the Spirit as the daily need of every Christian, not a gift of revelation to bring the Word of Christ.

10

THE NURTURE OF
THE CHURCH

Let us imagine that the Pastoral Search Committee of Faith Community Church has adjourned its first meeting, having decided that they need to take two steps back in order to move forward. They agreed that Faith Church should have a mission statement, but there the agreement ended. John Goforth insisted that a mission statement is about mission, and that the Great Commission makes evangelism the task of the church. Marian Schooler was not so sure. Her argument was that infants can't procreate, and that a congregation with so many babes in Christ needs nurture before it can reduplicate in witness. James Pew thought they both had it wrong. 'The church serves the Lord in worship,' he said. 'Everything else leads to that . . . to the glory of his name.'

Readers who have served on such committees may find this piece of fiction familiar, but they may remember how similar discussions had broadened everyone's understanding of the calling of the church. The church serves God directly in worship (as we saw in chapter 9), but it also ministers to believers in nurture, and to the world in witness. Each activity is part of Christ's charge; each needs the others.

Nurture of Father, Son and Spirit

While the church cannot be defined in terms of nurture alone, it cannot be understood without it: God the Father instructs and trains his children; Christ teaches his disciples; and the Spirit equips the saints to serve the nurture of the body.

The simplest biblical image of nurture is that of parental care. Among the Thessalonians, Paul was 'like a mother caring for her little children' (1 Thes. 2:7). Jesus, the good Shepherd, charged his penitent apostle Peter to feed his lambs and tend his sheep (Jn. 21:15–17). Pastors are shepherds who watch over their flock and nourish them from the Word of God (1 Pet. 5:2–3; cf. 4:11; Acts 20:28).

Peter pictures 'living stones' being fitted into the temple of which Christ is the chief Cornerstone (1 Pet. 2:4–6). Paul combines the figures of building and growth, as the Old Testament often does, when he compares the church to a cultivated field and a temple (1 Cor. 3:6–15). Fruit-bearing is an evidence of life (Ps. 1:3; Je. 17:8), and a goal of nurture (Mt. 7:20; Jn. 15:2; Rom. 6:20; Heb. 13:15).

Paul's image of the body of Christ offers profound insights for nurture: all the members are needed; gifts are for the body as a whole, and isolation is tragic; and diversity of function produces not division, but unity (Eph. 4:11–16).

The nurture of the heavenly Father

In Israel, the early education of children was provided by the mother, who also continued to train the girls (Pr. 1:8). Older boys, however, were educated primarily by their fathers, who taught them the religious and national traditions, including the stories and poems of the Scriptures, and such passages as the 'Shema' (Dt. 6:4–9). They also learned their father's occupation by working with him in the fields or the shop.[1] The father was a teacher as well as a protector and provider.

As a Father, God delivered Israel, his first-born son, from Egypt (Ex. 4:23), and taught him to walk in the wilderness (Ho. 11:1–3). That journey was a long educational field trip (Dt. 8:1–5). God gave his instruction at Sinai in his law; so, too, his word directed the course of their journey. The declaration that 'man does not live on bread alone but on every word that comes from the mouth of the LORD' refers to God's words of direction (Dt. 8:3b). God taught Israel by proving them, in order to show what was in their hearts (Dt. 8:2). He also disciplined them: 'as a man disciplines his son, so the LORD your God disciplines you' (Dt. 8:5).

God's fatherly instructing, directing, protecting, providing and correcting are constant themes as psalmists and prophets look back on God's dealings with Israel, and promise greater blessings to come (Ps. 23; 32:8–9; 103:6–19; 119; Ho. 11:1–4, 8–11; Is. 63:7–19; Heb. 12:5–11). God's grace claims Israel as his child; his nurturing love seeks the response of delight in his goodness (Ezk. 16:4–6).

The prophets lament the sins of Israel, but declare that God's purposes of love will not be frustrated. God seeks his unfaithful wife (Ho. 2:14–23), and even God's judgments have a disciplinary purpose. He will restore and reclaim a chastened son. The tenderest descriptions of God's love for his people are reserved for the relation that God will renew when he himself comes to be their Saviour (Zp. 3:17).

The nurture of the Son of God

As Lord, Jesus Christ undertakes God's nurture, calling the burdened to take his yoke and learn of him, the Wisdom of God (Mt. 11:29). Because he alone knows and reveals the Father, just as the Father alone knows and reveals him (Mt. 11:27), the Son provides the teaching of the Father. He is the Lord in whose training and instruction fathers are to bring up their children (Eph. 6:4). He is the Master, whose yoke is the yoke of Wisdom incarnate. 'Come to me . . . learn from me,' Jesus says, 'for I am gentle and humble in heart, and you will find rest for your souls' (Mt. 11:28–29). Christians are people of the Way (Acts 24:14, 22), the way traced by the footsteps of Jesus (1 Pet. 2:21), who shows the way and is the Way (Jn. 14:6). Our way through the wilderness (Heb. 4:8–11) is the way of the cross, for Jesus our Saviour is also our example. Christ teaches us as we follow him: obedience opens our hearts to understand; understanding kindles our zeal to obey.

The Reformation recovered the distinction between what Christ did for us and what he does in us. We are justified before God, not because of what we have done, or because of who we are, but because of what Christ has done for us and who we are in him. Yet Paul's fervent preaching that we are saved by Christ's righteousness, not our own, was matched by his zeal for the nurture of those who had received Christ's righteousness. He agonized to present every Christian perfect in Christ (Col. 1:28–29).

The work of Christian nurture will languish without a passion for holiness like that of Paul. Churches may attract outsiders by being 'seeker friendly'. Then, when surveys show that new members are dropping out, another minister is added to guard the back door by following up on non-attending members. Through that experience, many churches have recognized that training in discipleship has to be the *regular* ministry of the church to its members. The great missionary apostle saw church growth as growth in grace, wisdom and fruitfulness, *i.e.* growth in Christ (Col. 1:9–12; 1 Thes. 3:11–13).

The goal of nurture is to grow to maturity in the image of Christ, in whom the divine image in creation is restored. Christ, the Second Adam, has subdued all things and filled all things, transforming and fulfilling the calling of Adam and Eve (Gn. 1:28; Eph. 1:21–23; Col. 1:15–19). Those united to Christ become stewards in a world over which he is Lord. Sharing the distress of a creation that is not yet delivered from disorder and frustration, they work in hope, anticipating the joy of the new heavens and earth (Rom. 8:22–25). 'New Age' ecologists suppose that the earth must be saved by identifying with it. They therefore call for a return to a romanticized tribal animism.[2] Reverence all life, they say, including vegetable life (but not, apparently, human life in the womb). They fail to recognize that unless humankind is distinguished from the world of nature, human ecological management has no warrant. The restoration of God's calling in Christ does not yet restore Eden, but it does commission us to be gardeners, not ravagers of creation.

The renewal of God's image restores us as heirs of physical life, called to guard the structures of family, sexuality, personality and society that defend life. Yet even that task cannot be attempted apart from the nurture of spiritual life in the church as a heavenly society.

Full maturity in Christ brings stability in faith; mature

Christians are no longer 'blown here and there by every wind of teaching', but 'speak the truth in love' (Eph. 4:13–15). Christians who have matured in faith have 'knowledge of the Son of God' (4:13), and are 'built up in love' (4:16). They build each other up; they do not tear each other down (4:13, 16). Such growth is a process: growing into Christ the Head continues until he returns. It is growth together. The church does not aim at producing a few certifiable saints for the media. It seeks the growth of the whole body through the function of 'every supporting ligament'. Every Christian has a part to play in the maturing of Christ's church.

Yet participation by every Christian does not mean an egalitarianism of gifts. Some gifts are needed more than others; some, to be effective, require community recognition. The very difference in gifts enables the church to grow as an organism. Paul would have the church respect the functional priority of gifts for leadership, but show even greater love and honour to those whose gifts are more humble, recognizing the role of weaker members (1 Cor. 12). After all, we take our livers for granted, but we fuss over our hair so that its minor role will be recognized.

Paul gives priority to the teaching function in nurturing the body of Christ. Christ 'gave some to be apostles, some to be prophets, some to be evangelists, and some to be pastors and teachers, to prepare God's people for works of service, so that the body of Christ may be built up' (Eph. 4:11–12).[3] Edification is the purpose of Christ's gifts, and teaching the Word of Christ equips the church for that growth (1 Cor. 14:12; cf. 1 Pet. 4:10).

Discipline also advances nurture, a principle that applies to the family of God, as well as to children in the home (Eph. 6:4; Heb. 13:17). The New Testament often warns against the threat of false teaching (Rom. 16:17–20; Rev. 2:5), and requires the church to exclude it (2 Jn. 10–11; Rom. 16:17), and to deal with immorality (1 Cor. 5:3–13).

The nurture of the Holy Spirit

Only by diligent quenching of the Spirit can Christian education in the church become dispirited and dull. When it serves Christ in more than name, Christian education is, however, the field where the wind of the Spirit blows sweet and strong from the dawn of the new creation. Where the Spirit of the Lord is, there is freedom (2 Cor. 3:17).

How we have abused the word 'spiritual'! First we starved it with fasts and locked it in monastic towers; then we dragged it out to pour sentimental syrup over its wan frame and cover it with romantic feathers. Viewing such a bedraggled creature, we think, 'Before I become spiritual, I would like to live a little.' Even the advertising world has done the word more justice, and automobiles with 'spirit' offer life and excitement. But the Spirit of God is the Author of life in the first creation, and he is the Renewer of resurrection life in the world to come (Rom. 8:11). Those who have the first-fruits of the Spirit have already tasted the powers of the coming age.

Paul contrasts the life of the Spirit with intoxication. It is more, not less, exuberant, and knows none of the stupor of drunkenness. In the Spirit there is no opposition between nature and grace. The Spirit transforms the whole person, not merely the 'spirit'. Thus, Samson's strength is the gift of the Spirit; our Lord's body was conceived of the Spirit in the womb of the virgin.

'Come, Creator Spirit!' is a prayer for Christian education. To trace the work of the Spirit in creation and history is a spiritual task. To praise God with the labours of our hands from the field, the laboratory, the factory and the study is spiritual service. We do all to the glory of God. While not all that we do is worship in the special sense, and while not all is under the direction of the officers of the church, yet the whole life of the Christian grows in the service of Christ, and is a life of spiritual nurture.

The Spirit of life is also the Spirit of truth, and he brings together what secular education routinely separates. The dilemma of contemporary education is the contradiction between science and freedom. Science seeks to programme everything, but people would be free. Our conquest of nature has reached out into space, but it has also turned in upon human nature. Social engineering imagines controlling the minds of the living, shaping the genes of the unborn, and even freezing the dead for a scientific resurrection. Perfect liberty for science becomes perfect tyranny for humankind, for when humankind is free to determine everything, then humanity will be determined by those who control the crucial moment.[4]

Today, the secular mind, recoiling from the possibility of a Nazified science, turns instead to an irrational mysticism that shrouds another tyranny: possession by dark spirits.

The wisdom of the Spirit does not offer a supplement to the human mind, but challenges its autonomy at the roots. Knowledge that knows not God is folly, for the fear of the Lord is the beginning of wisdom. We are not computers, nor is wisdom only data-storage and problem-solving. Fellowship with the living God, and with the Spirit who searches the deep things of God, frees us to seek and possess knowledge. Such spiritual wisdom combines theory and practice, word and life.

The goal of nurture

The goal of the triune nurture of the church is found in God himself. It is to *know* the Lord, to *do* the Lord's will, and to *be* like the Lord.

1. Nurture in knowing the Lord

To know the Lord in the biblical sense means much more than to have information about him. Paul says, 'I know whom I have believed' (2 Tim. 1:12). His knowledge is that of saving faith, described by Jeremiah as the knowledge given in the New Covenant with the forgiveness of sins (Je. 31:33–34). Faith begins with the *truth* of God that replaces the darkness of *error;* faith *assents* to that truth, in contrast to the *illusions* of unbelief that rest on error; saving faith commits itself to the true God in *trust* that replaces the *idolatry* of unbelief. This trust defines faith, for the demons know the facts to be true – and shudder (Jas. 2:19).

Paul speaks of the legalistic self-righteousness that once fired his zeal to persecute the church. Now all that he once treasured he finds worthless, compared to the 'surpassing greatness of knowing Christ Jesus my Lord, for whose sake I have lost all things' (Phil. 3:8). To know Christ, Paul says, is to be found in him, to have Christ as his representative, paying the price of sin and bringing him to glory (3:9). It is also to know the power of Christ's resurrection, and to have fellowship with Christ as he shares in suffering for Christ, 'becoming like him in his death' (3:10).

For Paul, therefore, to know Christ included not only

confessing his deity (Phil. 2:6; Col. 1:15–16; Rom. 9:5), and trusting in his saving work, but also experiencing Christ's presence in his heart through the Spirit (Col. 1:27; Rom. 8:9–10). Suffering deepened that experience. Paul well knew that Christ's sufferings for him, and not his sufferings for Christ, atoned for his sin. Yet by following the Saviour in the way of the cross he found deep, even joyful satisfaction. Indeed, he served the Lord as his suffering servant who was made a light to the Gentiles (Is. 49:6, 8; Acts 13:47; 2 Cor. 6:2; Is. 52:15; Rom. 15:12). Knowing that Jesus had predicted a limit to the predicted woes of the Messianic age (Dn. 12:1; Mk. 13:19–20), Paul willingly accepted his sufferings, ready to carry more than his share for the church as Christ's body (Col. 1:24).[5]

But although Paul's ministry was unique, he calls on the church to join him in taking the cross, imitating him as he imitated Christ (1 Thes. 1:6; 2:14; 1 Cor.10:33 – 11:1).[6] To imitate the apostle is to say with him, 'To me to live is Christ and to die is gain!' (Phil. 1:21).

The knowledge of the Lord grounds all other knowledge in what the Bible calls wisdom. Reflection on God himself leads the psalmists to praise; reflection on God's revelation in the world develops wisdom. King Solomon was a scientist, studying botany from the cedar to the hyssop, and biology from soaring eagles to snails, snakes and fish (1 Ki. 4:33). He also analysed human behaviour and collected and wrote thousands of proverbs to summarize his findings. Solomon failed, however, when he became wise in his own eyes and forsook the law of the Lord. Nurture seeks growth in wisdom: knowing how to make daily decisions in the presence of God and the wisdom of the Spirit. You prove in practice that which pleases the Lord: learning his way as you drive your car, listen to the news, work at the office or talk with the family at dinner (Rom. 12:2). Paul emphasizes the importance of seizing opportunities to further the progress of the gospel (Eph. 5:15).

2. Nurture in doing the Lord's will

Knowing the Lord and gaining his wisdom cannot be separated from doing the Lord's will. The commitment of saving faith is a pledge of obedience. Christ calls disciples to follow him; those who find parents, children or possessions dearer than Christ

144

cannot enter the kingdom of heaven. When Paul speaks of the obedience of faith, he in no way obscures the fact that faith is trusting and receiving, not performing or meriting; but he affirms that faith involves conversion, turning from the service of one master to the service of another.

Heeding Christ's call marks the start of nurture; obedient faith marks growth to maturity. The author of Hebrews laments his readers' infantile lack of understanding (Heb. 5:11–14). They have not trained themselves to distinguish good from evil. The term for 'training' appears in the English word 'gymnast'. Maturity is gained, not just by compiling information, but by exercise, by living out doctrine in choices of obedience.

God nurtures his children through a process of proving as well as of instruction. Even Jesus, in his human nature, learned obedience through the things he suffered. God led Israel through the wilderness by a way designed to prove them. To serve the Lord in his work of nurture, we must take account of his curriculum in the lives of his people together and individually. Church education cannot be standardized to 'process' age groups from nurseries to nursing homes. It must enquire where people are in their pilgrimage, and what God is teaching them.

Paul teaches much about 'proving' the will of God. Proving is the path to wisdom. It brings understanding and obedience together, so that each deepens the other. We who build on the apostolic foundation have that revelation in Scripture, but we do not receive direct revelation as the apostles did, nor can we enquire of the Urim and Thummim in the breastplate of the high priest. We are called to prove in obedient experience what God has told us is pleasing to him. Such learning does not require infallible choices. God knows our weakness, and teaches us by our mistakes. He may show us our lack of commitment, or our failure to understand a scriptural principle, or the situation to which it was applied. Meanwhile, the Lord's hand on us makes even our mistakes work for our good.

God's nurture, as we have seen, includes correction. Without chastisement, his fatherly love would not be evident (Heb. 12:5–10). The church must not abandon its responsibility for discipline (Heb. 13:17), discipline that does not begin with official censures or excommunication, but with the personal accountability that exists among brothers and sisters in the Lord. But rigid authoritarian control exploits the fellowship of believers in a sectarian caricature of the church – Jim Jones's 'People's Temple' or the tragic community of David Koresh in Waco, Texas.[7] Leaders pervert discipleship when they make others *their* disciples. Jesus made it abundantly clear that those who would be 'first' must seek not prominence, but servanthood (Mt. 20:25–28).

Leaders who dominate others deny freedom of conscience in the Lord, directing lives by commandments that go beyond Scripture. Sometimes church covenants or by-laws legislate new rules, or alleged prophets or a prayer council may claim new revelation. It is not only the cults that attempt such control. Unaware of the power-seeking that underlies this abuse, some leaders presume to direct the lives and choices of others. They make their clients dependent on them and stunt their growth to maturity. Wise counsel provides scriptural precept and personal example, not manipulative control.

The Christian proves God's will in daily life by using natural and spiritual gifts to God's praise. Christian nurture aids God's servants in seizing opportunities to discover what their gifts are, and where to use them. While over-directedness has moved some Christian churches toward the cults, other churches have erred by indifference, or have supposed that Christian nurture applies only to spiritual gifts, or to serving at church suppers. Too often the church offers counselling only to those whose lives or marriages are already shipwrecked. Parents receive little or no assistance in the vocational guidance of their children. Educational and career choices are made under the direction of secular guidance counsellors who are unaware of the Christian origin of the very term 'vocation'.

3. Nurture in being like the Lord

Finally, nurture means growth not only in knowing the Lord and in doing his will, but in *being like him*.

Giving new life in Christ, the Spirit renovates our whole being. In the mid-seventies, Lawrence O. Richards gave a fresh start to Christian education in the United States with his *Theology of Christian Education* (Grand Rapids: Zondervan, 1975). Using the Gospel of John in particular, he defined the church as a community that shared the divine life, and was therefore called to make disciples by modelling the personal relationship of love. He insisted on the need for sound doctrine, but his use of *life* in John's Gospel suggested that a companion book could be written using the other pillar of John's Gospel, the *truth* in Christ. The written word of God is life-giving, the out-breathed word of the Spirit that gives new birth to the people of God (Jn. 6:63). Spiritual nurture, because it is God's own maturing of his children, is always growth in love toward him, love illumined by understanding what he tells us about himself.

Richards no doubt sought to correct the one-sided approach of traditional Christian nurture. Even when he wrote, however, most evangelical churches had abandoned the view of Christian education as indoctrination. The pendulum had swung far from arid intellectualism. Churches once 'fundamental' with reference to their basic orthodoxy are now more likely to be known as 'new life' congregations. The threat to Christian nurture now comes from the other extreme: the loss of ordered instruction in the Word of God.

Traditional 'Sunday School' moralism remains a problem, however, even in churches committed to evangelism. Teaching often consists in admonitions to be good, offered to restless children who already know the rules. The gospel is good news because Jesus Christ has the power to save and to renew. Only a Christ-centred message is a life-changing message. This is not to say that Christians have no need of instruction in the Ten Commandments. On the pop MTV channel in the United States, a 'special' concluded that 'The seven deadly sins are not evil acts but, rather, universal human compulsions that can be troubling and highly enjoyable.' Laurin Lazin, the producer of the programme, said she liked the topic because it dealt with human impulses and not a set of rules, like the Ten Commandments.[8] Against the climate of our age, children need to learn that sex must be pure before God, and not simply safe, in order to be OK. But to know the Bible's morality does not in itself bring either repentance or new life. To change our lives, the commandments must be heard as God's voice, spoken in God's plan to point us to Calvary.

Nurture in Christ is not a self-improvement programme to build self-esteem. The esteem we cherish is not self-esteem, but

147

our Father's esteem, extended to us not because we deserved it or earned it, but because in love he claimed us. True, we were made in his image, but like the prodigal, we had forfeited all the rights of sonship. The Father's amazing grace claimed us while we were without hope and without God in the world. God loved us enough to give his Son for us, and he loves us still. Nurture is rooted in our new position in Christ. Without hope there cannot be growth; without a new identity there is nothing to hope for.

God's royal grace that chose us in Christ before the foundation of the world brings us into a new status. We are all, male and female, sons in the Son (Gal. 3:28). That grace draws us to follow Christ's example and to reflect the same love. Knowing how we were forgiven and why, our righteousness must be like the righteousness that redeemed us – vastly more than just: overflowing with mercy and grace.

To be like Jesus, then, is to follow in the way of the cross, in the life of sacrificial love. Such righteousness is not reserved for apostles and for a few world-class saints: it is the calling of every believer. Peter asks it of servants of cruel masters, of husbands toward their wives (as well as of wives toward non-Christian husbands); Paul asks it of the Thessalonians as the Lord makes their love abound toward one another and toward everyone (1 Pet. 2:18 – 3:8; 1 Thes. 3:12–13). Indeed, they are not only to build one another up, to support the weak and be patient toward all, but they are to see that no-one returns evil for evil (1 Thes. 5:15). The apostles teach what Jesus taught in the Sermon on the Mount: the ethics of salvation by free grace.

The new life in Christ is a life of love, not 'sloppy *agapē*' – not sentimental gush, but strong sacrificial love, ready to pay the price of service. Cultivating such love requires practice, but it must flow from the deepest spring of devotion to Christ. More the fruit of prayer than of programmes, it is gained in obedience as the church serves the prisoner and the outcast, the lonely and the friendless, the forgotten in London, New York and Mexico City, the lost in Bangladesh, the starving in Africa – yes, and the neighbours across the street, those in the suburbs who have found no higher goal than money and amusement.

Church, home and school in nurture

In the Bible, parents are given a special responsibility: they are to bring up their children in the nurture and discipline of the Lord (Eph. 6:4). As their Creator, God claims the children, who bear his image and name: all life is his gift. In the Old Testament the first-fruit of the field and the flock was to be returned to God to acknowledge that all was given by him, and that his claim was on all (Ex. 13:12; Dt. 26:2). His most precious gift was children: 'Lo, children are a heritage of the LORD; and the fruit of the womb is his reward' (Ps. 127:3, ASV). That truth echoes in the names of many of our children, names that mean 'God-given': Theodore, Dorothy, Nathanael, Jonathan. God granted children to barren women, marking his grace in the history of salvation. Aged Sarah, Leah and Hannah all had special reason to thank God for his gift, and all pointed toward God's ultimate Gift to the Virgin.

The Lord claims the children not only as their Creator, but as their Redeemer. Since we and our children are alike sinners, God could claim us all in judgment. When that judgment was threatened against the first-born sons of Egypt, the sons of Israel could not be excluded. Through God's mercy, however, the avenging angel passed over the Israelite houses that had put the blood of the lamb on the doorposts. The first-born sons of Israel therefore belonged to God both by creation and by redemption (Ex. 12:26ff.). Mosaic legislation drove this point home. God continued to claim the first-born for himself as a sign that all belonged to him. That claim could be met by the Levites, given to the service of God in the place of the first-born sons of Israel. When the number of the first-born exceeded the number of the Levites, God instructed the Israelites to buy back their sons with the payment of five shekels (Nu. 3:40–51; 18:15–16). Christ himself met God's claim on the first-born when he was presented in the temple (Lk. 2:22–24).

When Israel followed heathen customs of ritual infanticide, God accused them: 'You slaughtered my children and sacrificed them to the idols' (Ezk. 16:21). In his promise of the great restoration, God said he would gather his sons from far and his daughters from the ends of the earth – 'everyone who is called by my name, whom I created for my glory, whom I formed and made' (Is. 43:7).

Jesus gathered the little children in his arms to bless them, *i.e.* to name God's name upon them in blessing (Mt. 19:13–15; Mk. 10:13–16; Lk. 18:15–17). He set a little child in the midst and said, 'For the kingdom of heaven belongs to such as these' (Mt. 19:14; Mk. 10:14; Lk. 18:16).

This special claim of God upon the children in his family underlies his charge for their nurture, a charge pointedly made to parents in both the Old and New Testaments. Bringing up children in the nurture of the Lord means acknowledging that they belong to him, and that he is bringing them up. As Jesus grew, that divine favour was evident: 'And the child grew and became strong; he was filled with wisdom, and the grace of God was upon him' (Lk. 2:40, 52).

Our total dependence on God's grace in this nurturing task does not eliminate accountability. Judgment awaits those who cause one of his little ones to fall into sin (Mt. 18:6).

To accomplish their task, parents are given authority over their children. Paul commands nurturing, but warns fathers not to abuse their authority so as to provoke resentment (Eph. 4:6). Parental authority does not mean that children belong to their parents. Neither in the womb nor out of it do parents have the right to dispose of their children as they wish; children are not exploitable property. Yet parents must exercise responsible authority, and the Lord commands children to obey their parents in him. Even Jesus was subject to his parents (Lk. 2:51). As his example shows, however, obedience to the heavenly Father comes first.

The promise of God's covenant with Abraham includes Abraham's responsibility to teach and direct his children and his household (Gn. 18:18–19) The famous Shema in Deuteronomy shows how household nurture was to be conducted:

> These commandments that I give you today are to be upon your hearts. Impress them on your children. Talk about them when you sit at home and when you walk along the road, when you lie down and when you get up. Tie them as symbols on your hands and bind them on your foreheads. Write them on the door-frames of your houses and on your gates (Dt. 6:6–9).

Such nurture goes far beyond formal instruction. The passage describes a life saturated with the Word of the Lord. Late and early, at home and on the road, God's law is a subject of conversation; it governs all thought and action. In the vastly different settings of contemporary life, how can parents provide such nurture?

Totalitarian systems always control education. Eastern European communist regimes imprisoned dissident parents and put the children in state-operated facilities for re-education. Western democracies still respect the precious right of parents to provide for the education of their children. Only as this right is exercised can it be preserved. Parents may still provide the environment for nurture that Deuteronomy describes. They are free to engage in home schooling, or to join forces with other Christian parents to establish and support Christian schools. When public education reflected Christian values, the need for distinctively Christian education was less evident. Now, however, public education has changed radically in the United States, and is changing in Britain. Secularism has driven all Christian religious instruction from public schools in America, and has substituted, in the name of moral education, its own religious values. At the same time, the identification of democracy with religious pluralism has led to a dogmatic insistence on the mythical character of all religions and to deep intolerance of any religion that claims absolute truth. Biblical teachings about sexual conduct and family structure are now viewed by the educational establishment as biases destructive of liberty. The National Education Association in the United States condemns home schooling programmes and demands that every teaching parent be licensed by the state and use a curriculum approved by the state.[9]

With the collapse of the family now taking place, the state school understandably sees itself as the only provider of the nurture that is so desperately needed. We must be thankful for teachers, including thousands of committed Christians, who face physical danger and frustration standing in the gap. We must understand, too, why liberal educators propose measures to broaden public education and to remedy social ills as they see them. We dare not forget God's common grace, still richly poured out on nations that deserve his judgment. Yet the effort

151

to claim for public education the work of nurture that families and churches owe to their children is an effort that can only destroy liberty and create the idolatrous cult of the state.

Christian education does not seek flight from the world, fearfully protective, like the home-school mother in the US who bought herself roller-blade skates so that she could spy on her children when they played with their public-school neighbours. The education we offer our children prepares them not only to face the anti-Christian forces of modernity and postmodernity, but also to understand our culture and to love those who do not share the faith. Through participation in community programmes, athletic and social, it seeks not to shield children from the world, but to prepare them for their calling in it. All this is part of the nurture of the Lord.

The Lord who entrusts his children to parents also entrusts them to the church. Pastors of the church have a special responsibility to the lambs of the flock. The Reformers took seriously the instruction of children: Luther's catechism provided for instruction by pastors. The Sunday School, first established by Robert Raikes in Gloucester, England, in 1780, opened a teaching function for lay men and women, aimed initially at evangelism and literacy. In America especially, the Sunday School has become the educational division of the church, with classes for all. The immense investment in plant and equipment has also opened the way to church day schools.

Churches run schools from kindergarten to denominational colleges and universities. Since the Bible commits the full training of youth to parents and not to those who govern the church of Christ, and since the church teaches the gospel and not physics, biology, or literature, Abraham Kuyper and others have favoured parental control rather than church control of general education. Charles Hodge, the American Presbyterian theologian, was prepared, however, to support church control of general education, provided that its educational direction and operation was given to educators and not to church governors. The relation of the spiritual overseers of the church to the activities of church members banded together for family nurture should be sympathetic and supportive, and ready to provide counsel, but should not be directive in the operational aspects of the school.

Whether the school be parent-controlled or under church sponsorship, it must reflect the biblical nurture we have sought to trace. Nurture is instruction, opening doors of knowledge on the truth about the world and the Lord. Nurture is proving, guiding Christ's youth in doing. Nurture is caring: offering both challenge and protection for growth in being. The school is rightly a shelter, a place for friendship, where students are known by name, where their identity is established among the people of God, and where their calling to serve the Lord is heard.

Christian education in the school and in the church prepares for courageous conflict and loving engagement, not just in the future, but daily. This world is the Lord's; his children, young and old, need not fear to face it with the hope and message of his gospel.

11

THE MISSION OF
THE CHURCH

The Lord who calls his church to worship and to nurture also sends it through the centuries and across the continents to witness for him.

The ecumenical movement that took form in the World Council of Churches began with mission conferences.[1] Under liberal leadership, however, missionary interest shifted radically. As early as 1928, the International Missionary Council, meeting in Jerusalem, was debating the 'why' of missions and discussing the merit of synthesizing Christianity with other religions in order to form a world faith. Debate continued at Madras in 1938, between Ernest Hocking, an advocate of religious synthesis, and Hendrik Kraemer, who defended a dialectical theology of revelation in which a 'No' as well as a 'Yes' must be directed to all world religions.[2]

In the sixties, the WCC developed the theology of the 'servant church', affirming that the church does not *have* a mission, but *is* mission: that the church exists only in mission.[3] For this view, the symbol of the WCC is singularly inappropriate: the church is not an ark of the saved delivered from a flood of judgment. Rather, it is the company of those who know that the whole world is saved, and can declare the world's salvation.

Predictably, the question became, 'What *is* the mission of the church?' At the 1966 World Conference on Church and Society in Geneva, it was said that the church's mission was to carry forward the work that God was doing in the world, namely, the liberation of the oppressed. The mission of the church was to support revolutionary movements by participating in them and bearing witness from within.[4] Gustavo Gutiérrez defined the theology of liberation as 'a theology of salvation incarnated in the concrete historical and political conditions of today'.[5] He reinterpreted Christ's ministry as a struggle for political justice, a struggle still continuing in God's liberating acts.[6] Theology did not summarize fixed truths; it became reflection on praxis, the socialized struggle of the servant church. The doctrines of Karl Marx, accepted as established social science, defined the salvation of the kingdom.[7] This revolutionary definition of mission redefined the theme 'Salvation Today' at the Eighth Conference on World Mission, held at Bangkok in 1973.

As we saw in the first chapter, the WCC Assembly in Canberra in 1991, which met after the discrediting of Marxism in Soviet Russia and Eastern Europe, planned its agenda to feature newer concerns, including those of feminists, environmentalists and advocates of other religions. Liberation theology again claimed Christ's cross as the sign of revolution.[8] But the Report also called for exploring 'the power of active non-violence for the transformation of society'.[9] Systemic evil was identified in the prevailing world economies and in ecological ravaging.[10] Caveats sprinkled through the Report qualified the more extreme positions.[11] Those who had hoped for a 'paradigm shift' that would find the mission of the church in its solidarity with the whole world (rocks, trees, animals and people) were only partly satisfied. The Report declared, 'A reconciled and renewed creation is the goal of the church's mission.'[12] To support this thesis, a Hebrew verb was mistranslated: 'We are charged to "keep" the earth and to "*serve*" it (Gen. 2:15), in an attitude of that blessed meekness which will inherit the earth.'[13] Since Western culture now touts animism as an 'ecology of the mind' far superior to Christianity, the Report seeks synthesis in the name of the Spirit. The 'spirituality of the land' that is found among indigenous peoples is said to offer new insights for a deeper understanding of 'a Spirit-centred theology of creation'.[14] Later, the caveat is added: 'However, sacralizing nature may lead us towards pantheism and to denial of the uniqueness of men and women as created in the image of God (Gen. 1:27).' The Report calls for continuing dialogue and encounter with non-Christian religions. Salvation is in Christ, though not only in him: 'We seek also to remain open to other people's expression of truth as they have experienced it.'[15] Indeed, 'The Holy Spirit, giver of life, is at work among all peoples and faiths and throughout the universe'.[16]

The agenda behind the conference surfaces throughout the text, but most statements are clothed in conciliar ambiguity. In a telling passage, opinion is said to be divided between the 'new cultural perspectives of emerging Christian voices' and what is called 'inherited faith claims'. The Report supports the new perspectives: 'We cannot turn our backs on them.'[17] Fundamentalism, however, is 'an intolerant ideological imperialism, closed to other approaches and realities'. Christian fundamentalists are lumped with non-Christian fundamentalists after the fashion of some media scripters who classify the 'Christian Right' with Muslim terrorists. On the other hand (again), Christians who are fundamentalist only in their approach to biblical interpretation are to be exempted from the definition.[18]

The confusing deliverances of the Canberra Assembly reveal the tensions between the evangelical convictions of many participants and the liberal agenda of the leadership. The tensions are not new: old questions come in new forms. Syncretism was the issue in 1928; it remains the great issue for today. Does mission seek to propagate the gospel or to reconcile religious faiths in mutual appreciation, so that the only heresy is the claim to exclusive truth? How the mission of the church is to approach non-Christians has always been of concern; the issue now is whether they should be approached at all.

Communication and transportation have shrunk our planet: bleeding, starving victims in urban jungles and remote villages appear on our living-room screens; millions in Third World poverty gain visions of affluence and seek entrance to the lands of their dreams. Millions more are not drawn but driven from

157

their homes. Ecological devastation contributes to the economic woes of the planet.

Again, intensified as they may be, the problems are not new. Every pioneer missionary met them at first hand, and shared the suffering they bring. Yet our new awareness gives old questions new force: What mission does the church have? Is it called to save the planet? To heal the sick of the world? To join wars of liberation to overthrow oppressive regimes? Our answer, as believers, must come from the Word of the Lord.

What, then, is the biblical theology of the mission of the church?

We have seen how completely the message of the Bible centres in God the Saviour. It is God who must come, because the human condition is hopeless, and God's promises are so great. We need God, not because we need his help to solve our problems, but because God's holy justice is our problem. Only he can make us right in his sight, and to do so he must bear our judgment, provide our righteousness, and transform our natures.

The 'new perspectives' in mission urge us to find a solidarity with all humanity, and indeed with all creation. Biblical theology has long taught the lesson of solidarity. We are all God's creatures, but our solidarity is solidarity in sin. Human lostness means alienation from the source of life. It also means doom. We, and all creation for our sakes, are under the deserved wrath and curse of God. Human pretensions to implement justice fall infinitely short of the execution of true justice. We rightly condemn wanton gang murders and calculated racist genocide, but we pass over the root of our own hatred of God, the God of love and justice. The first and great commandment is to love God with all our heart, soul, strength and mind. The second is like it because it derives from it: to love our neighbour as ourselves. David – betrayer, adulterer, murderer – can confess his crimes and yet pray, 'Against you, you only, have I sinned and done what is evil in your sight . . .' (Ps. 51:4).

Our fearful condition as lost sinners forms the dark horizon where God's grace brings the dawn of hope. In the Bible, salvation is God's mission to a lost world. It is God who seeks Adam and Eve in the garden; God who promises the Son of the woman who will crush the head of the serpent; God who warns

Noah, and calls Abraham in Ur and Moses at the burning bush. The book of Judges, the narratives of the books of Kings and the words of the prophets all point to the golden text of the Old Testament: 'Salvation comes from the LORD' (Jon. 2:9). God himself must come to bring his salvation. This is the *missio Dei.*

The church as the gatherers

God accomplishes his saving mission by sending his Son into the world. Jesus is the great Missionary, sent by the Father. As Lord, Jesus comes to gather his people, and to form his disciples as a company of gatherers. God had promised to deliver his sheep from the false shepherds. He promised to shepherd them himself, and to gather them from where they had been scattered (Ezk. 34:12). God promised, too, that his servant David would be prince among them in the day of his deliverance (Ezk. 34:24). Jesus announced that he was the true Shepherd, come to gather those the Father had given him, including the 'other' sheep that were not from the fold of Israel (Jn. 10:11–30). His sheep would hear his voice and recognize him, the Son of David who is also David's Lord. He is the Shepherd who will be struck down (Mt. 26:31; Zc. 13:7), the Good Shepherd who gives his life for the sheep (Jn. 10:11).

Jesus looked with compassion on the crowds of Galilee, seeing them as sheep without a shepherd (Mt. 9:36). Varying the figure, he longed to gather the people of Jerusalem as a hen would gather her chicks under her wings (Mt. 23:37). In his parables he also spoke of his gathering task. He described heaven's feast, and the refusal of God's summons by those who had been invited (Mt. 22:1–14). As God's Servant, Jesus calls guests to the supper, saying, 'Come, for everything is now ready' (Lk. 14:17). As the time for his crucifixion drew near, Jesus declared that his gathering would take place as he was 'lifted up' to the cross and to glory (Jn. 12:32).

Jesus came to gather, and to call gatherers, disciples who would gather with him, seeking the poor and helpless from city streets and country roads. Jesus said, 'He who is not with me is against me, and he who does not gather with me scatters' (Mt. 12:30; Lk. 11:23). Mission is not an optional activity for Christ's disciples. If they are not gatherers, they are scatterers. Some suppose that a church may feature worship and nurture, leaving gathering as a minor role. More often, Christians shrink from affirming such a position, but implement it in practice. Mission is reduced to a few offerings, the visit of several exhausted missionaries on fund-raising junkets, and the labours of an ignored missions committee. Such a church is actively involved in scattering, for the congregation that ignores mission will atrophy and soon find itself shattered by internal dissension. It will inevitably begin to lose its own young people, disillusioned by hearing the gospel trumpet sounded every Sunday for those who never march.

What is true of a congregation is true also of a Christian home. If a family fails to seek to gather friends and neighbours to Christ in hospitality and quiet witness, the children of the family will be scattered. We fail to bring up children in the nurture of the Lord if we fail to involve them in our efforts to gather others to the Saviour.

Jesus calls his disciples to bring in a harvest as field-workers, and to draw in nets as fishermen (Mt. 9:37–38; Lk. 5:1–11). These are heartening images. They labour in fields where the harvest is ripe: others have planted – and, indeed, he himself is the Sower – and they harvest his field. He is the Lord of the harvest. Prayer is the key to the mission of the church, for he will answer prayer by sending his labourers into his harvest. He is also the Lord of the sea; their nets gather the fish he has summoned. Jesus did not call his fishermen as they cleaned and mended their nets after fruitless hours of fishing; only when his command had filled their nets to the bursting point did he make them fishers of men.

Christ's commission to make disciples forms the climax of Matthew's Gospel. But the Great Commission at the end of this Gospel (Mt. 28:18–20) must not be isolated from the Great Constitution in the heart of the Gospel (Mt. 16:17–19). The words with which Jesus responded to Peter's confession show what it means to make disciples. Missionary churches may feature the Great Commission, and give little attention to the Great Constitution. The Church of Rome, on the other hand, has given more emphasis to Christ's words to Peter; those words, not the Great Commission, are inscribed around the entablature under the dome of St Peter's.

Both words of Jesus are part of the same Gospel. They must be understood together. The Great Commission of Matthew 28 requires the order Christ appointed for his church in the Constitution of Matthew 16. On the other hand, the Constitution of the church has a missionary purpose.

Mission expresses the purpose for which Christ came into the world, and the purpose for which he sends us into the world. His purpose is the purpose of the Father. We are called to mission, not only as disciples of Christ, but as children of the Father. Jesus teaches that the law of the Father's kingdom is love that is compassionate. The righteousness of the kingdom must exceed that of the Pharisees (Mt. 5:20). We are not to be more punctilious in legalistic observances, but we are to express the heart of the law in burning love to the Father, imitating his love of grace toward guilty and undeserving enemies (Mt. 5:44–48). Such love does not ask what it must do as a minimum, but rejoices in doing unrequired good. The compassion of the Samaritan does not ask, 'Who is my neighbour?' Rather, it displays the free love of a neighbour, reflecting the compassionate love of God (Lk. 10:24–37). We are to be merciful as our Father in heaven is merciful.

The heart of the gospel moves the church to mission and to deeds of mercy which have always been part of the Christian mission. The Christian who has tasted the compassionate love of God in Christ must ask the question put by Jesus: 'To whom am I a neighbour? I, to whom the Lord of glory became neighbour on the cross – who is it that now needs my compassion, the love that reflects the love of Calvary?'

The way of the kingdom is the way of seeking love. Jesus makes that clear in the parable of the prodigal son. The elder brother refused to enter the father's 'welcome home' party for the returning prodigal. In him, Jesus personifies the attitude of the Pharisees. They, like the heartless elder brother, are proud of their self-righteous service. Like him, they have no understanding of the father's joy in recovering the lost. They would not eat with tax-collectors and sinners, and faulted Jesus for doing so. That is why he told the three parables (Lk. 15). But Jesus knows the joy of heaven over one sinner who repents. In the parables of the lost sheep and the lost coin, he presents his own search of love. But in the parable of the prodigal son, Jesus

161

steps off-stage and replaces himself with a Pharisee. The full force of the parable comes when we reverse that substitution. What should the elder brother have done? Jesus, the true elder Brother, not only sits with prodigals at heaven's feast, but comes seeking them down the roads of far countries to find them in their pigsties. The gospel itself is the story of the seeking Saviour who knows the Father's love. If mission is lost, the gospel is lost.

Because Jesus sends us in his name and in the Father's name, we are not surprised that the Spirit sent by Christ moves and directs the mission of the church. Peter declared that the apostles were witnesses to the risen Christ, 'and so is the Holy Spirit, whom God has given to those who obey him' (Acts 5:32). Luke describes the entire missionary expansion of the church in apostolic times as the work of the Holy Spirit. It is the Spirit who launches the first missionary journey of Paul and Barnabas, as the leaders of the church of Antioch pray (Acts 13:2). The Spirit not only directs the apostle Paul forward, but even restrains him from certain areas in a divine plan (Acts 16:6–7). The Spirit empowers missionary preaching, equips apostles and evangelists as missionaries, and makes bold the saints to confess the Name.

The church as the gathered

The church not only goes, but it also draws. It is established on earth as the house of God, the place where his glory dwells, and to which the nations are drawn. God's praises rise from the new Zion, and the nations are called to join the song (Is. 25:6–8; 52:7–10; 60:1–3; Ps. 96:3). The church is prefigured in the house of God's dwelling in Zion (Eph. 2:21; 1 Pet. 2:5; cf. Heb. 12:22; Phil. 3:20). In Christ, God's promises are fulfilled; the door is opened for the Gentiles to be drawn in. Paul saw the offerings of the Gentile churches as a sign that the wealth of the nations was being brought to the Lord (Is. 60:5; Rom. 15:12, 16, 26–27).

The *identity* of the church is necessary for the *mission* of the church. Only as a holy nation, called out of darkness into the light of God's presence, can the church discharge its mission. Paul inverts the language of Moses describing disobedient Israel in order to describe the holy New Covenant people of God, shining as lights in the world (Phil. 2:14; Dt. 32:5). Peter affirms

the church's right to the titles of Israel, then describes the
church's witness of praise (1 Pet. 2:9–10). God's people now
include the Gentiles; in that new fact God's promise to Abraham
is at last realized, and, as the prophets promised, the covenant
relation is at last restored: 'I will . . . be your God, and you will
be my people' (Lv. 26:12; Je. 24:7; 2 Cor. 6:16).

This understanding of the church as the new and true Israel
in Christ must inspire our mission in the contemporary world.
The resurgence of ethnic communities and of ethnic nationalism surprises those who had supposed that electronic media
were uniting the world into a global village. No longer does the
public educational system in the United States seek the 'melting-
pot' goal that it once advocated. 'Multicultural' curricula
capitalize on the strength of ethnic loyalties to teach cultural
relativism – the position that cultures may be judged only by
their own value systems, and are therefore equally valid. Against
this background the *spiritual* ethnicity of the church binds
diversity in peace.

Christian churches in Africa, South America and Asia have
established their own identity, and are no longer bound to the
European and North American sub-cultures of the early
missionaries. The 'younger churches' of the mission lands are
now the growing and sending churches of the coming century.
Two crucial insights for mission flow from the Christian
'ethnicity' of the people of God. The first is the unity of the
new humankind in Christ, and their bonding into a people
bearing his name. In days of ethnic fighting in central Europe
and tribal warfare in Africa (not to mention the inner cities of
America), the 'peoplehood' of the church must become visible.
The transcending identity of the church does not erase ethnic
ties, but it bars them from demanding primary, and therefore
idolatrous, loyalty. Those who are united in the catholicity of
God's family, of Christ's kingdom and of the Spirit's fellowship
cannot in good conscience exclude from the table and roof of
brotherhood fellow-Christians from ethnic groups that are
hostile to their own. Certainly practice will mean more than
pious theory, but the theory, too, must be deeper. American
evangelicals have a tradition of individualism that sees the
church as a voluntary club for the converted. Until we have a
deep biblical sense of the corporate identity of the new people

of God, we will not be able to present the gospel of peace on the front lines of our 'culture wars'. The true drawing power of the church transcends the cultural enclaves of contemporary society to dissolve the hatreds of a fallen world in the love of Christ.

The church must also show how the gospel purifies cultures as it transcends them. The ideal of cultural diversity within the church means that we learn from one another, and appreciate the rich variety of human lifestyles. Unity in Christ does not suppress cultural expression. The leaven of the gospel in British and American culture has already demonstrated how much cultural distinctiveness may be carried along in the context of Christian conviction. One has only to open a hymnbook to see the variety of musical traditions that have entered the evangelical stream; the use of overhead projectors and desktop publishing promises more to come.

We have yet to reconcile the principles of church growth (that so faithfully preserve ethnic identities) with the principles of church unity (the new ethnicity of those in Christ). It is usually supposed that the first is necessary for mission, and that the second represents a later stage to be achieved by the spiritually mature. The church needs wisdom both to preserve and liberate, for it does not seek to loosen the ties of family, or to destroy ethnic identity. Yet it must not compromise its identity in Christ in order to attract the prejudiced. This denies the gospel at the very point where the world is watching.

The separating of mission

The Lord's gathering mission has a tragic context – division. From the first, God warns us that the supreme revelation of his love will bring the supreme hostility of human rebellion. The triumph of God's grace meets the hellish hatred of the human heart at the cross. The coming of the eternal Son opens wide the breach between penitent faith and proud unbelief, between those who are born of God and those who follow the Arch-rebel, the devil (Jn. 8:42–51). The feast is spread, but guests refuse the invitation; the net is drawn in, but the bad fish are discarded; the Word is sown, but weeds grow up in the midst of the wheat.

Paul knew that his gospel message was the smell of death to those who were perishing as well as the aroma of life to those who were being saved (2 Cor. 2:16). Not all are gathered in to the kingdom of God. Children come in, but a rich man goes his way; penitent tax-collectors are welcomed, but self-righteous Pharisees are excluded. Jesus came to bring not peace but a sword, dividing even the family circle by the ultimate claim of his kingdom. The root of the division remains: salvation comes, not by economic reform, political liberation or ecological steward-ship, but by faith in the Saviour, who is the Way, the Truth and the Life.

Witness is by life as well as by word, but never without the Word of God. The cutting edge of the sword of the Spirit is the telling of the Good News of Jesus Christ. Vast as is the indirect influence of the church as salt and leaven in the world, it must first hold forth the light of truth. We must consider the calling of the church in the context of contemporary culture, but its agenda is not that of the world. To accommodate its mission to the underlying assumptions of multiculturalism, radical femin-ism or even ecclesiastical ritualism is to repeat the mistake of the older liberalism by turning to another gospel.

With the New Testament picture before us of the church as gathered and as gathering, we must now consider the mission of the church in the world, first in relation to culture, then in relation to the state.

12

THE CHURCH
IN THE WORLD'S
CULTURES

'You mean to say that God doesn't want us going on cannibal raids?'

This response in a Bible study of Genesis 9 startled R. Daniel Shaw, a missionary to Papua New Guinea. 'Not being a cannibal,' he tells us, 'I had never considered this passage from that perspective.'[1] The Papuan saw the implications of the text: God is not pleased when we kill those made in his image. His Samo culture divided people into *Monsoon*, those who slept in the same longhouse; *Oosoo Buoman*, their allies; and *Ton*, those who spoke the same dialect; all others were *Hatooman*, enemies.

In the climate of modern multiculturalism, meeting the world-views of other cultures has become everyone's problem. Cultural change now requires us to cross cultural barriers in order to present the gospel across the street.

Christian attitudes to culture

What should be the Christian attitude to the world and its cultures?

As H. Richard Niebuhr and others have shown, very different

answers have been given throughout the history of the church.[2] Each has put forward scriptural passages to support its case.

Those who see the world and its culture as a threat appeal to the first letter of John and urge a strategy of avoidance:

> Do not love the world or anything in the world . . . For everything in the world – the cravings of sinful man, the lust of the eyes and the boasting of what he has and does – comes not from the Father but from the world (1 Jn. 2:15–16).

Avoidance is a matter of degree. Even a solitary hermit cannot abstain from all involvement in the world. On the other hand, Christians must simply say 'No' to many things in our pleasure-mad culture. Driving horse-drawn carriages on the highways of eastern Pennsylvania, Amish farmers give wide scope to that 'No'.

Many missionaries have taken the Christ-against-culture position, seeing the tribal or national cultures in which they evangelized as being completely hostile to the gospel. Individual converts, rejected by their own societies, joined their missionary mentors, sometimes in mission compounds where they adopted not only the culture but also the sub-culture of the missionaries. Since missionaries were, until recently, uncritical of their own culture, their activities promoted the colonialist expansion of the West. As the Third World shook off political control by colonial powers, it continued to resent economic colonialism but gave credibility to another form of Western domination: Marxist ideology.

Potent factors in missionary work, however, widened the horizons of dedicated missionaries. Language-learning meant culture-learning, and carried with it appreciation for the new culture. Seeking to approach people with the gospel, missionaries were also driven to understand better the values and structures of their own culture. The success of Don Richardson in finding powerful cultural analogies for presenting the gospel to tribal cultures led him to believe that every culture has a providentially prepared key that will unlock it for the truth.[3]

Some other church leaders throughout the centuries have argued for an opposite strategy. Instead of withdrawing from the world, the church should join it. Did not the apostle Paul seek to be all things to all men so that by all means he might win some (1 Cor. 9:20–21)?

The apostle himself, however, was not prepared to sacrifice the truth of the gospel in order to conform to culture. He refuted the Judaizers, who synthesized the gospel with Judaism by adding works to faith for justification, and compelled Gentile converts to become circumcised Jews. And the early church did not accept the Gnostics' effort to conform the gospel to Hellenistic culture.[4] Writing when he did, Niebuhr thought that the pansophic theories of that age had vanished. He could not have imagined how closely the current New Age movement would replicate ancient Gnosticism and seek to win Christians to the same heresies.[5]

The various synthesizers of the gospel with culture have followed all the cultural movements and popular philosophies since the Enlightenment: the older liberalism of Schleiermacher and Ritschl, Christian existentialism and process theology, and, more recently, deconstruction and theological relativism.

Adaptation to tribalism has produced multitudes of sects in Africa, each incorporating some elements of biblical teaching.[6] In China, the Boxer Rebellion began with a movement that drew elements of Christianity into Chinese culture. Governments have attempted to co-opt the Christian church: Hitler's *Volkskirche*; the recognition and control of the Christian church by Communist China as the 'Three-Self' movement; the infiltration and manipulation of the Russian Orthodox Church by Stalin.

The Roman Catholic Church represents a third approach to mission. Thomistic theology holds that fallen sinners can build from God's general revelation a structure of theology that is true, though incomplete. This natural theology needs only the addition of the supernatural truth of the gospel in order to gain a saving knowledge of God. Appeal is made to Paul's words that 'since the creation of the world God's invisible qualities – his eternal power and divine nature – have been clearly seen, being understood from what has been made' (Rom. 1:20). Does not Paul also appeal elsewhere to a heathen poet to refute idolatry (Acts 17:28)?

The 'two-level' approach in Catholic mission was strikingly

169

illustrated in the ministry of Matteo Ricci, the Jesuit missionary who began his work in China in 1583. He was successful in reaching the Chinese governing élite, and even the Emperor. He commended Christianity to the Chinese scholars by showing its conformity to natural law, the principles of which, he claimed, were in their own classics. His use of the classical term *Tien tsu* (Lord of Heaven), or even *Tien* (Heaven), for God, led to a controversy that raged for a century and ended with the exclusion of all Catholic missions from China when the Emperor insisted on the use of *Tien* and the Papacy at that time forbade it.[7]

Yet other Christians maintain the sharp distinction between the church and the world, but view the world with indifference rather than hostility. Looking expectantly for the return of the Lord, they do not flee the world but ignore it. They point to Paul's words to the Corinthian church, where he says the time is short, and that Christians should regard life's relationships with detachment, not using the things of the world to the full, 'For this world in its present form is passing away' (1 Cor. 7:31).

In practice, this has led to a split in American evangelical life. Since the world cannot be avoided, evangelicals have lived and flourished in it, but found little application of Christian principles in the market-place or their neighbourhoods. To be sure, there is now a growing consciousness of the erosion of Christian and family values that were once taken for granted in the secular world. Governmental support for abortions and for homosexual lifestyles has roused evangelicals to social action, yet on the whole they still live in one world on Sunday and in another on weekdays. This has been possible because of the individualism that marks evangelical life.

Luther's doctrine of the two kingdoms seemingly separates life in the world from life in the kingdom of grace. He asserted: 'There are two kingdoms, one the kingdom of God, the other the kingdom of the world.' Those who confuse the two put wrath into God's kingdom, and mercy into the world's kingdom, 'and that is the same as putting the devil in heaven and God in Hell'.[8] Niebuhr defends Luther, describing the Reformer's attitude to culture as that of paradox. Luther, he points out, did more than any leader before him to emphasize obedience to Christ in daily life, urging education in languages, arts and

170

history as well as piety, and putting music next to theology as a noble gift of God. All vocations were spheres of service to God: commerce, politics and even soldiering were part of a common life dedicated to God.[9]

Luther's doctrine of the two kingdoms has been used to build walls not only between church and state, but also between science and religion, reason and revelation. Fundamentalists built the walls while they waited for the imminent return of Christ; evangelicals huddle behind them, vainly seeking to shelter an emotional faith while conceding more and more to the demands of secularist culture. Separation between private faith and public concerns has become the price of religious toleration. So long as faith touches only what takes place in a house of worship, and does not impinge on what is said or done outside, secularized democracy may grant it a licence as harmless.

A final approach to the world is not simply to fight it, join it, build on it, or try to ignore it, but to change it. Jesus compared the working of the kingdom to the action of leaven in a lump of dough: it continues until the whole lump is leavened (Mt. 13:33). In a similar figure, he likened his disciples to salt (Mt. 5:13). Nor is the working of the kingdom always hidden. The disciples are the light of the world, a city set on a hill that cannot be hid (Mt. 5:14).

Augustine declared that culture was to be transformed by the gospel.[10] When he turned away from the Manichaean view that matter was evil, he began to emphasize the goodness of the created world, and of created human nature. Though human nature is perverted by sin, the structures of human life are not evil in themselves. Further, God's redemption through Christ changes life and its relationships. 'Everything, and not least political life, is subject to the great conversion that ensues when God makes a new beginning for man by causing man to begin with God.'[11]

The gospel and cultures

How, then, is the church to transform life in the world without becoming a kingdom of this world?

To understand the mission of the church in the world we

171

must better understand the relation of the gospel to the cultures of the world.

The Bible's use of terms for 'world' is not simple. As God made it and keeps it, the world is good. God pronounced it very good at the time of creation, and he promises the restoration of a new heaven and earth (Ps. 24:1; 50:12; Pr. 3:19; Je. 10:12; Acts 3:21).

As a rebellious world, however, it is bad. The people of the world have become God's enemies (Ps. 17:14; Jn. 15:19). The world became the domain of the devil (Jn. 14:30; 1 Jn. 5:9; Mt. 4:8; Eph. 6:12–13). The present time is an evil age (Gal. 1:4; Eph. 2:2; Col. 2:8), in which 'worldliness' is an enticement to sin (Rom. 12:2; Mt. 16:26; 2 Tim. 4:10; Gal. 6:14).

Yet the world, as a lost world, is both doomed and spared. It is doomed by God's judgment against it (Jn. 12:31; 17:19; Rom. 3:19). It is spared, however, in God's longsuffering mercy, and it is made the object of God's love.

The statement of John 3:16 that 'God so loved the world' does not view the world as desirable. Satan sees the world as desirable, and he tempted Jesus to give up his Father for the glory of the world, but Jesus would not give up his Father for all the world. When the Father gave up his Son for the world, he was not doing what his Son refused to do. God does not see the world as Satan presented it. He does not need or covet the world; rather, his holy wrath threatens it. John 3:16 does not reflect on how big the world is, but on how bad it is. The marvel of grace is that the holy God could direct his love toward a world of sinners who deserved his curse (*cf.* Jn. 1:29; 2 Cor. 5:19).

This fallen, broken world is now Christ's world. It is the theatre of his redemption (1 Cor. 4:9; Rev. 5), the place of his mission, over which he has total authority for the accomplishment of his saving work (Mt. 13:38; 28:18–20; Jn. 8:12; 17:15–18). The rule of Christ will bring this present world to the glory of the world to come (1 Cor. 15:22–26; Rom. 8:19–20; Acts 3:20–21; Rev. 21:1). He will come again in glory to judge the nations and form a new universe (Mt. 24:14; Acts 1:11; Rom. 16:26; 2 Thes. 1:7–10; 2 Pet. 3:10).

What the Bible says about the world guides us in understanding the cultures of the world.

The term 'culture' may mean 'high culture', the habits and

tastes of the social élite; it may denote material culture, the learned mastery of environment shared by a people (the pottery of a bronze-age culture); or it may mean the common values that guide community behaviour, and form its climate of opinion. Underlying the values in the latter definition are the religious assumptions and convictions that are the inner core of every culture. Human beings are cultural beings because they are made in the image of God. Human culture is a socially assumed and transmitted pattern of thought and life developed around a scheme of values. While rebellion and apostasy may enshrine idols, or even develop atheistic assumptions, the function of such convictions is inescapably religious.

God has assigned a cultural task to his image-bearers: they are to fill the earth as God's stewards, beginning with the cultivation of Eden where God had placed them. The fruitfulness of the Garden and the abundance of animal life make their task easy, and there is promise of future development – God has provided gold and precious stones in the land of Havilah (Gn. 2:11–12). Artistry as well as husbandry is in view. God's blessing accompanies his charge: labour begins under the sign of God's sabbath rest.

Yet the key to the blessing of Eden is God's presence there, and his speaking to Adam and Eve. Their environment is not chaos or a silent planet, but the Garden of God. The 'cultural mandate' defining human stewardship is under the sign of the tree of life – the promise of God's final blessing of fellowship and sonship beyond the initial period of testing. God gives that tree; it is not Adam's prize horticultural hybrid. Its test is sheer obedience to God with respect to abstinence from another tree.

God's commands are formative for the 'culture' of Eden. History is not blind fate under astral dominance, nor is it evolutionary progress. Perfected fellowship with God is the goal of human history set before us in the Bible; it is a goal to be reached through God's blessing. Emil Brunner has pointed out that Christianity has proved culturally fruitful not in spite of, but because of, the fact that it has sought a higher goal than cultural fruitfulness. Cultural benefits follow in the train of those who seek first the kingdom.

With the fall, the activities that were commanded in the cultural mandate come under the curse. Yet even the curse implies that God's calling remains: Adam's painful labour will subdue the earth; Eve's travail will fill it. Moreover, through the travail of the woman, One will be born who will receive the sting of the serpent but who will also crush its head (Gn. 3:15).

With the fall, the apostasy of culture appears: Cain the fratricide builds a city to bear his son's name; the proud architects of Babel anticipate Tyre, Nineveh and Babylon. Exalting man's name invites divine judgment (Gn. 11:4; Is. 13:19; Ezk. 27:3; 28:2; Dn. 4:30; Na. 3;). Metals are smelted, swords can be made, and Lamech sings his arrogant hymn of hate (Gn. 4:23–24). The kingdoms whose cultural riches Satan will show to Jesus begin to rise like beasts out of the sea.

God preserves culture, even under judgment. He marks Cain, sparing his life. Cultural achievements in the line of Cain are recognized and valued. In Sumerian mythology, the gods bring down the elements of material culture. In the Bible, they are the products of human toil and inventiveness: Jabal raises cattle and Tubal-cain fashions copper.

As well as the expulsion from the Garden, there are two other divine judgments described in Genesis that mark the continuance of culture in a fallen world. First, the flood checks the rampant violence of evil, but does not eradicate its infection. Following the flood, God's forbearance is pledged in his covenant; under the rainbow, human life continues, protected by his ordinance. Yet the united capacity for proud evil is so evident among the descendants of Noah that God's judgment falls again, this time at Babel. The division of languages divides cultures and peoples and ends the threat of one world in totalitarian revolt against God. God's division of the peoples prepares for the call of Abraham and the establishment of a people of God to bear his promised blessing to all the families of the earth. As we have seen, Israel was constituted as a separate people. God's covenant established a new spiritual core for Israel's life, expressed in moral values, and marked by the external separateness of the laws of purity. The spiritual character of covenant culture flowered in the psalms and songs of Israel. In architecture, as in other aspects of culture, Israel was dependent on the surrounding nations. Solomon's royal wisdom marked a pinnacle of achievement in statecraft, literature and natural science (1 Ki. 4:29–34), but he needed the help of Tyrian craftsmanship to complete the temple he built for the worship of God (1 Ki. 5:7–12; 7:40–47).

Israel's apostasy brought divine judgment, but the promises of God became only greater, for God himself must come if the dead bones of Israel's captivity are to live again. The prophets describe a glorious future in which the curse will be gone, the fields will be bursting with fruit and the cultural mandate will be fulfilled in the context of devotion and praise.

Jesus Christ, who comes to bring salvation, also fulfils the heart of the cultural mandate. Paul pointedly declares that Christ not only has dominion over all things, but that he fills all things (Eph. 1:23; 4:10; Gn. 1:28). The Second Adam has completed the calling of the first in both aspects. His dominion is shown, not through elaborate technical means, but by the immediate exercise of his power. He did nothing to redesign Galilean fishing craft, but simply walked on the water to reach his disciples in the storm.

No cultural achievements are needed to complete Christ's work or to provide for the new order at his *parousia*. The church does not fabricate an international super-culture. It is called to penetrate and preserve the cultures of this world so that all peoples may hear and heed the good news of Christ's kingdom. God's people are to labour to relieve distress and to promote peace and justice, but they cannot hail such efforts as bringing salvation.

Jesus calls his disciples to seek first his kingdom and to trust the provision of their Father in heaven. In consequence they sit lightly to cultural loyalties. Christians look beyond the immediate; they possess as not possessing, 'For this world in its present form is passing away' (1 Cor. 7:31). Paul could be a Jew to the Jews and a Roman citizen to the Gentiles (1 Cor. 9:19ff.). He could speak Aramaic to a Jerusalem crowd and Greek to a Gentile official. But Paul serves Christ, knowing that in Christ there is neither Jew nor Greek, barbarian, Scythian, bond or free. These identities have not disappeared, but they can no longer demand first loyalty.

To be sure, a tension remains. The spiritual renewal of the gospel does liberate a man or woman for living, and for the use of God's rich gifts in cultural pursuits. The Reformation changed the understanding of work, and opened the joys of

175

music, art, science and industry to the common people who had been ignored by the Renaissance élite. But at the same time, the new understanding of the gospel gave a focus as well as a purpose to life. Cultural achievement is not life's final goal.

The goal is to advance God's saving rule on earth. The way is that of the cross; full triumph awaits Christ's return. His church that now shares in his suffering will then share in his glory. Like Israel in captivity, the church will pray for the peace of the city where they dwell as resident aliens' (Je. 29:7; cf. 1 Tim. 2:2), but they have no abiding city here; they seek the Jerusalem to come (Heb. 13:14). Until then, their spiritual weapons have the power of Almighty God to accomplish his purposes of redemption (2 Cor. 10:3–6).

In the pursuit of holiness, in the proclamation of the gospel, in the service of the poor and friendless, the church of Christ builds a spiritual culture, a foretaste of the kingdom to come. Life is transformed in a community living in love for God and for neighbours. No poetry can compare in power with the simple glory of fervent prayer; when the deeds of men and women are revealed before the face of God, what hidden beauty will appear! The deeds that store treasure in heaven are the real achievements of human culture in this present age. The true cultural significance of Martin Luther's translation of the Bible into German was not the strengthening of German literary prose, but the impact of the opened Word of God on the German people. No battle in human history had the 'world-historical' significance of Christ's solitary combat with Satan in the wilderness – with the exception of Christ's triumph on the cross. In his footsteps, the pilgrim church of Christ is called to a lifestyle of obedience under testing. Cross-bearing is the work of the highest spiritual culture.

As the Christian mission presents the Christian gospel, the cultures of the world will affect both the way the gospel is presented and the way it is received. 'Contextualization' has become a major concern for the missionary church.

Claiming a modern understanding of culture, some have criticized the mission of the church as a remainder of colonial imperialism. Paul J. Achtemeier describes the crisis that comes from the 'discovery of the historically conditioned nature of human culture and understanding, and the corresponding inability to assume that what was true in the past must inevitably be true for the present as well'.[12]

The 'discovery' that all truth – like milk cartons – needs to be dated leads to a rejection of the truth claims of the Christian mission. The theology of the gospel is described as the 'myth of a nomadic desert tribe' enforcing patriarchal dominance, or as one among many Hellenistic saviour cults. The exclusive claims of the gospel are seen as fracturing the quest for understanding among the manifold cultures of the world. Dogmatic cultural relativism has, of course, a difficulty: it affirms absolutely that nothing can be affirmed absolutely.

The Christian answer to relativism is theological: the reality of the Creator God. He is both Creator and Interpreter. Made in his image, we have a relation to his created universe that is not illusory. He is free to reveal himself in time and space, and in the languages of the cultures that develop in human history. Christian theology takes seriously the cultural contexts in which God's revelation is given, and the Christian mission takes seriously the cultural contexts it addresses. Hermeneutical studies have reminded us that our own culture has an impact on both tasks. But so does God's Word have an impact on all languages and cultures. Confronted with God's revelation, our own understanding changes, and we alter our assumptions. Not a circle, but a spiral of clearer reception and communication of the message results. God has made his truth communicable; he calls us to 'think his thoughts after him'.[13]

Human autonomy cannot escape meaninglessness; the centre will not hold. Existential commitment, whether individual or societal, offers no remedy. Jean-Paul Sartre's *Nausea* exposes, but cannot resolve, the absurdity of the hero of the absurd. Meaninglessness cannot provide a basis for morality.[14]

Our understanding of history and culture, mistaken as it often is, yet has meaning because we live in a real world and God is not dead.

Culture and mission

Mission is God's action. In commissioning his church, Christ gave assurance of his presence and power. We go where the Lord is already at work. He preserves all things and sustains his image in us so that the gospel call reaches creatures capable of religious response. Although morally dead because of separation from God, the sinner remains human, and is addressable in human language. The very survival of ordered human culture shows the Lord's restraint on the disintegration of sin. Because culture is bound up with humanness, mission must not attempt to destroy it.

Efforts to flee from culture will end in building other cultures, often legalistic or mystical. Defining church life by resistance to worldly customs has created counter-cultures that list cultural taboos. In the 1930s, fundamentalist piety in the United States came to be defined by its ban on a list of 'worldly' practices: dancing, theatre or movie attendance, card-playing, smoking, drinking alcoholic beverages. Yet a checklist of these admittedly dangerous practices creates a curious negative dependence on the very worldliness it seeks to avoid. Abstinence from practices that may not, in all cases, be sinful cannot replace the willing obedience of love that seeks the glory of Christ in every activity of life.

Mystical withdrawal from the world may also depend on what it rejects, fashioning ascetic disciplines that are culturally shaped. Niebuhr finds a distrust of the God of creation and of nature in the immanentistic spiritualism of Tertullian's Montanism, spiritual Franciscanism, and inner-light Quakerism.[15]

The problem with the Christ-against-culture approach is not that it finds some cultural practices objectionable, or even that it discerns an anti-Christian bias in the spiritual core of a culture. Rather, it fails to take adequate account of what Calvin and later Reformers spoke of as God's *general* or *common* grace, by which God works among fallen humankind to restrain sin and evil and to promote a measure of moral and civic order. Calvin says that in the midst of the total corruption of human nature 'there is some room for Divine grace, not to purify it, but internally to restrain its operation'.[16] God not only controls the wicked so as to defend and bless his people;[17] he also dispenses particular graces 'in great variety, and in a certain degree to men that are otherwise profane'.[18] Calvin, a scholar in the classics, found much to admire in the writings of Stoic moralists and esteemed the virtues of pagans. He praises God for all relatively good actions, although he recognizes the fatal flaw in actions that ignore the love of God, and do not seek his glory.[19] Human culture in this fallen world has customs that tend to preserve life, to offer some protection to the weak, and to reward virtue.

Scholars of missions have debated whether cultures should be understood as organisms or aggregates. Is the Kwakiutl culture of Alaska described by Ruth Benedict, for instance, a systemic whole, or is it a collection of unrelated bits united by the accidents of history and given coherence in practice?[20] Not all customs are dictated by physical environment. The *mana* of a Polynesian chief rendered sacred every spot where his foot rested, so that at last, to avoid sequestering any more island real estate, the chief had to be carried everywhere.

Organic views of culture are necessary in order to explain cultural patterns. Cultures provide more than rules for life; they develop life systems in which the rules make sense. Every culture has at its core a view of life and the world that is fundamentally religious, and that is expressed in social order as well as sacred practices. Yet no culture joins all its customs and social wisdom in one harmonious whole. Further, it is precisely at the heart of a culture that rebellion from God will be most evident. The Sawi people laughed and applauded the treachery of Judas in betraying Christ.[21] Their culture had been shaped by the glorification of deceit and treachery. In more subtle but not less perverse ways, every culture reflects sinful pride and rebellion.

Cultures, then, like people, are notably inconsistent. They are neither an aggregate of unconnected elements like marbles in a bag, nor are they seamless garments of systemic consistency. The elements and structures of culture have a history that reflects God's dealings with a people.

The apostle Paul traced the degrading of worship over the centuries (Rom. 1:18–32). As humankind rejected God, God gave them up to their own lusts, withdrawing the restraint of his common grace. The history of God's encounter with human beings and their cultures continues, and is now under the rule of Christ, the Son of God. The wrath of God is revealed anew in Christ's authority; even more God's goodness and saving righteousness are revealed through Christ (Rom. 1:17). God keeps revealing himself in nature, including human nature. Paul argues that the knowledge of God that people cannot escape

179

renders them guilty. Their altar to an unknown God confesses the very God they seek to escape. In his overview of the Christian approach to non-Christian religions, missionary theologian J. H. Bavinck asks the key question: 'What have you done with God?'[22] Have these religions promoted him to be a high God who may be safely ignored? Have they merged him with the stuff of the universe so that god is all, and all is god? Have they screened him behind a ceiling of legal rules, split him into male and female principles, or renounced him for a host of spirits? They have always done something to avoid the God whose creation testifies afresh with every sunrise.

The missionary approach of the church joins in an encounter that is already in progress. God confronts his creatures, much as they seek to escape, and preserves them in his image so that cultural structures remain. The mythologies that peoples weave as barriers to God also divide them from one another. Humanism has approved all the discordant mythologies of the world's peoples and is still discovering how anti-humanistic most of them are. Further, people believe their own myths, not the humanist myth of multi-cultural relativism; they are fundamentalist adherents of their own mythology. Yet cultures are not autonomous islands, nor is truth provincial. Culture reflects the image of God in his creatures; language opens a highway, and every culture is subject to transformation by the power of the truth.

Languages may be translated; the 'generative power' of language found in its metaphorical nature shows that language is not a prison, but a road.[23] If a language lacks the terms to communicate what the original biblical languages convey, that lack does not open an unbridgeable chasm. Circumlocutions can skirt the difficulty, metaphors may be coined, expressions may be borrowed from the biblical languages or other languages, and defined by their usage in the biblical context.

No language or culture is opaque to the gospel. Every culture is tainted with human apostasy, every language reflects that bias, but every culture may be transformed by the gospel, and every language made a vehicle for the gospel and for a redeemed understanding of life and the world.

Cultural and linguistic diversity enriches our understanding of God's revelation in both nature and Scripture. God's revelation both used and transformed Near Eastern and Hellenistic culture in the inspiration of Scripture. It is not necessary to be a shepherd to appreciate the meaning of pastoral figures in the Bible. God's revelation is not so much super-cultural as infra-cultural: the revelation of the divine Logos from whom culture-creators derive their being. The effort to express the revealed truth of the gospel in other languages and other cultural contexts inevitably opens new perspectives on that revelation itself.

The Christian who travels may be surprised to see pigs wander through an African church service, or to hear the Scriptures chanted by Muslim converts, but be moved to praise, sensing the multicultural universality that springs from the unity of God's truth. At Pentecost the divisions of Babel were overcome. The apostles spoke no heavenly language, or even a spiritual Esperanto as one universal language, but the many languages of their world. Yet their message unified divided peoples and formed a new humanity in the church. Commenting on the 'contextualized' theologies that have arisen – African, Asian, black, Hispanic – Bruce Nicholls wisely observes: 'The truer they are to the givenness of biblical theology the more complementary and the less contradictory they become.'[24]

Scripture is the norm for evaluating culture. Stephen Neill lists cultural practices that the Bible condemns outright: idolatry, witchcraft and sorcery, female infanticide, abortion, the killing of twins, cannibalism and head-hunting in New Guinea, private vengeance and blood feuds in Arabia, ritual prostitution in India, even cattle-raiding as a way of life among the Masai of Africa.[25] Other practices not condemned categorically by the Bible are so transformed by the biblical message as to remove them from the practice of the church: slavery, the caste system, polygamy, polyandry and tribalism. Still other cultural patterns, neither condemned nor discountenanced in the Bible, are still subject to the transforming and patterning power of the gospel message: customs in eating, drinking, marriage, dress, bathing, etc.

In the dynamic approach of the mission of the church, the witness of both word and life encounters the peoples of the world. A new word is spoken, the powerful word of God's mercy, calling them to repentance and faith. The Spirit who speaks

181

through the Word employs the formative power of language. As the message rises on the horizon of a culture, its light reveals not only the sin of the individual, but the twisted structures of the culture itself. Often this leads to a power encounter. In the eighth century, Boniface, the first missionary to Germany, chopped down the oak of Thor at Geismar in Hesse.[26] As Stephen Neill has pointed out, the Germans would understand this act of defiance as a trial by ordeal (like that of Elijah on Mount Carmel). Since Boniface destroyed the sacred oak with impunity, his God must be stronger than Thor. Boniface respected their culture; he did not insult the people to whom he preached: he challenged their god. But his chopping down the oak undercut the creed of their culture, beginning a long process of cultural transformation.

Paul's gospel for the nations trumpets the dawning of a new age – not the 'Age of Aquarius', but the time of Christ's lordship when God's Word goes out to the nations that had lived in 'the times of ignorance'. The gospel still summons the peoples to shed the fears and burdens that all cultures know too well, and to grasp a promise beyond imagining.

Spoken witness is confirmed by the testimony of life (1 Cor. 4:9, 16; 11:1; Phil. 2:14–16). Before missionaries can speak a sentence in the tribal language, their lives can speak volumes. By returning to the Auca tribe that had speared her husband to death, Elisabeth Elliot eloquently lived out the gospel of grace. Resident missionary families have long been the cutting edge of approach in tribal areas, and now, too, this is true in urban population centres. Although the living witness of the church is absent or hidden for a distressingly large proportion of the world's peoples, shifts in population and student visas have brought unreached people to communities where the church is present. Millions of refugees and political exiles can observe the life of the evangelical churches for the first time. Without the obedient life of Christians, the opportunity for witness will be lost, and the world will throw the gospel invitation back into the church's face in mockery. The scandals of TV evangelists in the United States have made the point unforgettable.

Where, then, should a missionary begin in approaching people with the gospel? Is there a key, a point of contact?

Scholars have given us a baffling array of different answers.

Eugene Nida finds language the point of contact. Hendrik Kraemer says it is in the life of the missionary. J. H. Bavinck gives God's general revelation as the area of contact, while Karl Barth puts it in God the Holy Spirit. Matteo Ricci appealed to the 'natural theology' of the Chinese classics. Bruno Gutmann made contact by identifying with African tribal life, 'going native'. Cornelius Van Til taught that the image of God in man is the point of contact. Are these different answers all in response to the same question? There are, in fact, different questions.

We may ask a theological question: what does God's Word teach us about the situation of lost humanity and how the gospel can touch them? This is the most basic question about the point of contact. It is true that all people are made in the image of God and are therefore addressable by him. They are all sinners, with darkened understandings, but they are confronted by God's general revelation and preserved by his common grace. We know this in principle without yet knowing anything in particular about the people group we would reach. Note how some of the answers above reply to this question.

Building on that foundation, we may ask another question: What have these people done with God? This is asking not how does God see them, but how do they see God. It addresses the religious core of their culture (even atheism is a religious attitude). The point of contact calls for contrast, but contact must be made. Krishna worship needs to be taken seriously, and its devotion understood, so that Christians can show why they cannot adopt Hinduism and make Jesus another avatar like Krishna. Some people – Muslims, for example – relish religious discussions. Others may think of themselves as not religious. Our approaches will differ, but basic religious commitment must be addressed, or even professed conversion may prove superficial.

A third question is not so deep but it is much broader. We ask, 'Who are you?' in the more usual sense. Apart from religious commitment, where is the person in society? What people group is addressed, and what is the role of the individual? 'Point of contact' in this sense has to do with knowing language and customs, and with establishing rapport over cultural, social and personal barriers.

The point of contact at each of these three levels –
theological, religious and cultural – applies to the missionary
approach in both word and life. For instance, the steady
effectiveness of 'tent-making' missionaries shows the impact of
the witness of life in lands where public Christian witness is
forbidden and proselytizing severely punished. On the other
hand, the 'word only' witness of radio and literature may reach
populations whose only Christian presence is in underground
church groups.

The following chart highlights some of the key issues that
arise at each of the three levels when mission takes place,
whether by life or by word.

Aspects of approach in mission

	'Broader' approach (Life)	'Kerygmatic' approach (Word)
Theological level	Created being: image of God Cultural task Fall: disruption, curse Common grace	Created understanding: language Religious capacity Fall: depravity in understanding General revelation
Religious level	Encounter in life Worship: ethics of Christian community Cultural transformation in the Christian community	Encounter in witness: addressing pattern of unbelief Contact with cultus: critique or confrontation Direct and indirect approach
Cultural level	Contextual life of the church Establishment of rapport over cultural, social and personal barriers	Contextualizing the message Establishment of communication: Bible translation, style in preaching, teaching

184

A strategy of approach may focus on just one of these three levels.

Some strategies adopt a direct approach, aiming straight at the basic situation of those addressed, as theologically defined. Since we know the real condition and need of lost sinners, why not address it directly? An extreme example of this was an early missionary in East Africa who travelled from village to village with a phonograph and a recording of John 3:16 in Swahili. He did not know the language of the tribes, but he knew the message they needed. The same conviction moves the missionary who keeps just the reference 'John 3:16' on camera at sporting events in the United States.

Other strategies are aimed at the religious beliefs of non-Christian peoples. Raymond Lull, the medieval Franciscan missionary to Islam, developed a logic to show the unity of all truth and used it in disputations with Islamic scholars in an effort to win them to Christian faith. Since Thomas Aquinas wrote his *Summa contra Gentiles*, many specific systems of apologetics have been developed to deal with adherents of various sects and non-Christian religions.

Still other strategies are more contextualized, aimed at specific social situations and cultural interests. If we draw a diagram and put the target of approach as a bull's-eye, we might designate the centre as the theological core of culture; the next ring as the cultus of the people, their system of religious observances; and the outer ring as the social and cultural customs that carry out the core commitments.

The advantage of a strategy aimed at the bull's eye is the economy of time and the frankness of confrontation that it employs. There are serious weaknesses, however, in using the abrupt 'Brother, are you saved?' approach. The basic issue is raised, but the response may not be brotherly. Many who pray the prayer after being led through the 'Four Spiritual Laws' of Campus Crusade have little understanding of the significance of what they have done, or of the price of discipleship. The direct approach is often needlessly offensive, brushing aside all personal interest and viewing people only as objects of evangelism, like scalps on the soul-winner's belt.

Focusing on the religious affiliation of a person or group may still be too general. It may also miss the mark for those whose religion is nominal or unorthodox.

A strategy aimed at the outer ring wins a hearing by taking a person or group seriously, appreciating their culture, and listening synpathetically to their problems. The danger is that the evangelist may never get to the core issue, or that by the time he gets there, he will have shown so much tolerance and sympathy that the confrontation will be neither acceptable nor believable.

In practice, however, strategy is seldom limited to one level. Because cultures are inconsistent and broken, many cracks run from the periphery to the centre. On a long plane flight I might begin by showing personal interest in a seat companion, seeking to spiral in toward more substantive discussion, but make little progress. At this rate, I may fear, the plane will land before I communicate any gospel at all. But then, in conversation about personal concerns, I learn that the stranger is flying to attend the funeral of his father from whom he was alienated for most of his life. A crack has opened that leads from peripheral matters to the core of my companion's convictions.

In all concern about the strategy of approach, one fixed point remains: mission is the work of God. His Spirit prepares the way, opens the heart and brings the message and the hearer home.

13

THE KINGDOM,
THE CHURCH AND
THE STATE

On a cold November day in 1095, a French Pope, Urban II, stood in the fields of Clermont, France, to address an assembly of thousands. Princes, knights, bishops, priests and monks heard his resounding voice call them to holy war against the Turks who held Jerusalem. In those days before television, the Pope had to provide his own graphic description of the tortures and atrocities committed by the infidels against Christians in the Holy Land. Who should avenge these wrongs, who recover the holy places, if not the French, the flower of Christian chivalry? Let them remember Charlemagne and his successors 'who destroyed the kingdoms of the pagans and planted the holy church in their lands'.[1] They must recover the Holy Sepulchre from the hands of unclean nations.

Since fighting each other was both vocation and avocation for his knightly hearers, the Pope challenged them to redirect their killing. 'If you must have blood, bathe in the blood of infidels . . . Soldiers of Hell, become soldiers of the living God!' The crusades undercut the mission of the church to Islamic lands for a millennium, for they committed the Christian faith to a *jihad*, a holy war under Christ's banner. This betrayed the mission of the church in the world; armed might cannot advance the kingdom of the Lord Jesus, who had made Peter sheathe his sword. Jesus told Pilate that he was indeed King (Jn. 18:37), and he does not lack royal power. The God-man is Lord of all: his salvation brings judgment as well as redemption (Ps. 96:13; Jn. 5:21–23); his rule in heaven now governs all creation, and he will put down all evil for ever (1 Cor. 15:24–28; Heb. 1:4; Col. 2:15; Phil.2:9–11). Yet Jesus told Pilate that his kingdom is not of this world, otherwise his servants would fight to defend him and to bring it in (Jn. 18:36). What does Jesus mean?

Christ's kingdom of grace and glory

Christ's kingdom is a kingdom of grace and of glory. The cross is the way of his saving grace. His disciples did not understand this; to them Messianic salvation meant political deliverance from the Romans. In Herod's prison, John the Baptist was dismayed that Jesus did not use his power to bring in the judgment (Lk. 7:18–19). He sent his disciples to ask Jesus, 'Are you the one who was to come, or should we expect someone else?' (Lk. 7:20). Jesus sent John's disciples back to him as witnesses of the Messianic miracles that fulfilled prophecy (Is. 35:5–6; 61:1). He added a word for John: 'Blessed is the man who does not fall away on account of me' (Lk. 7:23).

Jesus was in fact telling John, 'Trust me to bring in my kingdom my way.' Had he brought judgment, Jesus could have spared neither Herod nor any sinner, not even doubting John. Jesus came in the flesh not to *bring* the judgment, but to *bear* it; not to slay with the sword of his lips, but to receive the nails in his hands and the spear-thrust in his side. In no other way could his kingdom come and God's will be done in earth as in heaven. The kingdom established by grace must be advanced by grace, then consummated in glory. Not by political power, but by the power of the Spirit, is the gospel carried to the nations.

Glory as well as grace defines Christ's kingdom. For him glory has already begun, and by his Spirit from the throne we begin to taste it (Rom. 14:17). The glory that will appear when he appears is a glory in which we already rejoice in spite of our trials (1 Pet. 1:7–8; 4:14; 2 Cor. 3:18). Not through a political utopia enforced by the sword will Christ judge and renovate the earth, but by his return in glory. Our salvation is nearer than when we believed, because Christ's coming is nearer. We have the down-payment on glory in the presence of the Spirit as we wait for the kingdom that is to come.

The church as the community of Christ's kingdom on earth is a theo-political order.[2] While all things are under the rule of Christ, it is his *saving* rule that constitutes his kingdom (Col. 1:13). The church is the heavenly *polis* on earth, the new humanity whose hearts are circumcised by his Spirit. Its breadth reaches out to all peoples; its depth renews the heart (Je. 32:39; Ezk. 11:19). The 'ethnicity' of the church as the new Israel of God underscores its communal reality, which is not diminished but enhanced because it is spiritual. We have no abiding city here; the church cannot be identified with the kingdoms of this world (Heb. 13:14). But we do have a city with foundations, whose builder and maker is God; the church exercises heavenly citizenship in the fellowship of the saints (Heb. 11:10, 16; 12:28; Phil. 3:20). The community exists on earth, but it is governed by the keys of the heavenly kingdom, with spiritual, not physical, sanctions (Mt. 16:19; Rev. 3:7).

As a company of heaven-bound pilgrims, the church does not wield the sword (Jn. 18:11, 36). It *need* not fight, for God's kingdom needs no human weapons; it *may* not fight, for (as the Crusaders learned) the sword cannot bring kingdom salvation. Our weapons are spiritual, and the more potent for that reason (2 Cor. 10:4–5; Eph. 6:12–18; 1 Cor. 4:8). Nor may the church attach itself to worldly conceptions of honour and power.

Jacques Ellul refers to an incident that is sometimes adduced as a prime example of the absurdity of theological speculation: while the Turks surrounded Constantinople, the Byzantines were busy debating the doctrine of the Trinity. But, asks Ellul, 'What, in the final analysis, is really important for the whole of mankind – that Jesus is indeed the Christ? – or that the Turks defeated the Byzantines in the early 15th century?'[3] The sword cannot decide ultimate questions.

Sad to say, the church has often sought the advantage of the sword by handing it to the state to wield on its behalf. This was the practice in the long history of the Inquisition, beginning in 1163 when Pope Alexander III urged bishops to seek out heretics and the secular princes to punish them.[4] In Calvin's

Geneva, the church condemned Servetus, but it was the city magistrates who burned him. The Crusades were preached by the church, but it was troops of European princes who did the fighting.

Church–state relationship

How, then, should the church relate to the state?

The church, while a company of pilgrims, is also an embassy of Christ's kingdom, representing the authority of Christ. By his command, the church teaches Christians to be subject to the state. We are to render to Caesar that which is Caesar's (Mk. 12:13–17; Tit. 3:1; Rom. 13:1–2). This is not an option or a strategy, but an obligation. God ordains government to establish his purposes (Rom. 13:3–4). Like others, Christians benefit from the order that governments bring. Indeed, our evangelistic task is aided by civil peace (1 Tim. 2:1–7), just as the *pax Romanum* offered Paul opportunity for his journeys. Our service to God includes obedience to civil authority for conscience's sake (Rom. 12:1–2; 13:1–2).

The fact that governments are authorized by God does not guarantee that their actions will be just. Daniel's prophecy likens world empires to beasts rising out of the sea; the book of Revelation also depicts pagan government as a threatening Beast (Rev. 13 – 14). Christian obedience to the state cannot be blind. When the state commands what God forbids, or forbids what God commands, we must obey God rather than men (Acts 5:29). Jesus warned his disciples that they must suffer before magistrates for his sake (Mk. 13:9).

Nor are Christians necessarily called to suffer state persecution in silence. Jesus called Herod 'that fox' (Lk. 13:32); John the Baptist rebuked the same notorious king for his incestuous marriage (Mk. 6:18); Paul remonstrated against illegal procedures in his hearing before the Sanhedrin – although he apologized for calling the high priest a 'whited wall', because of the respect due to his office (Acts 23:3). The Christian may criticize, but stands before a magistrate in meekness and respect, to give a reason for the hope that is within him or her (1 Pet. 3:15).

Church, family, society and state

The church witnesses to the righteousness of the kingdom, penetrating society like leaven or salt, but it is not identified with the world it touches. The church is neither competitive nor correlative to the family, to the state, or to other societal institutions. These are the forms of life in the world, from which the church is distinguished.

It is a mistake to suppose that the invisible church finds institutional expression not only in the visible church, but also in the family, the state and various societal groups.[5] The church is the form that Christ has appointed for the community of those who confess his name; in the church alone, the body of Christ is made visible in this world.

In patriarchal times, the kingdom was ordered in the form of the family; later it had the form of a state (Israel); now it has the outward form of a societal institution. In each case, however, the form that God appointed has clear differences from the secular institutions that it resembles. The Lord overruled patriarchal family structures to choose the heir of the promise (Isaac, Jacob, and then Joseph). Later, God's covenant at Sinai created a

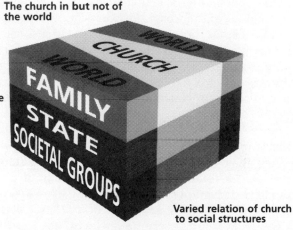

The church in but not of the world

Forms of social life in the world

Varied relation of church to social structures

The church in the world

191

unique nation, shaped by God's laws and under his rule. The Lord limited Israel's expansion and barred treaties with other nations that would deny its theocratic basis. Unlike other voluntary societies, the church is not freely organized by its constituents, but, like the patriarchal family and the covenantal nation, it is theocratic in its basic structure.

In the history of redemption, the forms that God appointed for his church show continuity of development. The family is not outmoded or dissolved, but drawn into the church community; family relationship is transformed within a spiritual family, the fellowship of the saints. Though God judges Israel, he does not abandon his covenant. Paul shows the continuity of the Old Covenant with the New, using the organic image of the one olive tree from which the natural branches are broken off and to which the wild branches are grafted (Rom. 11:16–21). While 'not all who are descended from Israel are Israel' (Rom. 9:6), the church continues the true Israel of God, the real and spiritual circumcision promised by the prophets (Phil. 3:2–4; Eph. 2:11–22).

Continuity does not mean identity, however, for renewal and fulfilment require change. Though the church is both a family and a nation in the spiritual sense, it does not have the form of a patriarchal family, or take its place as a Christian nation among the nations of the world. As God's family, it models Christ's love in the closest bonds of human relationships; as God's new humanity, it rebukes the pride and intolerance of modern nationalism, showing a unity that transcends cultural and ethnic distinctions. No matter how tragically the church may fail to demonstrate the holy love of the kingdom, its mandate remains.

Christian reponsibility in politics

Zeal for the righteousness of the kingdom will witness to the values that society must uphold. If Paul insisted on honouring the pagan totalitarian state of his day, he would find the democratic state, leavened by centuries of Christian influence, no less worthy of respect and support. Since democracy gives its citizens a voice in government, Christians have the responsibility of their privilege to participate. There is every reason for the general office of the church ('laity') to consult together on political issues. So, too, the special officers of the church must provide biblical guidance and wisdom to assist in Christian analysis of political questions. The church has a prophetic role to perceive and expose ethical questions that underlie political issues. Where God has spoken in condemning sin, whether sodomy or financial exploitation, the church cannot be silent. Under Communist and Fascist rule, the church of Christ has repeatedly paid the price for applying Christian doctrine to political wrongs. In democratic regimes also that price has been – and will yet be – exacted.

Yet Christian involvement in political life does not cancel out the spiritual form of Christ's kingdom. Calling the state to righteousness does not mean calling it to promote the gospel with political power or to usher in the last judgment with the sword. Christians are not free to form an exclusively Christian political party that seeks to exercise power in the name of Christ.[6] That would identify Christ's cause with one of the kingdoms of this world. Political action on the part of Christians must always be undertaken in concert with others who seek the same immediate objectives.[7] Such objectives, promoting life, liberty and the restraint of violence, are the proper goals of civil government. They are not the goals of faith and holiness that Christ appointed for his kingdom.

Here the question of an established church arises, particularly with regard to the Church of England. It has been said that 'King Henry VIII froze the Church of England'.[8] The shift from the Pope to Henry as the 'Supreme Head of the English Church and Clergy' (1532) established the government of the church before it had completed the process of internal reformation. The later Puritan effort at reform disintegrated in civil war and ended with the Restoration of Charles II. The break with Rome was not due merely to Henry's marital interests, but to the political influence of the papacy in the appointment of bishops. Henry's claim to headship over the church sought the interests of national sovereignty, not the perfecting of scriptural church order.

Many privileges of the established church have since become merely ceremonial: the right of the Archbishop of Canterbury to crown the Sovereign, religious services associated with events of national life, the Sovereign's required communion in the Church. The parish system, however, still gives each parishioner the right to be married, to have a child baptized, and to be buried with benefit of clergy. Since there has been little practice of discipline, Britain's nominal faith stands like an empty church edifice marking the graves of the past. The drift has not been checked by the curriculum for Christian religious education in the schools, desirable as that might seem when compared with the incredible exclusion of all reference to biblical teaching in the public schools of the United States.

The authority of the Crown over the Church remains, now exercised, not by the Sovereign as a member of the Church, but by the Prime Minister and the Cabinet. These are not necessarily Christians, and they could appoint non-Christians as bishops and university professors to train the clergy. (The Prime Minister can appoint but cannot consecrate bishops.) Church law requires the approval of Crown and Parliament even in regard to matters of faith and worship. In 1928, the House of Commons rejected a revision of the *Book of Common Prayer* presented by the Convocations of bishops and clergy.

Today, a pragmatic shift has given the church more independence, according greater authority to a synodical structure with houses of bishops, clergy and laity. Few are satisfied with the remaining authority of the state over the church, particularly in view of the increasingly pluralistic population of England. Even an established church need not be so subjected, as the Church of Scotland shows. The spread of Anglicanism overseas also demonstrates that it need not be under the British Crown.

Advocates argue that only an established church has freedom from the limiting distinctives of a denominational body, and can be simply the church catholic without credal definition.[9] This assumes that the 'assent' of the clergy to the Thirty-Nine Articles means only that they were somewhat useful in the sixteenth century, and that the genius of the Church of England is its doctrinal inclusiveness. Liberal denials of basic Christian doctrine, however, need no Crown or hierarchy for shelter. Denominational headquarters of free churches now offer the same doctrinal pluralism. They will tolerate all possible views, except, perhaps, the views of those who find such tolerance intolerable.

Change in the form of the Church of England seems inevitable. Only great changes in practice, though not in theory, have kept the system viable. The Lion of royalty has lived long without teeth; it would be foolish to predict the end of the established church. Yet practical as well as principial problems point to complete independence of Christ's church from the sovereignty of the state. Church government is exclusively spiritual; its officers are chosen from among its members because of their spiritual gifts. No part of the kingdom rule of Christ over his church can be delegated to the state and enforced by the sword.

The patriotism is misguided that sees the United States or the United Kingdom as a Christian nation composed of God's elect and entitled to his favour and blessing. Such a claim is patently false, and illegitimate even as an ideal. Christ's kingdom is not typical and preparatory, like the kingdom of Israel; it is realized and ultimate. All that is less than loving God with heart, soul, strength and mind, and one's neighbour as one's self, is totally excluded by the new law of love. That is why the ultimate enforcement of Christ's law must be brought about, not by political power, but by his own judgment at his appearing, and by the total transformation that will make his bride spotless for the wedding feast of glory.

Christians must favour a limited role for government: to support life and restrain evil, but not to enforce the righteous living that is the standard of morality for Christ's church. Salvation does not now come by the 'redemption' of the political order, but by the new birth that brings lost sinners into the kingdom of God.

John Stott, in a book as weighty as it is brief, makes this last point in contrast to liberation theology and to statements of the WCC Assembly in Bangkok, 1973, on the theme 'Salvation Today'.[10] He reminds us that Jesus came on a rescue mission 'to save sinners' (1 Tim. 1:15). That salvation, Stott declares, is not socio-political liberation.[11]

At the same time, Stott seeks to emphasize social action in the mission of the church. While some would make social action a *means* to evangelism, and others view it as a *manifestation* of evangelism, Stott urges that it be seen as a *partner* to evangelism.[12] He reasons that 'The Great Commission neither explains, nor exhausts, nor supersedes the Great Commandment' of love to God and neighbour.[13] As Christ came into the world to serve, so

195

we, as his disciples, are to serve human need wherever we encounter it, loving our neighbour as ourselves. 'Mission' describes everything the church is sent into the world to do, including the political dimension of social concern.[14] While our love of neighbour is first expressed in our desire to share the gospel (2 Cor. 5:14, 20), it does not stop there, but extends to all human needs, including political needs.

We must appreciate the truth of Stott's contention that the Great Commandment controls all our service of the Lord, and that we are called to serve him in many vocations, not simply in evangelistic work. But we must not forget the difference of which Stott also reminds us: the difference between the salvation that Jesus came to bring at his first coming and the salvation he will bring when he comes again. Jesus did not join Jewish freedom fighters to oppose the Romans, nor did he empty the prisons of Palestine. Social action may oppose evils that God hates, but it cannot bring the salvation that Christ lived and died for.[15] The mission of Jesus had a particular focus – to be the Saviour of the world (1 Jn. 4:14). He came to serve; the heart of that service was to give his life a ransom for many (Mk. 10:45). Even the miracles of Christ were *signs*, as Stott points out.[16] Jesus healed to reveal himself, and to point to the deeper salvation he came to bring.

When we consider whether social action is part of the mission of the church, we must keep to the limit that Jesus set. The weapons of the church are spiritual, not physical; the kingdom is not to be advanced by the sword. Speaking of a proposed evangelical strategy for the evangelization of Britain, Stott says, 'Perhaps it should also be concerned not only for evangelism, but for mission in the wider sense. Or maybe this is a job for the Shaftesbury Project or the Festival of Light or some other organization.'[17] His hesitation is wise, and revealing. Describing the political dimension of social concern as including 'the quest for better social structures in which peace, dignity, freedom and justice are secured for all men', Stott adds, 'And there is no reason why, in pursuing this quest, we should not join hands with all men of good will, even if they are not Christians.'[18] The critical point here is that we not only may, but *must* co-operate with other citizens when we seek to use the levers of political power. We do so, not as citizens of the heavenly Jerusalem, but of an earthly nation. Christians may not band together in the name of Christ to use the political weapons of the world to fight the spiritual battle of the kingdom. There is a love of divine benevolence that sends rain on the just and unjust, and there is a duty for Christian citizens to show that love to others. Yet the line must be drawn between the ministry of mercy that is part of the mission of the church, and the reach for political power that would destroy the church by politicizing it.

We have considered the ministry of the church in worship, nurture and mission, and have reflected on the relation of the church to culture and to the state. In the next chapter we look at the structure of the church itself, and at the scriptural principles that can guide us in discerning the normative features of church organization.

14

THE STRUCTURE
OF CHRIST'S
CHURCH

Critics of 'churchianity' hold that institutional structure freezes the flowing streams of the Spirit. The task of the church is indeed spiritual, as we have seen: to worship God, to nurture the people of God, and to bear witness to the world in mission. Yet no less spiritual are the means that Christ has provided by which we are to achieve these three goals. The Spirit of Christ brings order, as well as ardour.

The means of ministry

In every task of the church, the *ministry of the Word of God* is central. It is the Word that calls us to *worship*, addresses us in worship, teaches us how to worship and enables us to praise God and to encourage one another. By the Word we are given life and *nurtured* to maturity in Christ: the Word is the sword of the Spirit to correct us and the bread of the Spirit to feed us. In the *mission* of the church, it is the Word of God that calls the nations to the Lord: in the teaching of the Word we make disciples of the nations. The growth of the church is the growth of the Word (Acts 6:7; 12:24; 19:20): where there is a famine of the Word, no expertise in business administration or group dynamics will build Christ's church.

The three goals of the church are to be sought not only through the Word, but also in the obedience of love. When they are so sought, a *ministry of order* will result. The Lord rejects the *worship* of those who honour him with their lips, but who do not love and honour him in their hearts and lives (Is. 29:13). We *nurture* one another by deeds of love, not just by sharing Scripture texts. In the *mission* of the church, deeds and words combine in our witness (Phil. 2:15). Love that is real requires accountability, and accountability means order. The discipline of the church appears in the love that Christians show for one another, in encouraging, counselling, asking, 'How are you doing?' and looking for an answer.

As God's Word grounds our ministry in faith, and the order of the church commits it to the ministry of love, so the *ministry of mercy* opens the door of hope. Love is the fruit of faith, and hope springs up when love serves human distress and need. The miracles of Jesus were signs of hope, for they showed his compassion and his purpose in delivering us from sin's curse.

Mercy appears in our *worship.* The gifts for the poor in Jerusalem, for instance, were an offering to the Lord (2 Cor. 9:12–15; see Phil. 4:18). We cannot *nurture* one another if we will not help one another (Jas. 2:15–16). The *mission* of the church that proclaims Christ's love of compassion also shows compassion for the sick and the poor.

The diagram opposite demonstrates how the three means of ministry outlined above intersect with the three goals of ministry. (This forms the base for the three-dimensional diagram that appears on page 209.)

The forms of ministry

With the goals and the means of ministry before us, we may naturally ask about the forms of ministry. How is the service of the church ordered? What authority does it exercise? Who is to conduct the ministry? Is there an organization chart?

Apparatchiks are never popular, and if political and business paper-shufflers are bad, ecclesiastical clerks and clerics can be worse. The blight of church bureaucracy, however, is not just

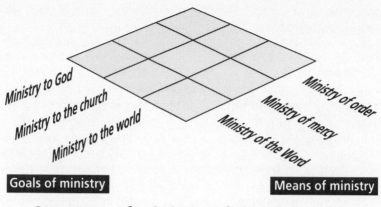

Goals of ministry

Means of ministry

Structure of ministry of the church (1)

paper-shuffling; it is the tyrannies that have been built over denominational life. Occasionally church members stage a revolt, as in 1991 when the 203rd General Assembly of the Presbyterian Church (USA) rejected a shockingly permissive report on human sexuality. More often, decrees from denominational headquarters go unchallenged until at last churches seek relief by leaving the denomination.

Such abuses move many Christians to reject all church structure, whether at the denominational or local level. Yet, if formal structures are refused, informal ones will gain their own validity in practice. Churches that reject denominational connection will often form their own connections by participation in parachurch structures: an inter-church mission conference to co-ordinate missionary activities, a Sunday School union, the Christian education curriculum of a US Christian publisher, the activities of Youth for Christ or Campus Crusade.

Local leaders will gain recognition in spite of the most egalitarian efforts at simple brotherhood. The danger of setting aside biblical principles appears when the church is organized after an alien model – that of an entrepreneurial business, for example, or of the military. It is all too easy for such a church to operate under the direction of an ecclesiastical chief executive officer, exercising an authority that a Borgia Pope might envy.

1. Church authority

Our understanding of the government of Christ's church must begin with the Lord himself and his *kingdom authority*. He is the Head of the church; his rule is unique and incomparable. A second principle derives from the first. The church shows the *organic life* of Christ's body: it lives as an organism, not just an organization. The third principle is no less essential. The church is not like the kingdoms of this world, for it is organized for service, not dominion. All government in the church is *stewardship*: *i.e.* its leaders are servant-managers, who use their authority only to advance the interests of those they represent and serve.

Some forms of church government reflect these principles better than others, yet even the best form of church government is an empty shell if these principles do not grip the hearts of those who lead and those who follow. Better by far are imperfect structures in the hands of devoted servants of Christ than the most biblical form of church government practised in pride or in a loveless and vindictive spirit.

Christ exercises his absolute authority on behalf of his body, the church. His rule over the church differs from his rule over the universe, for it is his saving rule: he frees his people from the power of the devil (Col. 1:13–14). All authority in the church belongs to Christ. From his place of authority at God's right hand, Christ gives the keys of his kingdom; he validates in heaven what is done in his name on earth. Church government cannot modify his Word by deletion or addition (Rev. 22:18–20; Gal. 1:8, 12). Because its power is declarative, not legislative, it may not invent new doctrines or require practices that have no scriptural foundation.

The rule of Christ is made effective by his Spirit, through whom he illumines our understanding of his Word, and gives us wisdom to apply it to the changing circumstances of our lives. As we have seen, the process of applying the Word of Christ to new situations and different cultures leads to deeper insights into Christ's teaching. Through the Spirit, too, Christ guides his church in its service. The rule of Christ through his Word and Spirit is not the dead hand of human tradition reaching from the past. Rather, by his living truth and the abiding presence of his Spirit the Lord governs, guides and refreshes his people.

Because Christ's saving kingdom is spiritual, not temporal, the power given to the church must also be spiritual. The government of the church cannot use political sanctions or physical force (Jn. 18:36–37; Mt. 22:16–21; 2 Cor. 10:3–6).

Church authority, grounded in the Word of Christ, is also limited to it. Christian obedience to church rule is obedience in the Lord, for his Word governs the church, not the other way round. The conscientious freedom to disobey remains if the government of the church commands anything contrary to the Word, which is open to all. (Such freedom also applies, as we have already seen, when the church goes *beyond* the Word in matters of faith or worship.)

The Protestant Reformers protested against the abuse of authority in the Roman Catholic Church, because its teachings were in part against Scripture (including its teaching on the need for good works with faith for justification; and on the mass as a renewed sacrifice); and in part adding to Scripture (the Virgin Mary's sinlessness and mediatorial place; the papal claims to temporal authority; and the system of indulgences). Another issue was also involved: if the Pope possessed apostolic authority, the Catholic Church could add tradition to Scripture, for it had in the Pope not only an infallible interpreter of Scripture and tradition, but a Vicar of Christ who could still add to the apostolic teaching on which Christ established the church. The Reformers denied to the Pope the apostolic authority given in the completed canon of Scripture.

Modern abuse of ecclesiastical power continues: it may bind on the church the 'political correctness' of secular society, or it may enforce total control over subjugated disciples. But the drift of modern society takes the opposite direction. Church members frown at the suggestion that the church should have authority beyond that of a club to make its own rules.[1] That Christ expects the keys of the kingdom to be used in the discipline of the church runs counter to the notions that religion is a matter of private opinion, and that religious association is optional.

Spiritual power, however, is more, not less, effective than

physical power. Equipped with the keys of the kingdom, church government represents the authority of Christ the Lord, who will judge the living and the dead. Though church government is fallible in applying Christ's Word, Christians must submit to it (Heb. 13:17; 1 Cor. 4:21; 2 Cor. 13:2, 10). There is a recognized fellowship of believers, to which others who believe are added by baptism (Acts 2:41, 47). Within this fellowship, rule is exercised by those with recognized gifts (Acts 20:28; 1 Tim. 5:17; 1 Cor. 12:28), and Christians are to respect that rule (1 Thes. 5:12–13). Those who sin are to be corrected, and if they refuse to hear the church through its officers, they are to be excluded from the fellowship (Mt. 18:17–18; 1 Cor. 5:13; 2 Thes. 3:6–7, 14–15; 1 Tim. 1:20; Tit. 3:10–11).

Solemn as the authority of the church is, it is *gospel* authority. The disciples misunderstood when they wanted to call down fire from heaven on a Samaritan town (Lk. 9:49–56). Paul asked for discipline reluctantly, since his calling as an apostle was to build up, not to cast down (1 Cor. 10:8). Even excommunication does not pronounce God's anathema, for part of its design is to reclaim the erring brother (1 Cor. 5:5; 2 Cor. 2:6–7; Gal. 6:1).

The model of church order is organic. The body of Christ is made up of members who are dependent on one another in the exercise of the life they have from Christ. Paul presents the unity of the Spirit in the great variety of gifts granted to the church (1 Cor. 12). Peter also describes the 'multi-hued' gifts with which the church is endued, and defines two classes: gifts of speaking God's Word and gifts of serving (1 Pet. 4:10–11). To be effectively exercised, some gifts require recognition by the community. This is particularly true of the gifts for rule (Rom. 12:8; 1 Cor. 12:28; 1 Tim. 5:17). Publicly recognized gifts differ only in degree, not in kind, from gifts possessed by every believer. This is denied by the Roman Catholic Church, which teaches that the common priesthood of the faithful and the hierarchical priesthood 'differ essentially and not only in degree'.[2] Vatican II labours to recognize the place of the laity, and their sharing the offices of Christ as Prophet, Priest and King. But the hierarchical structure remains: only the priest in Holy Orders 'effects the eucharistic sacrifice and offers it to God in the name of all the people'.[3]

Jesus contrasted the brotherhood of his disciples with the hierarchical attitudes of the rabbis (Mt. 23:7–12). Paul applies the same principle to those who were proud of their spiritual gifts at Corinth (1 Cor. 12). Differing gifts do not divide, but unite, for their exercise is mutual. The governing of the church is a shared responsibility. Any Christian man or woman who rebukes a fellow-believer participates in the governing of Christ's church. Without the support of the whole body, the work of those with greater gifts for leadership would not be effective, or even possible. We submit to the authority of others while exercising our own.

Organic mutuality requires the joint exercise of church authority. Jesus did not choose one apostle but twelve, and sent them out two by two as witnesses. The Roman Catholic Church, by misconstruing the place of Peter in the apostolic company, and by claiming that the Pope is Peter's successor, gave to the Pope 'full, supreme and universal power over the whole church, a power which he can always exercise unhindered'.[4] The bishops cannot exercise such authority without the Pope, but he can exercise it without them.

Peter surely did not exercise papal authority in the book of Acts, where he was not even chairman of the Christian council which met in Jerusalem (Acts 15:13–22). Paul and Barnabas appointed a plurality of elders, not just one bishop, in the churches that they planted (Acts 14:23). James advises one who is ill to call for the elders of the church (Jas. 5:14).

The recognition of metropolitan bishops after the apostolic age has been defended as a proper improvement, necessary to defend the apostolic faith and preserve church unity against threatening heresies.[5] Presbyterians, insisting on the sufficiency of Scripture, maintain that by precept and example the New Testament presents a church order in which a plurality of elders join in governing the church. Episcopalians find in the angels of the seven churches in Revelation early evidence of singular bishops. Presbyterian practice, they note, has strayed from Presbyterian principle, since the 'superintendents' of Scottish Presbyterian history could pass for bishops by another name. (Most are agreed that 'bishop' and 'elder' are two terms for the same office in the New Testament.)

In any case, Scripture teaches mutuality in the exercise of the gifts of the Spirit as a major principle in the ordering of the church.

Church government is organized for service, not dominion. Church office serves both the Lord and his people. The Old Testament concept of elders as representatives of the people was not simply carried over from patriarchal societies. It was founded by God's command when, in response to the plea of Moses, the Lord told him to assemble seventy elders acknowledged by the people to share with him the burden of judging Israel (Nu. 11:16). These elders were set apart to their office by a gift of the Spirit. They were not only judges, but also spokesmen for the people (Dt. 19:12; 21:19; Ex. 3:16; 4:29; 24:1–2; 1 Sa. 8:4; 2 Sa. 5:3).

In the New Testament, they are still called 'elders of the people' (Mt. 21:23; 26:3, 47; 27:1). When Luke, who has spoken of the elders of Israel in his Gospel (Lk. 22:66), first mentions elders of the church in Jerusalem (Acts 11:30), he assumes that their office and function will be understood. Those elders meet in the Christian council, just as Jewish elders met in the Sanhedrin (Acts 15).

While chosen and recognized by the people, church elders receive their authority through the Holy Spirit who called them, endued them, and appointed them for service (Acts 20:28). Service, not power or prestige, is the purpose of church officers, as of all believers. The Christian follows his Lord in the way of the cross. Jesus repeatedly reversed the disciples' thinking. They sought worldly greatness – places of honour in his kingdom; but he asked if they could drink his cup of suffering, and told them that he came, not to be served, but 'to serve, and to give his life a ransom for many' (Mt. 20:25–28).

Peter learned that lesson, and he later warned elders not to lord it over those entrusted to them, but to be examples to the flock; more than others they must gird on humility, as Jesus girded on a towel to wash his disciples' feet (1 Pet. 5:3, 6).

No teaching of Jesus is more easily grasped; none is more basic for Christian living; none is more often forgotten, betrayed, and resisted. Yet it remains the hallmark of Christian leadership; without it, the Lord's order for his church collapses in shambles. Church government is the rule of Christ's kingdom of grace and sacrificial love. Without that love, church rule can become the worst kind of oppression, that which destroys the soul.

2. Church office

All Christians, called to belong to Christ and equipped to serve him, hold office in his church. That office receives public recognition when a believer makes a public profession of faith and is welcomed by the church. The vows that are exchanged are an induction into an office that angels might envy: Christ's calling to bear his name before the world. The particular gifts of a believer need not be identified, for they do not require public recognition to be effective. Yet, few or many, they function in the body's worship, nurture and witness.

The Christian attitude toward the world and its culture helps define this general office of Christians. To advance Christ's kingdom defines the Christian's life. No Christian can store personal faith at home while pursuing money and power in a secular occupation. Loyalty to Christ's calling demands sacrifice in the market-place.[6] The Christian struggles to overcome the disorder of sin and to preserve and develop God's world. In management or as an employee, the believer can show the meaning of work that serves the Lord. Christian witness consists of not only making the occasional comment at the office, or willingness to suffer loss when doing right, but also the quality of the work of the Lord's servant in the Lord's world (Col. 3:22–24).

Yves Congar, a pioneering Roman Catholic writer on the theology of the laity, once described three positions of the layman in the church: sitting, kneeling and reaching for his wallet.[7] How well do church programmes serve the laity that supports them? Do they assist the general office, not only in the work of the church, but also in the broad fields of ministry in the world?

Certainly need-based programmes have multiplied: parents meet to share their burdens and joys, addicts support one another in their struggles, singles and those shattered by divorce share experiences. Christians also organize by vocation: there are national parachurch societies of Christian lawyers, doctors, nurses, college and university students, broadcasters, publishers, educators, professional golfers and others. Some larger churches have begun to encourage the forming of groups of writers, musicians, teachers, lawyers and health professionals.

Although no aspect of modern life needs informed understanding more than the obligations of Christian citizens, evangelical churches have practically ignored this ministry, perhaps because they are aware that the church does not seek to wield political power. Government actions do challenge Christian morality, and informed witness by Christian citizens requires consultation, not only to perceive the threats, but to reflect on a response that glorifies the Lord.

Local vocational groups have the advantage of frequent meetings where involved Christians can share their problems and opportunities. Another great advantage of church sponsorship, whether by one congregation or a number, is the support and involvement of church pastors and teachers – who may expect to gain more from such meetings than they contribute.

In all of this the place of the family is unique, since it is incorporated into the form of the church as the family of God. It holds the primary role in Christian education, supported by the ministry of church and the school. Today's developing home-schooling revolution may radically alter the understanding of Christian parents and children as to the place of the home in education.

The diagram on page 201 showed the intersection of the goals of the church's ministry (worship, nurture and witness) with the means of ministry (the Word, order and mercy). To that two-dimensional chart a third dimension may be added as we now consider the *agents* of ministry, *i.e.* those to whom the work of ministry is committed.

The broad base of the three-dimensional diagram is the general office of believers. Growing out of that general office are the special offices of the New Testament. Exalted above both general and special office is the unique, mediatorial office of Christ, the Head of the church.

The general and special offices share all the goals and means of ministry. The ministry of the Word is carried on by both offices, since the special office differs from the general in degree and not in kind. The use of the Word in evangelism, nurture and worship is part of the daily calling of every Christian. (Think of the diagram as a three-dimensional solid,

208

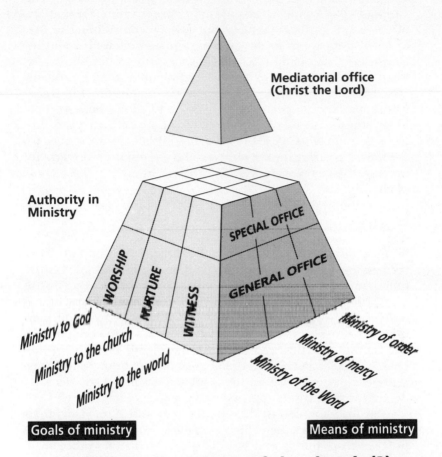

Structure of ministry of the church (2)

and the ministry of the Word as a slice across the front.) All Christians participate in the ministry of order within community life, not only in their families, but also by contributing to the order of the church in its witness, its loving discipline, and its Christ-centred worship (the middle slice of the pyramid). In the same way, the ministry of mercy is committed to all Christians (the last slice). It is part of the work of mission, for while Christians have a special responsibility to direct benevolence toward those who are of the household of the faith, they are also to do good to all (Gal. 6:9–10; 1 Thes. 3:12; 5:15). In witness to the world, in caring for the saints and in the offerings brought in worship, the mercy that reflects Christ's mercy marks the service of all his people.

Special offices in the church rise from Christ's calling, for he has endued some of his disciples with serving gifts to a high degree. Some of these gifts need public recognition in order to be used effectively (the gift of governing, for example). This recognition by the community discerns the call of Christ. Calling, gifts and office go together. Christ grants the gifts of the Spirit in his calling. An individual may be aware of Christ's call before the gifts are evident, or the presence of the gifts may bring awareness of the calling. When people see the evidence of fruitful ministry, they extend the outward call to office in the church. Grades gained in a theological college or university may represent performance on the academic level, but the decisive demonstration of gifts appears in the service of the church.

The diagram shows the mediatorial office of Christ as detached from all other office because it is unique. We do not proceed from the special offices to the Mediator's office by a gradation similar to that between the general and the special office. That separation could be misleading, however, for Christ, though highly exalted, is not detached from his church, but is intimately joined to it by his presence through the Spirit.

The special offices all seek the *goals* of ministry, but they may be distinguished by the *means.*

The New Testament recognizes special gifts for the proclamation of the Word. Paul was an apostolic missionary, driven to preach Christ where he had not been named (Rom. 15:20). Others shared this missionary calling, and are called apostles (as sent ones: Acts 14:14; Rom. 16:7; 2 Cor. 8:23), or evangelists (as

210

preachers of the evangel: Eph. 4:11; 2 Tim. 4:5). Still others are called pastors or teachers (Acts 13:1; Eph. 4:11; 1 Cor. 12:28; Jas. 3:1). While they would also be involved in evangelism as preachers of the gospel, their central calling was the building up of the body of Christ.

We have seen that the apostles, in the narrow sense of 'the twelve', were the foundation stones of the church, providing through the Spirit the revelation of the person and work of Christ, and the 'pattern of sound words' that established the church in the truth (Eph. 2:20; 3:3–5; Gal. 2:8). As recipients of revelation, they were joined by New Testament prophets.[8] When their task was completed, and the final revelation of Christ, the Son of God, had been given, the calling of the apostles and prophets was fulfilled, although apostles in the broader sense (missionaries) and evangelists continued to carry the gospel to those who had not heard.

With regard to the ministry of order, the New Testament speaks of those who are recognized in the church as having gifts for rule or government. Paul distinguishes this gift from teaching in 1 Corinthians 12:28; in the context he is making the point that not all have the particular gifts he is listing. Similarly, in Romans 12:8 he identifies a distinct gift of rule. In his pastoral instructions to Timothy, we read that elders are to be honoured, but 'especially those whose work is preaching and teaching' (1 Tim. 5:17).

We have noted that the office of the elder in Judaism was carried over into the Jewish Christian church. The term refers either to seniority or to office. In 1 Timothy, Paul had been speaking first of older men (1 Tim. 5:1). He goes on to speak of one group among older men, the group of those who rule (5:17). Ruling *well* is inserted because Paul is speaking of those to be honoured. He is not, however, making the major distinction between church governors who do a good job and those who don't, nor is he implying that those who rule well would get double honour, while those who botched it would come off with single honour. The double honour of which he speaks is most likely the honour due to them as older men plus the honour due to them as rulers in the church. (It could also be honour plus honorarium, see 5:16).

In any case, this passage and others in the New Testament

211

indicate that among the elders who rule in the church, there are some who also labour in the Word and in teaching. That was also the case in Israel: 'the tradition of the elders' (Mt. 15:2) refers to teaching elders. Honoured older scholars were called 'elders', and their pupils 'sons of elders'.[9] The Sanhedrin consisted of chief priests, scribes and elders (Mk. 11:27; 14:43; 15:1; Mt. 27:41). The term 'elders' could refer to all the members of this council as the 'elderate' (*presbytery*: Lk. 22:66; Acts 22:5; 1 Tim. 4:14); it could also designate the non-priestly members (Mt. 26:3; 27:10), or the lay members in distinction from both priests and rabbis (Mk. 11:27; 15:1; Lk. 20:1).

In short, then, the gift of teaching distinguishes pastors and teachers from other church elders with whom they share ruling authority in the church. The major difference between Jewish and Christian practice lay in the distinctively spiritual authority claimed by church governors. The church could appoint elders to settle financial disputes between members (1 Cor. 6:1–7), but no Christian body of elders could issue letters like those furnished to Saul the persecutor by the Jewish 'presbytery' at Jerusalem (Acts 22:5).

The third *means* of ministry in our diagram, that of the ministry of mercy, also claims a special office, that of the deacon. The New Testament uses the term 'deacon' (*diakonos*), like the term 'elder', in both broader and narrower senses. In the broad sense, every Christian is a servant of Christ (Jn. 12:26). In a special sense, Paul calls himself God's servant (2 Cor. 3:6; 6:4; Eph. 3:7; Col. 1:23, 25), as are Apollos (1 Cor. 3:5), Timothy (1 Thes. 3:2; 1 Tim. 4:6) and other fellow-servants with the apostle (Col. 1:7; 4:7). Christ himself fulfils the role of Israel as the 'servant of the circumcision' (Rom. 15:8).

In another special sense, *diakonos* is used to describe a special office in the church distinct from that of the gospel ministry. This is the case in 1 Timothy 3:8–13 and Philippians 1:1 and also, it would appear, in Romans 16:1.

The establishment of the office of the deacon in the church is often traced to the initiative of the apostles that is described in Acts 6. As the church grew rapidly, so did the difficulties in administering relief to impoverished widows. Christians from the Greek-speaking Jewish community complained that their widows were being neglected in the daily distribution of food.

The apostles, who had been administering all the affairs of the community, saw that they should not be leaving the ministry of the word, their distinctive calling, to serve (*diakonein*) tables. They therefore asked the brethren to choose seven good men from among them, full of the Spirit and of wisdom, whom they could appoint to administer relief. The seven chosen all have Greek names: it would appear that the church was ready to put the entire administration into the hands of members of the Greek-speaking community so that they could not feel excluded. The seven chosen were brought to the apostles, who laid their hands on them, blessing them for this ministry.

It is not clear, however, whether the office of the deacon began with the seven. Certainly Stephen and Philip, at least, had gifts for the ministry of the Word as well as for administration, and Philip is called an evangelist (Acts 21:8). It would seem that this marks the first division of office in the church of the New Covenant, and that the choosing of the seven provided for eldership as well as the diaconate. This is supported by the fact that the offering for the poor in Jerusalem is conveyed by Paul and Barnabas to the elders (Acts 11:30). The account of Acts 6, and the broad use of *diakonos* in the letters, has therefore led to the conclusion that deacons are assistants to the ministers of the Word, rather than officers charged specifically with the ministry of mercy.

The use of the verb in the New Testament, however, favours understanding diaconal ministry as works of mercy, often in serving food (Mt. 4:11; 8:15; 25:44; 27:55; Lk. 8:3; 10:40; 12:37; 17:8; Jn. 12:2; Rom. 15:25; *etc.*).[10] The noun *diakonia* has a similar usage, especially when it speaks of service to the saints (Lk. 10:40; Acts 11:29; 12:25; 1 Cor. 16:15; 2 Cor. 8:4, 19–20; 9:1, 12–13; Rom. 15:25, 31). Further, in distinguishing gifts of the Spirit, Paul mentions gifts for the ministry of mercy, and does so in passages concerning office (Rom. 12:8, 13; 1 Cor. 12:28–29). The term 'helps' in 1 Corinthians 12:28 (NIV, 'those able to help others') is used in its verbal form to describe helping the weak with the income from labour (Acts 20:35). In Romans 16:1–2 the term *diakonos* is joined with the concept of ministering to physical needs.

The use of the *diakonia* terminology points to the conclusion that the deacon serves not the bishop or elder, but the saints.

213

The pyramid structure, showing an area of ministry in each block, helps us understand how the blocks are related, and it can enable us to identify which one might need attention.

At one time, mission was viewed exclusively as the work of the special office of an evangelist or missionary. 'Mission', in this sense, would include only one block of the pyramid. The diagram, however, reminds us that witness is a whole *slice* of the pyramid: the ministries of order and mercy also have a part in the mission of the church; the general as well as the special office is charged with mission. Mission clinics, hospitals and Christian relief agencies express the compassion of Christ that accompanies the gospel offered in his name. Christians will join with others in supporting agencies able to rush relief to victims of famine or disaster. They may also join with others seeking to change political and economic causes of deprivation. Yet what Christians do together as the Lord's people must be done in the name of Jesus. Even when that help is refused, along with the gospel, the church continues to seek doors of opportunity.

The exclusion of Christian missionaries from many countries has forced the church to use less direct means of presenting Jesus Christ. 'Tent-making' missionaries have sought employment in business, technology and education in countries that prohibit open evangelism. Their presence and testimony provide an entrance for the gospel. This ministry of the church's mission appears in the diagram as the ministry of order carried out by the general office. While verbal witness may be limited, the presence and example of Christians and of Christian families shine as a light in the world.

15

THE MINISTRY
OF WOMEN IN
THE CHURCH

Debate continues in Britain and the United States concerning the ordination of women to church office.[1] Rapid social change and the pressure of feminist movements have heated up the discussion. An egalitarian view denies any role differentiation between men and women, and minimizes physiological differences: for instance, women boxers are hailed on television. Pleading the offensiveness of generic male pronouns, women's movements have changed English usage: contemporary style now adopts 'gender-neutral' language. Major Bible translations have followed this style within limits; and some theologians refer to God as 'he/she/it'.[2] If biblical exegesis on these issues was once conducted by males who assumed male superiority, the current literature now reveals new prejudices.

Biblical teaching on the issue may be quickly adjusted by discarding those passages that appear to bar women from ruling office in the church, as being evidence of male prejudice. Paul Jewett distinguishes between what Paul said as an apostle from what he said as an unreformed Jewish rabbi.[3] Others discredit passages in 1 Timothy and Ephesians as non-Pauline, or reject them as interpolations.[4]

Evangelical scholars who accept the authority of canonical Scripture raise different questions. In passages where Paul seems to subordinate women, he also discusses such matters as head-coverings and braided hair (1 Cor. 11:3–16; 1 Tim. 2:9– 15). Are not his instructions restricted to their cultural context?[5] The literary and cultural context of these passages requires detailed consideration, of which there is now no lack![6]

First, Paul seems to bar women from ruling office or teaching authority in the church (1 Cor. 14:33b–36; 1 Tim. 2:8 – 3:7; Tit. 1:5–9). In the Titus passage, the qualification for a bishop is given: he must be the husband of one wife, with children who are believers. To the church at Corinth Paul gives instructions that apply to 'all the congregations of the saints'. He declares:

> Women should remain silent in the churches. They are not allowed to speak, but must be in submission, as the Law says. If they want to enquire about something, they should ask their own husbands at home; for it is disgraceful for a woman to speak in the church (1 Cor. 14:34–35).

The directions given to Timothy are also explicit:

> A woman should learn in quietness and full submission. I do not permit a woman to teach or to have authority over a man; she must be silent (1 Tim. 2:11– 12).

But an apparent counter-indication appears in Paul's same letter to the Corinthians (1 Cor. 11:5, 13). If women are to be silent in the churches, why does Paul give instructions about head-covering when they pray or prophesy?

Again, in Galatians 3:26–29 Paul says that all who are baptized into Christ have been clothed with him. 'There is neither Jew nor Greek, slave nor free, male nor female, for you are all one in Christ Jesus' (3:28).

Does not the apostle state a principle here, drawn from the heart of his theology, that removes all sexual distinctions from ministry in the Lord and in the church?

Apostolic theology of order in the church

Paul's theology centres on the realization of God's promises in Jesus Christ, the fulfilment of the history of redemption. He turns to this framework to support his instructions regarding men, women and church order. He appeals to the creation order, to the curse and the resulting ordinances of God for a fallen world, and to the restoration and renewal that have taken place in Christ.

Paul affirms the primacy of man over woman in creation as his rationale for requiring the submission of the woman: 'For Adam was formed first, then Eve' (1 Tim. 2:13). In 1 Corinthians 11:3–16 he develops this, speaking of propriety in worship:

> Now I want you to realise that the head of every man is Christ, and the head of the woman is man, and the head of Christ is God . . . A man ought not to cover his head, since he is the image and glory of God; but the woman is the glory of man. For man did not come from woman, but woman from man; neither was man created for woman, but woman for man (1 Cor. 11:3, 7–8).

Paul is not just accommodating to the current culture in order to win respect for the Christian community. He is urging the church to express in its cultural context a fundamental principle revealed in God's creation order. The headship of the man over the woman he compares to the headship of Christ over the man, and the headship of God over Christ. What Paul means by the headship of God over Christ is evident from 1 Corinthians 15:27–28.[7] All things are finally put under Christ, except God himself, to whom the Son is made subject. Because of Adam's role as head and image-bearer, it was by his sin, not Eve's, that death passed upon all his descendants, except for the Virgin-born second Adam (Rom. 5:15–19). Adam served as the representative head of humanity even in the Garden of Eden, when humanity was the couple.

At the same time, Paul warns against making this distinction in creation the only factor in God's ordering of the relation of man and woman. He adds:

In the Lord, however, woman is not independent of man, nor is man independent of woman. For as woman came from man, so also man is born of woman. But everything comes from God (1 Cor. 11:11–12).

In their fellowship in Christ, men and women need each other. Perhaps by adding 'in the Lord' Paul is linking creation with the incarnation of Christ. In creation the woman did not exist without the man, for Eve was formed from the body of Adam ('woman came from man'). In the incarnation, the new Man came from woman alone in the Virgin birth ('man is born of woman').

Paul finds in the Genesis creation account God's order for the relation of the sexes. He takes note of the creation of Adam in the image of God. Adam himself bears God's image; he does not bring only half of the image into his marriage with Eve. Paul's emphasis on Adam as the image-bearer points to Christ as the final Image-Bearer (1 Cor. 15:49; 2 Cor. 4:4; Col. 1:15; 3:10; cf. Rom. 5:14, 19). Paul also affirms that Eve bears the full image of God, for she came from Adam and shares the divine image that is the glory of Adam (Gn. 1:27; 1 Cor. 15:48–49).[8] Paul stresses the dignity of the woman in the marriage relationship, where man and wife become one flesh, so that in loving his wife, the husband is loving himself (Eph. 5:25–31; Gn. 2:23–24). He is one with her, and she with him in analogy to the relation of Christ and the church. So, too, Paul cites the command of the Decalogue that children should honour their fathers and their mothers (Eph. 6:1; Lv. 19:3).

Paul, then, teaches both the headship of the man over the woman and the interdependence of the man and the woman. It would be a mistake to suppose that the second statement cancels the first.[9] Rather, it qualifies the first by showing that the subordination is with respect to roles, not being. So, too, Christ, the God-man, is subject to the Father, although as the divine Son he is equal with the Father.

Paul applies God's creation order to the customs of head-covering. There were differences in culture between Greeks and Romans. (Roman men covered their heads in worship, Greeks did not. Corinth, as a Roman colony, presumably reflected both customs.)[10] Paul asked for a unified practice. He does not command simple obedience to apostolic authority (*cf.* 1 Cor. 14:37), but appeals to their own judgment as to what was proper, and to the practice of the other churches. Nevertheless, he grounds practice in the divinely established order.[11]

The apostle's reasoning also takes account of the fall, and of God's curse on the fallen world. Under the curse, Adam still subdues and develops the earth, but what was once delightful gardening now becomes exhausting labour. Eve, the mother of all living, fulfils the creation command to fill the earth. But she now knows pain in the agony of child-bearing. The Genesis passage concludes: 'Your desire will be for your husband, and he will rule over you' (Gn. 3:16). This sentence is clarified by a similar one, where the Lord warns Cain that 'Sin . . . desires to have you, but you must master it' (Gn. 4:7).[12] The desire of the woman will be to dominate her husband, as she did in giving him the forbidden fruit, but that desire will be frustrated, because by God's appointment and decree the man will retain his headship. Paul's appeal both to the creation account and to God's judgment after the fall calls attention to the connection between the two. The subordination of the woman's role does not begin with the fall, nor does it cease in the New Covenant people of God. Rather, all is transformed by the love of Christ, so that the rule of the husband seeks the wife's good, and the pain of child-bearing is fellowship with the Saviour.

Paul refers to the fall as well as to creation to support his command that a woman should not teach or have authority over a man (1 Tim. 2:12). After saying, 'For Adam was formed first, then Eve,' he adds, 'And Adam was not the one deceived; it was the woman who was deceived and became a sinner' (1 Tim. 2:13–14). Some make Adam the greater sinner, since he disobeyed God more deliberately, *i.e.* without the crafty inducements of the serpent (*cf.* 2 Cor. 11:3). But this cannot be Paul's thought here, for it would not support the point he is making. But neither is he saying that women are to be subject to men because their sex is more gullible. Rather, his emphasis reflects the whole account of the fall, including God's words to Adam: 'Because you listened to your wife and ate from the tree . . .' (Gn. 3:17). Eve's initiative reversed the relationship that she should have maintained with Adam. She decided to eat of the tree, and Adam followed her. When the Lord pronounced the curse against the woman, he reinstated a relationship that Eve had reversed in her sin.

The false teaching that Timothy was to oppose at Ephesus included a rejection of marriage and a ban on certain foods (1 Tim. 4:3). Perhaps this was connected with the teaching of Hymenaeus and Philetus that the resurrection had already taken place, so that Christians were now free from family constraints (2 Tim. 2:18; *cf.* 1 Tim. 1:20). These 'things taught by demons' may also have influenced the behaviour of certain women who 'turned away to follow Satan' and made a career as gossips and busybodies (1 Tim. 5:13, 15).[13] False teaching that proclaimed 'resurrection' liberation from family structures may account in part for the counter-emphasis that the pastoral letters put on maintaining godly households, and on the importance of the woman's role in the home (1 Tim. 3:2, 4–5, 12; 5:1–16; 2 Tim. 1:5; 3:6–7, 15; Tit. 1:6, 11; 2:2–6).

In this context we may understand Paul's statement that the women 'will be saved through child-bearing – if they continue in faith, love and holiness with propriety' (1 Tim. 2:15). Since the woman Paul has been speaking of in 2:14 is Eve, he may be alluding to *the* child-bearing, *i.e.* the promise that the Seed of the woman would crush the head of the serpent (Gn. 3:15; *cf.* 4:1, NKJV). Paul's words about child-bearing in 1 Timothy 5:14, however, indicate a different meaning: that women, including young widows, should not 'turn away to follow Satan' (being deceived as Eve was), but rather lead godly lives as wives and mothers (as Eve later did). By accepting motherhood, a godly woman, in contrast to the gossiping idlers described in 1 Timothy 5:11–13, fulfils a calling from the Lord, and commends the faith to others.

Paul orders the life of the church according to principles found in the Genesis account of creation and the fall. These principles, however, are part of God's revelation of promise, pointing to Christ. Christ fulfils the law and restores what was lost in the fall. Because God's own Son became a sin offering, we have been delivered from the power of sin, and sin has been condemned, 'in order that the righteous requirements of the law might be fully met in us, who do not live according to the sinful nature but according to the Spirit' (Rom. 8:4).

But to be in Christ means more than restoration. It means a new creation that partakes of Christ, and of the Spirit of glory. In Christ a new order begins, anticipating the kingdom to come.

> You are all sons of God through faith in Christ Jesus, for all of you who were baptised into Christ have clothed yourselves with Christ. There is neither Jew nor Greek, slave nor free, male nor female, for you are all one in Christ Jesus. If you belong to Christ, then you are Abraham's seed, and heirs according to the promise (Gal. 3:26–29).

This text is at the centre of debate about the role of women in the church.[14] Some hail it as 'The Magna Carta of Humanity', a magnificent vision that the apostle Paul, unfortunately, does not always keep in view.[15]

In the context, Paul's point is that we cannot be found righteous in God's sight by keeping the law (Gal. 3:11). Salvation by grace was God's promise to Abraham, realized in his one Seed, Jesus Christ. The law, given centuries after the promise, did not contradict it, but proved the need for it. God's people were under the law as under a tutor, led forward toward the promised inheritance of the Spirit through faith. Paul restates the key principle of his theology: representative union with Christ. We are righteous in God's sight because we are in Christ, because we have 'put on' Christ, and have title to his sonship. As Abraham's seed in Christ, Gentiles inherit the blessing of Abraham, the promise of the Spirit through faith (Gal. 3:14, 29). Therefore, it is fair to say that in Christ the Son there is neither Jew nor Greek. In Christ, believing Greeks are fellow-citizens with the saints, i.e. believing Jews (Eph. 2:19).

Paul's main point is made when he declares that the distinction between Jew and Gentile is transcended in Christ. But he goes on to indicate that in Christ all other distinctions are also transcended: in Christ there can be no bond or free, no male or female. Again, the point is that these distinctions, so important in our daily lives, are transcended by that union with Christ that is the means of our justification. Just as there is a sense in which we are all Jews in Christ, there is a sense in which we are all free in Christ, and a sense in which we are all male in

221

Christ, for in Christ we are one (*heis*, masculine). For Paul, union with Christ means that we are not simply children of God, but sons of God.

This passage is illumined by a similar text in 1 Corinthians 12:13:

> For we were all baptised by one Spirit into one body – whether Jews or Greeks, slave or free – and we were all given the one Spirit to drink.

As in the Galatians passage, Paul alludes to baptism, the sacrament of our saving union with Christ. He goes on to describe a new diversity within the unity of the one Spirit and the one Body. That diversity is not defined by distinctions between Jew and Gentile or between slave and free (for they have all drunk of the one Spirit), but rather by differences in the gifts of the Spirit and in the ministries that these gifts enable. Being a Jew or a Gentile would not determine who should govern in Christ's church. Neither would being a slave bar one from exercising the gift of administration (1 Cor. 12:28).

Is this, then, not decisive for the issue of women in office? Could not Paul have added 'whether male or female' in 1 Corinthians 12:13, as he did in Galatians 3:28? When it comes to office in the church, is not being male or female as irrelevant as being Jew or Gentile, slave or free? Many recent writers have concluded that Paul did not work through the implications of what he says here, but endorsed a ban on women's exercise of authority that ran contrary to his own deepest theological principle.

Yet it would be mistaken to suppose that a contradiction is involved here. The relations that are transcended in Christ are not all transcended in the same way. The difference between Jew and Gentile was appointed by God in the Old Covenant; it was transcended when Christ fulfilled the covenant promise. The difference between slave and free had no such place in God's saving plan, but was the result of human exploitation. The difference between male and female, however, is part of God's creation order, and, to understand how it is transcended in Christ, we must take account of that order.

The accompanying diagram indicates the levels that apply to

222

the ordering of Christ's church. God's *ordinances* for the fallen world still apply, for the church still lives in that world and must obey God's commands for it, *e.g.* in submitting to human government. At the same time, the church has experienced the *restoration* that Christ brings. Daily work, the labour of child-bearing: these are not a curse for the Christian – they have become part of Christ's calling. Further, the church tastes not only the joy of restoration, but the beginning of renewal. With the coming of the Spirit there is a foretaste of glory; a *heavenly order* has already begun, but it is not yet the order of the New Jerusalem. This distinction is critical for understanding how the form of the church differs from the form of the final kingdom. In the church, the ordinances of *creation*, restored in Christ and renewed by the Spirit, are still applicable. This does no prejudice to the reality of our union with Christ; it only recognizes that we are not yet in the church triumphant. The *parousia* and the *consummation order* are yet to come.

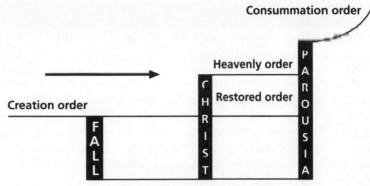

Levels of order in Christ

The family of God

The restored and renewed form of the church appears in Paul's figure of the household and family of God. As the national form of the Old Testament people of God is transformed in the church as the new Israel, so the family form of God's covenant with the patriarchs is transformed in the New Covenant church as the family of God. When Paul requires that a candidate for

the office of bishop direct his own household well, the
connection is immediate, for the task of caring for the church
is directly analogous to that of a father in a household. If a man
does not govern his own household well, how shall he take care
of the church of God (1 Tim. 3:5)? Paul wrote to Timothy so that
he 'will know how people ought to conduct themselves in God's
household, which is the church of the living God, the pillar and
foundation of the truth' (1 Tim. 3:15).[16] In God's household
older men are to be regarded as fathers, younger men as
brothers, older women as mothers, and younger women as
sisters (1 Tim. 5:1–2). Paul asked the Corinthians to imitate him,
for though they might have ten thousand tutors in Christ, they
had only one father, for 'I became your father through the
gospel' (1 Cor. 4:15). He describes his fatherly care of the
Thessalonians:

> For you know that we dealt with each of you as a father
> deals with his own children, encouraging, comforting
> and urging you to live lives worthy of God, who calls
> you into his kingdom and glory (1 Thes. 2:11–12).

The Lord has designed an order in his church for accomplishing the goals of worship, nurture and witness. That order is
not the imperial structure of the Roman empire, or the fraternal
order of the Masons, the Rotary Club, a labour union or a
farmers' co-operative. Neither is it the hierarchical order of a
business organizational chart. It is the order of the extended
family, not under the direction of a patriarch, but served by a
council of elders.

Underlying this form of organization is all that the Bible
teaches about the fatherhood of God with respect to his
children, those born of the Spirit, who are brothers and sisters
in Christ.[17] Because God is Father, his children are family:

> For this reason I kneel before the Father [patēr], from
> whom his whole family [patria] in heaven and on earth
> derives its name . . . (Eph. 3:14–15).

No earthly fatherhood can replace God's. Jesus told his
disciples that because they had one Father they were all

224

brethren, and no holy 'father' should be named among them (Mt. 23:8–12). Yet the care of church leaders must be a fatherly care, for they, like Paul, watch over the family of God. To the guidance and protection of a shepherd, serving the flock under Christ the chief Shepherd (1 Pet. 5:1–4), every elder must add compassionate, tender, fatherly care for God's family. The elders are examples to the younger men, and the younger men are to show humility by submitting to those who are older (1 Pet. 5:5). Older women are examples to younger women, training them in godly living (Tit. 2:3–5). Widowed elderly women with a reputation for good works have their own recognized place in the household of God (1 Tim. 5:9–10). Paul mentions the faith and instruction of Timothy's mother Eunice and his grandmother Lois, through whom he gained the knowledge of the Scriptures (2 Tim. 3:15).

The Lord is a Husband as well as a Father to Israel. These two images are drawn together in the allegory of Ezekiel, where the Lord adopts an abandoned newborn, then marries her when she is grown (Ezk. 16). But usually the figures are distinct, and the marriage image supports the family image in determining the structure of the church. *Representative* union with Christ transcends sexual identity, so that in Christ we are all *sons* of God. On the other hand, *vital* union with Christ is portrayed by the personal fellowship of marriage union, in which man and woman become one flesh. Our union with Christ unites us to each other as the *bride* of Christ. When Paul instructs the church about the role of husbands and wives in marriage, he keeps shifting from the human relationship to that which it symbolizes, the relation of Christ to the church (Eph. 5:22–33). The authority of Christ over the church supports the headship of the husband in marriage, but the love of Christ for the church shows how that headship is to be exercised: not in selfish dominance, but in self-giving, sacrificial love. Paul invests so much in this analogy, making marriage so solemn and marvellous that it is easy to see why he would preserve the relationship of husbands and wives in the ordering of the church as the family of God.

Again, the conviction of the apostle that the church is the bride of Christ has implication for office. As rule in the church reflects God's fatherly claim, it also reflects the claim of the Lord Christ as Bridegroom. Paul shared the Lord's jealousy for the church, zeal that drove him in his struggle to present the church as a spotless virgin to Christ (2 Cor. 11:2; *cf.* Eph. 5:27). The Lord's holy jealousy for his bride, like his fatherly care for his household, requires the church to respect the structure of the family. Those who watch over the church in Christ's name represent the authority of the Father in the family of God and of the Son in claiming his Bride. The Spirit is the Spirit of fatherhood (*Abba*) and of sonship.

The family structure, as established from creation, provides the model for the church. Is that structure egalitarian in the New Testament? Craig Keener argues that it is, basing his claim on Ephesians 5:21, 'Submit to one another out of reverence for Christ.' He interprets the following verse, 'Wives, submit to your husbands as to the Lord' as an *example* of mutual submission, so that Paul could as well have made the husband the example, 'Husbands, submit to your wives as to the Lord.' Paul does not put it that way, Keener explains, because he is sensitive to custom. Nevertheless, Paul's position is radical. Husbands are to submit to their wives, masters to their servants (but not, he acknowledges, parents to their children).[18]

Keener recognizes another possibility: 'Paul would then be saying that all Christians should submit to one another, but that they should submit in different ways, as detailed in his list of duties in 5:22 – 6:9.'[19] (Even in that sentence Keener inserted an 'all' that is not found in the text.) Because he finds an absolute mutuality of submission in the general statement of 5:21, he rejects what otherwise would be a compelling interpretation. Indeed, when Keener seeks to come to terms with the following verses where Paul compares the wife's submission to her husband to the church's submission to Christ the Saviour, Keener does allow for radically different ways of submission. 'The wife recognizes her husband as "head" in terms of submitting to his authority (5:22–23), but the husband recognizes his headship in terms of loving and serving his wife (5:28–30).'[20]

If, in that last statement, the 'serving' of the husband is modelled on the serving of Christ in his work as Saviour, Keener is well stating Paul's precise point: that relations of authority and submission, while not removed, are radically transformed by the gospel. Christ the Saviour remains the Lord of the church. The relation of Christ and the church is not egalitarian. Jesus washed his disciples' feet, but John prefaces his account of that service by reminding us that 'Jesus knew that the Father had put all things under his power, and that he had come from God and was returning to God' (Jn. 13:3). After Jesus had finished, he reminded the disciples that they rightly called him 'Master' and 'Lord'. If he, in his exalted role, washed their feet, how much more ought they to wash one another's (Jn. 13:13–17)!

It is astonishing that Paul so distinguishes husband and wife (who are 'one flesh') as to compare the husband to Christ, and the wife to the church. He does not say that the husband should surrender his headship, but that he should exercise that headship by loving his wife and being ready to die for her, as Christ loved and died for the church. The path of sacrificial love to which a husband is called is not an egalitarian rejection of responsibility for caring for his wife, but the faithful service of Christ as one charged with withholding nothing to advance her growth in radiant holiness ('in this same way', Eph. 5:28).[21]

The way in which the relation of slave and free is changed by Christ needs attention if we are to see how it differs from that of male and female. The two are often seen to be analogous. It is argued that if the commanded submission of a slave to a master is no longer binding, but was applicable only in the culture of Paul's world (not 'transcultural'), why should the submission of a woman to her husband be now binding (transcultural)?

Although submission is required of wives, slaves and children in the household codes of the New Testament letters, the three relationships are not analogous in other respects, nor, as the texts show, is the submission the same. Keener acknowledges the difference with respect to children. There is no less difference between the submission of the wife and the obedience of a slave. Marriage is divinely instituted; there is no such divine warrant for slavery. For that reason, a slave may seek freedom (1 Cor. 7:21), and a master is always free to liberate a slave. It is wrong, however, to dissolve the marriage relation that God has joined together (Mk. 10:6–12). A Christian wife should not separate even from an unbelieving husband (1 Cor. 7:13; 1 Pet. 3:1).

Not only does slavery lack a divine warrant; the transformation of relationships that the gospel brings subverts slavery.

227

Hearty obedience, offered as to the Lord, undercuts exploitation and becomes a slave's ringing testimony to his freedom in Christ. His suffering under a harsh master is fellowship with Christ, who felt the lash for him (1 Pet. 2:18–25). Paul does not command Philemon to free his slave, but shows how the relationship between master and slave has been transformed.[22] Onesimus has become a beloved brother, doubly dear to Philemon: the literal translation is 'in the flesh and in the Lord' *i.e.* both as a slave and as a brother (Phm. 16). Transformed by Christ, slavery becomes a bond sanctified by Christ's love. Philemon is to receive Onesimus as a 'partner' (*koinōnos*, a term cognate to 'fellowship'); Onesimus, an apostolic assistant, was to be received as the apostle himself.

Christian masters are to show the same care for their slaves that their slaves show toward them, not threatening them, but together serving the Master in heaven (Eph. 6:9). Precisely because there is neither bond nor free in Christ, the social condition of bondage may continue in a way that is completely transformed for the Christian. In holy irony, the victory of the cross transforms society. A transcultural ethic undergirds these instructions to slaves and masters: the love of Christ does not demand rights but displays the royal submission of the Lord of glory. That ethic will not sanction a slave revolt in the Roman empire, but it will so transform the attitudes of society that slavery itself will be removed. Other forms of socially sanctioned exploitation have succeeded slavery, but the Christian secret remains. Serving the Lord is the service of the free; it confounds exploitation by cheerful love.

Why, then, does not the loving submission of the wife and the sacrificial love of the husband subvert the structure of authority in the marriage relationship?[23] Because slavery is an enforced relationship that is altered in its *essence* by mutual love, while marriage is itself a relationship of love ('one body'), a relationship brought by grace to fulfil God's design in the roles appointed by his creation.

The analogy between marriage and slavery raises another question: if a slave may be eligible for ruling office in the church, in spite of his role in a household, why is a woman ineligible for such office, even though she does not exercise headship in the home? The answer, as we have seen, lies in the great difference between the two institutions: a divine pattern on the one hand, and human exploitation on the other. If Onesimus, as a brother beloved, should hold office in the church, and should his new fellowship with Philemon alter his role as a servant in the household by his service in the gospel, so much the better. Love has transformed the very nature of slavery.

But for a woman to exercise rule in the church would undermine the order for the family that God has established. Christ's love transforms the nature of marriage, not by dissolving the role relations by which marriage is constituted, but by bringing them to fulfilment in the amazing model of Christ and the church.

Paul's instructions for order in the church as the family of God are consistent with his instructions for life in the home, and with his teaching regarding the gifts of the Spirit and the foretaste of the life to come. As in the home, women in the church are to be subject to male headship, and are not to exercise authority over men (1 Tim. 2:12; cf. 3:4; Eph. 5:22–33). The teaching office in the church exercises authority through the ministry of the Word (2 Cor. 12:29; 1 Tim. 5:17; 2 Tim. 3:14 – 4:5; cf. Heb. 13:7, 17). For that reason, he does not permit women to teach in the church. While teaching and exercising authority are separately forbidden in 1 Timothy 2:12, Paul's mention of the exercise of authority serves to explain why teaching is not permitted. While the word 'man' may be the object of both 'teach' and 'exercise authority', it is authoritative teaching that is forbidden.[24] This is evident from the context of 1 Timothy 2, where Paul is giving instruction on prayer and appearance in public worship. Paul does not bar a woman from communicating biblical truth to her husband when she asks him at home about the examination of a prophet in the assembly (1 Cor. 14:35). Paul knew the teaching capabilities of Lois, Eunice. and Priscilla. It is authoritative teaching in the public assembly of the church that involves the ruling function.

To apply this teaching in the diversity of times and cultures requires wisdom. In a variety of informal circumstances, women may teach children, other women and men as well, provided that the teaching not be of the authoritative sort that would disrupt apostolic order. It is not arbitrary to distinguish between classroom teaching in educational institutions and the author-itative instruction of an ordained teacher of the church, engaged in the exercise of his office. In lay activities such as Sunday school, opportunities abound for the use of women's gifts in teaching. A writing ministry allows women free exercise of teaching gifts. Yet the distinction remains: those not called as authoritative teachers of the church, men or women, serve the church in a different capacity from those who are so called. Rule in the church always aims at encouraging all Christians to grow in the use of the gifts the Lord provides.

How, then, can Paul permit women to pray and to prophesy, if they must be silent in the assembly (1 Tim. 2:12; 1 Cor. 11:5; 14:34)? The silence Paul asks is not silence for its own sake, but in reference to the issue of authority. The requirement of silence in 1 Corinthians 14:34 seems to apply to the participa-tion of women in the examination of a prophet, where an authoritative decision is to be made.[25] The 'silence' of 1 Timothy 2:12 is also in the context of authority. In the case of prophecy, the difference is not that prophecy is less authoritat-ive than other forms of speaking or teaching, but the contrary.[26] When a woman has the prophetic gift, she speaks the word of the Lord. Her authority is not her own but the direct authority of the Lord. The fulfilment of the prophecy of Joel, proclaimed by Peter at Pentecost, provided the gift of prophecy to both men and women, in harmony with the gift of the Spirit to all the people of God. That Paul recognizes this gift, but yet in the same letter insists on the deference of women to male leadership in the church, shows the importance which he attaches to the continuing order of the church, even in the midst of the outpouring of spiritual gifts that marked the apostolic age.

With respect to prayer, the situation is different yet again, for prayer does not bring God's authoritative word to the church, but addresses the praise and petition of the church to God. Public prayer must be ordered, as must all parts of the service, but it is not restricted to those who rule in the church, or to men alone.

The church is the family of God, and with apostolic authority Paul teaches implications with respect to the roles of men and women (1 Cor. 14:37). His teaching collided with false teaching in his day, and it collides with the spirit of our time in the West.

230

At stake is not only church order, but the form of the family and of its values. The New Testament shows that the church and the family stand together.

Women in ministry

To maintain the biblical perspective, we cannot be content with a legalistic defence of a proper church order, but must grasp the total renovation of relationships brought about by the Spirit of Christ. Paul recognized that the gifts of the Spirit were granted to the whole body of Christ, to women as well as to men. He speaks of Euodia and Syntyche as his fellow-workers in the gospel (Phil. 4:2–3), along with Priscilla and Aquila (Rom. 16:3). *Iounian* in Romans 16:7 is a woman's name, translated Junias in NIV. (While it could be an abbreviation of the masculine name 'Junianus', examples of this are rare or lacking.) Andronicus and Junia, presumably husband and wife, were Paul's relatives and Christians before him; this noted missionary couple was imprisoned for the gospel (perhaps even along with Paul).[27]

Women supported the work of Christ and the apostles; others assisted Paul, and were well known in the churches he established. Were they deacons in the apostolic church? Many who recognize the continuing force of the apostle's instructions about the role of women in the church conclude that he denies the office of deacon to women.[28] Two passages, however, seem to indicate the contrary. The clearest is Romans 16:1–2:

> I commend to you Phoebe our sister, who is [also] a servant [*diakonos*] of the church in Cenchrea, that you may receive her in the Lord in a manner worthy of the saints, and assist her in whatever business she has need of you; for indeed she has been a helper of many and of myself also (NKJV).

The terms *diakonia* (service, ministry), and *diakonos* (servant, minister) are used in both broad and specific senses in the New Testament, reflecting the wide use of the verb *diakoneō*. The noun *diakonos* may mean any disciple of Christ as his servant (Jn. 12:26); the verb may describe the ministering of officers of the church in general (where *oikonomos*, steward, is the noun; see 1 Pet. 4:10). *Diakonos* may also refer specifically to ministers of the gospel, with their ministry of the Word particularly in view (Rom. 12:7; 1 Cor. 3:5; Col. 1:23; 1 Thes. 3:2; 2 Tim. 4:5). Yet it is also used of deacons in distinction from bishops (Phil. 1:1; 1 Tim. 3:8).

C. E. B. Cranfield concludes that the form Paul uses in Romans 16:1 speaks of 'deacon' in the official sense.[29] The present participle of the verb 'to be' is regularly used to identify an office (Jn. 11:49; Acts 18:12; 24:10). The addition of the name of the church in Cenchrea fits this identification: 'Phoebe our sister, being also deacon of the church in Cenchrea . . .'[30] If *diakonos* were being used in the general sense of 'servant' we might have expected 'servant of Christ'.

The reference of *diakonos* to an office is further supported by the fact that Paul goes on to describe how Phoebe fulfilled the office. She was a 'helper' to many, including the apostle himself. The Greek term *prostatis* was sometimes used in the sense of 'patron', someone with the social position and means to protect the defenceless.[31] Perhaps Phoebe's 'business' at Rome included the legal defence of widows or orphans.

The charge Paul gives the Roman church concerning Phoebe does not merely commend a friend to their fellowship. He formally requests recognition for Phoebe, and full support for her activities. How do we define 'office' if not as a function that requires public recognition for its proper exercise? If Paul had not called Phoebe a *diakonos* at all, the fact of his commending her for support by the Roman church in her work indicates that she was entitled to formal recognition in any case.

A second New Testament passage appears to refer to women as deacons:

> Women in like manner must be grave, not slanderers, temperate, faithful in all things (1 Tim. 3:11, ASV).

This verse occurs in a passage that gives the requirements of church officers: first bishops (1 Tim. 3:1–7), and then deacons (3:8–10, 12–13). Verse 11 is located in the middle of the passage that describes the deacons. Clearly this is not a description of women in general: the verse describes either women who are deacons or women who are wives of deacons. The NIV settles the question by translating 'wives' and inserting a possessive pronoun which is not found in the Greek text, *i.e.* '*their* wives'. It offers the other possibility in the margin by translating 'women' as 'deaconesses'.

An argument against referring this text to the wives of deacons is the fact that there is no similar description of the wives of bishops in the preceding verses. The absence of the possessive pronoun is also significant. More striking is the use of 'likewise' or 'in the same way' (*hōsautōs*), which was used in verse 8 to relate the requirements of deacons to those of bishops. Evidently three parallel sections of qualifications are aligned: for the bishop (3:1–7), for deacons 'likewise' (3:8–10), and for women 'in the same way' (3:11). This mention of deacons' wives comes before the requirements for male deacons are resumed in the next verses (3:12–13).

Further, the requirements listed for the women in 3:11 are remarkably parallel to the requirements for deacons in general (3:8–10). Paul seems to point out that these requirements apply to women deacons as well as to men, before going on to describe the further requirements for men, and then concluding with a statement of the reward of faithful diaconal ministry.

Since Paul excludes women from authority in the church (1 Tim. 2:11–15), and presents order appropriate to the 'household of God' (3:15), he makes no provision for women when he gives the qualifications for the office of bishop. Women are not called to rule in the family or in the family of God. But Paul does make provision for women in the office of deacon, and recognizes Phoebe as active in that office.

The strongest counter-argument on the Timothy passage is that deacons are to rule their children and houses well (3:12). Does this require only that a male deacon is to be a good father and husband, or does it imply that the deacon is also to exercise rule in the household of God? This is the parenthetical argument in connection with the bishop (3:5): '(If anyone does not know how to manage his own family, how can he take care of God's church?).' While used there for the function of a bishop, the term 'take care of' is broad. In the parable of the good Samaritan, it describes the care that the Samaritan provides for the wounded man. If the same parenthetical remark were made

233

for the deacon, it could apply to diaconal service.

We may feel disappointed that the first letter to Timothy describes the qualifications of the offices more explicitly than their functions, yet we must not forget that the offices of bishop/elder and deacon are different, and that, in this letter and elsewhere, rule is a distinguishable function for which gifts of the Spirit are provided (1 Tim. 5:18; Rom. 12:8; 1 Cor. 12:28). The difference between those who rule and those who serve is indicated in the very names of the offices. A man who is a deacon serves the church in the ministry of mercy. In this role he must have a good reputation in the church and in the community, which implies faithfulness in his other roles, particularly in his family responsibilities. This requirement does not seem to imply that he, like the bishop, is to be a ruler of the church. (The 'likewise' linking qualifications of bishop and deacon cannot be pressed without also linking the 'likewise' of women as deacons.)

The brief descriptions of diaconal office in the letters are not the only clues we have on the ministry of mercy in the early church, and of the participation of women in it. The women who accompanied the disciples and provided for them presented an original example of diaconal service. Dorcas, at Joppa, was 'always doing good and helping the poor' and there was a company of widows associated with her (Acts 9:36–39).

John Calvin saw a close connection between women as deacons and the ministry of widows described in 1 Timothy 5:3–16.[32] According to Calvin, the support that enrolled widows received from the church (1 Tim. 5:16) was a fixed stipend, half the remuneration of elders. Calvin's connection of widows with women deacons may be too close; Phoebe does not seem to have depended upon relief funds from the church. But the breadth of the term 'deacon' suggests a wide variety of benevolent and support functions, activities in which women had a prominent role.[33]

A great barrier to the recognition of women as deacons has been the assumption that all ordination in the church is to ruling office. If deacons are ordained, it is supposed, they must be called to rule. But ordination, accompanied by the laying on of hands, is a blessing that invokes the presence of the Spirit for the work to which the individual is set apart. Such blessing is fitting for any work on behalf of the church, whether it be rule or service. Parents bless their children; the pastoral benediction, pronounced in a worship service with uplifted hands, is also a renewed 'ordination' of the people of God to their service in the general office of all believers. Paul asked the Roman church to recognize Phoebe, not only as a deacon of the church of Cenchrea, but also as one authorized to discharge a mission in Rome. He charges the church to aid her in her ministry. The church today must recognize its Phoebes and see that their ministries are carried forward.

16

THE GIFTS
OF THE SPIRIT
IN THE CHURCH

The twentieth century has confronted the church with the importance of the presence and gifts of the Spirit. Pentecostal and charismatic movements have spread throughout the world, establishing new denominations and attracting followers by the millions within established churches. Statistician David Barrett has estimated that by the middle of the 1980s there were more than 330 million Pentecostal/charismatic church members in the world, *i.e.* 21% of Christian church membership.[1] His estimate included more than 80 million 'postpentecostals' and 'postcharismatics', but growth-rates make that figure conservative for the mid-nineties. Peter Wagner calculates that between 1979 and 1984 charismatic Christians increased at a rate that would yield 457% growth in every decade.[2]

Three 'waves' have been identified in this charismatic revival – the Pentecostal, the charismatic, and the 'Third Wave'.[3] Peter Wagner describes Third Wave charismatics as those who want the 'signs and wonders' of charismatic manifestations without the theology or labels of the Pentecostal/charismatic movement. 'Third Wavers' hold that: 1. baptism in the Spirit occurs at conversion, not as a second work of grace; 2. the filling of the

Spirit is repeated; 3. speaking in tongues is not a sign of Spirit baptism, but a gift for ministry or prayer; 4. service rather than spiritual experience is the mark of the anointed Christian; and 5. the terms 'charismatic' and 'Spirit-filled' are divisive, implying a separate class of élite Christians.[4]

The remaining distinctive of this broadened charismatic wave is its insistence that the apostolic 'signs and wonders' continue after the apostolic age. Wagner defines the movement by these manifestations, holds that they are abundant and irrefutable, and that spectacular growth is linked to them, though not principally due to them.

By rejecting baptism of the Spirit as the definitive second work of grace, distinct from conversion, the Third Wave diverges from Pentecostalism, which grew out of the Wesleyan holiness movement. There are strong biblical reasons for joining the gift of the Spirit to the beginning of the Christian life. Our study of the gift of the Holy Spirit at Pentecost has reminded us of the Old Testament promises fulfilled by that event. The filling of the Spirit was promised for all the people of God, in contrast to the power of the Spirit given to a few in the Old Covenant. Pentecost brought the distinction between the Old Covenant and the New, not between 'average' Christians of the New Covenant and a spiritual élite. In his Pentecost sermon Peter claims the promise of the gift of the Spirit to all whom the Lord calls: 'all flesh' – young and old, male and female, near and distant: 'The promise is for you and your children and for all who are far off – for all whom the Lord our God will call' (Acts 2:39; Joel 2:28–29; cf. Ezk. 36:25, 27; Is. 44:3).[5] Commenting on Acts 2:38, John Stott says that the gift of the Spirit 'is as much an integral part of the gospel of salvation as is the remission of sins'.[6]

In Acts, Luke traces the fulfilment of the prophecy of John the Baptist (Lk. 3:16) and Jesus' promise to baptize with the Spirit (Acts 1:4–5). Through the Spirit Christ's disciples would be his witnesses in Jerusalem, Judea, Samaria and across the earth (Acts 1:8). The Spirit fell on the whole company of Jewish believers at Pentecost (Acts 2:1–4); on the Samaritans later (Acts 8:14–17); and on the Gentiles in Caesarea (Acts 10:44–48). These narratives do not describe a second-blessing experience that all these people received, but show the inclusion of Jews, Samaritans and Gentiles in the new and true people of God.

The gift of the Spirit marks all Christians, not a separate class of 'anointed' Christians. In each case, groups of people are baptized in the Spirit.

Paul's letters emphatically support this, for he teaches that anyone who does not have the Spirit does not belong to Christ (Rom. 8:9). The Spirit is received by the hearing of faith (Gal. 3:2, 14), and all God's sons possess the Spirit of sonship (Gal. 4:6; Rom. 5:5; 8:14–16). John's Gospel records the promise of Jesus that he will not leave his disciples orphans, but will come to them in the Spirit (Jn. 14:18).

But what of the passages in Acts that seem to describe the reception of the Spirit on the part of those who are already disciples? In Acts 8:14–17 the Samaritans receive the word of God from the preaching of Philip and are baptized, but they do not receive the Spirit until Peter and John come from Jerusalem, pray for them and lay hands on them (Acts 8:4–24).

James Dunn explains that the Samaritans had not come to clear faith in Christ until Peter and John appeared. Reflecting on the Samaritan expectation of a royal Messiah (*Taheb*), he reasons that their enthusiastic reception of Simon's claims (Acts 8:11) may indicate their readiness to receive the message of the kingdom in their own context, with deficient understanding of it. They gave Philip the credence they had already given Simon the sorcerer (Acts 8:6, 9–10). When Luke describes their faith he does not say that they believed in the Lord, but that they believed Philip, who preached the good news of the kingdom (8:11).[7] Luke immediately describes the faith and baptism of Simon in the same terms (8:13). Clearly, Simon's faith was deficient: his heart was not right with God (8:21–22). The contrast appears: the Samaritans come to genuine faith and receive the Spirit; Simon receives the curse.

Another possibility is that the Samaritans were believers in Jesus, just as the disciples were before Pentecost, but that the Lord withheld the gift of the Spirit until the apostles appeared, so that they might signal the breaking down of the wall between Jew and Samaritan in the church. Through the laying on of the apostles' hands, Samaritans are welcomed into the apostolic fellowship.

Another Acts passage cited to demonstrate a second work of grace is the account of the twelve disciples at Ephesus who

239

received the Spirit with the laying on of Paul's hands (Acts 19:1–7). Again, Dunn makes a persuasive case that they had not come to faith in Christ until Paul explained the gospel to them.[8] Luke does speak of them as 'disciples', and Paul asked if they had received the Spirit when they believed. But Luke here (for the only time) uses 'disciples' without the definite article. He does not say 'certain of *the* disciples' to indicate a group within the community of 'the disciples' at Ephesus. Rather, his expression implies that they did not belong to that company of disciples, an implication supported by their ignorance of the most basic Christian matters. Many in those days considered themselves disciples of Jesus in some sense.[9]

Paul's question as to whether they received the Spirit when they believed indicates surprise and uncertainty. They appear to be disciples, but do not evidence the presence of the Spirit. Paul's second question shows that he was not thinking of the gift of the Spirit as a second blessing, 'Into what then were you baptized?' (NKJV). He does not suppose that they lacked an additional gift; he suspects that they did not have the primary gift, the conversion experience sealed by baptism in the name of Jesus. Assuming that baptized Christians have the Spirit, he goes back to basics, and instructs them as to the difference between John's baptism and belief in the One who was to come after John, Christ Jesus. They are then baptized in the name of Jesus, Paul lays his hands on them, and they receive the gift of the Spirit, marked by speaking with tongues and prophesying. The book of Acts, no less than the letters of Paul, sees the gift of the Spirit as the possession of the New Covenant church.

The Spirit is both Giver and Gift, present as Lord and as the Source of all blessing. Dwelling with us, individually and as a community, the Spirit forms us in the image of Christ, renewing our created capacities. All that we are is his: we cannot sharply distinguish between new supernatural gifts of the Spirit and 'natural' gifts renewed by the Spirit. We have nothing that we have not received.

The Lord has fashioned his church as an organic body. The gifts he grants are not given for their own sake; their presence does not support pride, or their absence justify envy. When the gifts are in any way detached from the fruit of the Spirit in the service of love, they become distracting noise, attracting attention but accomplishing nothing (1 Cor. 13).

The major question is not the nature of the gifts, but their use in building up the saints and carrying the gospel to the world. All the charismatic gifts were abundant at Corinth (2 Cor. 12:12), but their display did not win the apostle's praise, or advance the work of the Lord in that city. Paul had to rebuke them and point to the 'more excellent way' of love.

Yet the issue of the continuance of 'signs and wonders' remains one of watershed importance in Christ's church. When the Westminster Confession declares that these extraordinary gifts have ceased, does it presume to limit the power of God, and to block the Pentecostal power of the church?

Apostolic signs

We must recognize, first, that the gifts, calling and office of the apostles marked the foundational era of Christ's church. We have already considered the uniqueness of the apostolic office as witnesses to what Jesus said and did, and as recipients of revelation after his resurrection.By a unique intervention of the risen Lord, Paul was called as the apostle to the Gentiles. Although not one of the twelve, he was a true apostle, granted authority by Christ who had appeared to him, so making him a witness of the resurrection. Paul was the 'last' of the apostles, the last to be added to the 'master builders' and foundations of the church (1 Cor. 3:10; 15:8; Eph. 2:20).[10] No later generation could produce eye-witnesses of the resurrection of the Lord.

Paul's calling as an apostle was validated by the miraculous signs he could perform, the 'signs of an apostle' (2 Cor. 12:12).[11] These signs marked the continuity of their witness with the miracles done by Jesus. Jesus appealed to his miracles as being the works of his Father (Jn. 5:19, 30–40). He would not produce miracles for their own sake just because his enemies demanded them (Mt. 12:39). They were done in compassion, as he bore our sicknesses and carried our diseases (Mt. 8:17). They were also signs and, in John's Gospel, often combined with discourses that explain their symbolism. The feeding of the five thousand, for example, is followed by Christ's discourse on the bread of life. Peter, preaching at Pentecost, declares that 'Jesus

241

of Nazareth was a man accredited by God to you by miracles, wonders and signs, which God did among you through him' (Acts 2:22). Christ's miracles revealed his authority, his person, and the meaning of his saving work.

The miracles of Jesus, then, were not done at random; they fulfilled the Father's plan. He changed the water to wine at a wedding feast, not at the bidding of Mary, but as a sign that when his hour was come at the cross he would supply the wine of the Messianic banquet. By his comment to Mary, Jesus made the miracle a sign, not merely of his power as Creator, but of his coming death as Redeemer.

Luke highlights the continuity of the signs of the apostles with the signs of the Lord. As we saw earlier, Peter's 'Tabitha, get up!' in the raising of the dead echoes Jesus' words 'Little girl . . . get up!' (Acts 9:40; Mk. 5:41; Lk. 8:54). Peter, after healing the lame man at the temple gate, made it clear that the miracle was done only in the power and name of Christ, through faith in that name (Acts 3:12–16).

Although there were seasons when many miracles were done by the apostles, they were not continuously in evidence. Paul's thorn in the flesh was not removed, and he left the sick Trophimus behind at Ephesus. But his miracles, and the gifts that were granted through his ministry, were signs of his apostleship. The same rationale for miraculous signs is given by the author of Hebrews:

> This salvation, which was first announced by the Lord, was confirmed to us by those who heard him. God also testified to it by signs, wonders and various miracles, and gifts of the Holy Spirit distributed according to his will (Heb. 2:3b–4).

Note that this passage includes gifts of the Holy Spirit along with signs and wonders as certifying the apostolic witness. The connection of the gifts with apostolic signs also appears in the Corinthian passage (2 Cor. 12:12). Paul is forced to defend himself against charges of the 'super-apostles' who had so captivated the church. With strong irony he compares his ministry with theirs. Only he could perform the signs and wonders that mark an apostle, and only he could provide the richness of gifts that the Corinthian church enjoyed. He reminds them that they were in no way inferior to other churches – a fact of which they were all too conscious, when it came to the manifestation of charismatic gifts! They were not inferior, for they were the fruit of the apostle's ministry. His preaching, his prayers and the laying on of his hands had been used to bring a rich enduement of charismatic gifts upon the church at Corinth.

The New Testament provides us with the reason for the signs and wonders worked by the Lord and his apostles. They attest God's revelation in Jesus Christ, and its transmission through witnesses of his resurrection, inspired to communicate his word to the church. Miraculous demonstrations of God's power have not been uniformly present in the history of redemption. They mark eras in God's saving work: the exodus, the beginning of the prophetic period, and the climax of redemption in the coming of Christ.[12] The signs wrought by Moses attested his authority as the law-giver, bringing the word of God to Israel; the miracles of Elijah and Elisha showed the authority of the word and of the prophets who spoke the word in a time of apostasy.

But everything prepares for the coming of Jesus Christ. His miracles are done in his own power, as the Son of the Father, by the word of his command. They show that the Lord himself has come, the Lord who completes his work of redemption, and makes the apostles the foundation of his church, giving them his word and signs to work in his name.

Miracles, then, have meaning, attesting Christ's finished work and the apostolic foundation of the church. Apostolic miracles sealed the final revelation given in Christ, preserved for us in New Testament Scripture. The signs of an apostle were not random miracles, but the supernatural heightening of gifts that continue to attest the work of the Spirit. The healing power of Christ continues in answer to prayer offered in the Spirit (Jas. 5:15). In the apostolic sign, however, the Spirit immediately restored to full health, signalling the Lord's presence and power. Peter says, 'Tabitha, get up' (Acts 9:40), and the Lord restores life to the dead.

The same heightening that produced the sign of miraculous healing also operated with respect to God's word. By the unction of the Spirit, the Lord's evangelists and pastors today regularly

243

proclaim the word of God. But in the apostolic gifts of prophecy and tongues, words of the Lord were directly inspired by the Spirit. Believers today may exhort one another in psalms, hymns and spiritual songs, but by the apostolic gift, inspired psalms and songs brought the revelation of the Lord for the founding of the church among the nations.

The cessation of the apostolic signs does not mean the cessation of the gifts of the Spirit. The saints still possess the graces that were supernaturally heightened in the miraculous gifts. Jesus pronounced a special blessing upon those who would believe without seeing. He continues to bless those who no longer seek for signs, but rejoice in the gifts and fruit of the Spirit by which the Lord continues to show his presence with his people.[13]

The gift of tongues

The gift of tongues has had a central role in the development of the Pentecostal and charismatic movements. Pentecostal theology made the gift the necessary evidence of the baptism of the Holy Spirit. Speaking in tongues was the 'initial evidence' that the empowerment of the Spirit had come.[14] 'The Pentecostals maintained that a Holy Spirit baptism, validated and evidenced by "speaking in tongues", was a normative post-salvation religious experience that was available to all Christians.'[15]

While this gift was identified with that mentioned in 1 Corinthians 12:10 and 30, its presence as an initial gift was distinguished from its later possession. The focus on tongues has diminished in some charismatic churches, but remains the characteristic outward mark of the movement.

Some critics, finding Luke's account confused, doubt the historicity of the Pentecost event.[16] Was the event inside or outside? How could people hear their own language among such a crowd? What attracted the crowd to start with? Dismissing Luke as a writer of theological fiction, they conclude that we can deduce nothing as to linguistic phenomena. Luke, to be sure, was not writing a film script for a re-enactment of Pentecost. Whether the disciples began in an upper room and moved to a housetop; whether a falling tongue of fire might attract public notice; whether there were people in the crowd who could follow someone speaking their native tongue in a crowded place: these questions will hardly trouble those who recognize the reality of divine intervention. Luke sees theological significance, as well he should; for him theology is not a matter of literary imagination, but of divine revelation.

The book of Acts presents the speech miracle at Pentecost as a miracle of languages. The languages and dialects spoken that day were the mother tongues of Jews who had returned to Jerusalem from their places of residence during the dispersion. The theological significance is plain. The coming of the Spirit reverses the judgment of Babel; the glory of the Lord is proclaimed at Zion in the divided tongues of earth.[17] The missionary vision of the Psalms is fulfilled. Although the hearers are Jews, they know the languages of the nations; the gospel addresses the nations that had sheltered them.

Israel, disobedient to the word of God, had tasted the bitter judgment of exile. They had mocked God's prophets for babbling the ABCs of judgment, and would hear babbling indeed – the strange tongue of foreign invaders occupying their land (Is. 28:11–13). At Pentecost, the sign of judgment became a sign of blessing: in Jerusalem, in the dialects of the nations, the praise of God sounded forth. Jewish tradition linked Pentecost with the giving of the law at Sinai;[18] the law, it was said, had been given in seventy languages, so that 'every people received the law in its own language'.[19] We cannot say that this tradition was earlier than the second century, but the event at Pentecost has the meaning that was assumed in such traditions: that the word of the Lord addresses the world.

Critical scholars usually assume that speaking in tongues at Corinth was like the modern phenomenon, understood to be ecstatic or syllabic speech without linguistic structure. They then assume that the tongue-speaking at Pentecost was the same, and that Luke described it as the use of languages in order to make the point that the gospel and the church were for the world. But Luke describes current languages that could be catalogued (Acts 2:6, 8, 11).[20] If we accept the accuracy of Luke's account, the question of its relation to tongue-speaking at Corinth remains. Different languages were spoken at Pentecost, so were different languages perhaps also spoken at Corinth?

It would be strange indeed if Luke's later references in Acts

to speaking in tongues (Acts 10:46; 19:6) describe a phenomenon different from tongues at Pentecost. Luke tells us that Paul
laid hands on the disciples at Ephesus who proceeded to speak
in tongues (Acts 19:6). In Luke's account, those disciples
received the gift that had been granted at Pentecost, and Paul
was the apostle through whom the gift was given. The gift of
tongues that came through Paul's ministry in Corinth would not
be different from the gift that came through his ministry in
Ephesus.

Further, this presumption of continuity in the gift of tongues
is supported by the language Paul uses in 1 Corinthians. The
term *glōssa* usually means 'tongue', either the physical organ or
the 'language' spoken by the tongue (*cf.* the English 'language'
derived from the French *langue*, tongue). *Glōssa* has the meaning 'language' in the Septuagint references to Babel and in Acts
2. There are other Greek words to describe babbling: *battalogein*,
for example (Mt. 6:7).

Again, as Donald Carson has emphasized, there is a close
connection between speaking in tongues and interpretation.[21] A
glōssa, language, is to be *interpreted*. Often this word simply means
'to translate', but where the broader sense of giving the meaning
is in view, it still assumes that the speech to be interpreted is
interpretable, that it has linguistic meaning. Without that
meaning, 'interpretation' would not be interpretation at all but
an utterance without connection in *meaning* to the 'tongue'.

Still further, Paul's appeal to Isaiah 28:11 points to tongues as
a sign to the unbelieving (1 Cor. 14:21), assuming that the
tongues spoken in Corinth correspond to the tongue to be
spoken in judgment on Israel, the foreign language of the
Assyrian invaders, not understood by the Jews.[22] In the same
section, Paul says that he would rather speak five *words* in church
with understanding than ten thousand *words* in a *glōssa* that
could not be understood (1 Cor. 14:19). Obviously he thinks of
his own tongue-speaking as the utterance of words, words that
form part of language structure.

The arguments against understanding tongues as languages
in 1 Corinthians are not convincing. Cyril Williams has held that
Paul could not say of a *language* that it is addressed to God with
no man understanding (1 Cor. 14:2).[23] But Paul is describing a
situation in which no interpreter is present. If an interpretation

were given, whether by one who possessed that gift or who knew the language that was spoken, the utterance would not be for God alone, but also for others to whom the message was brought.

It might appear that Paul's comparison with musical instruments in 1 Corinthians 14:7–11 fits only with sounds that are not part of language. He does argue that musical instruments played with indistinguishable sounds would not have significance (14:7–8). Yet his point is not to describe tongues as composed of sounds that are not distinct, but as sounds that the hearer cannot distinguish, that are not readily understood (*eusēmos*, 14:9). This is clear from the context. He is favouring prophecy over tongues unless there is interpretation. When he applies the point, he says that every 'voice' has meaning: a 'voice' is patterned sound, whether musical or linguistic. (The term *phōnē* may mean 'voice', 'sound' or 'language'. It is used in parallel with *glōssa* in the Septuagint of Genesis 11:7.) He does not mean that 'tongues' are sounds without words, but that there are many language systems in the world, and one who does not know the meaning of a language cannot communicate, but must relate as a 'barbarian'. The language barrier to communication in tongues may be removed by interpretation (14:13).

Much has been made of Paul's reference to the tongues of angels (1 Cor. 13:1), as though we might assume that most tongue-speaking, then and now, is utterance in the languages of the heavenly host. Yet Paul is not affirming or implying that this is the case. His language is hyperbolic: no degree of tongue-speaking is of value without love; even if one were to speak the very dialects of heaven without love, it would be in vain. In any case, even if one might speak a language of heaven, a language is still in view.

The nature of glossolalia in Corinth is important because it is well established that contemporary tongue-speaking does not have linguistic structure, and that the phonemes used in it are the phonemes to which the speaker is accustomed in the language or languages already known.[24]

If the references in Corinthians are to the speaking of languages, and tongues today are not languages, then the claim that current 'tongues' are legitimated in Scripture fails. Paul's command that speaking in tongues is not to be forbidden applies then to speaking in languages, not to speaking in syllables. The issue is particularly acute with respect to interpretation, for if the tongue has meaning and can be interpreted, and a genuine interpretation is provided, then God is speaking to his church in our day. Since the tongue-speaker was not aware of the meaning, the meaning did not originate with the speaker, but was contained in the Spirit-given message; that message is then interpreted infallibly (or at least reliably) by one with the gift of interpretation.

Some object by arguing that there could be language systems not fitting the pattern of natural languages which could convey specific meaning. Computer programmes can encode language in almost any predetermined form: in units of six letters or in binary numbers, for example, and can defy the detection of patterns by continually shifting the master code. Angels might speak in cryptograms. Our failure to discern a pattern in apparently random syllabic babbling only indicates our lack of angelic intelligence rather than the meaninglessness of the utterance.[25]

It would be foolish to limit the possibilities of encoding in angelic speech. It does seem unlikely, however, that Paul would speak of ten thousand *words* in a tongue if he had in view speech that was encoded and not verbal. He does think of that which is uttered by the tongue as language; his statement, 'unless you utter by the tongue speech easy to be understood . . .' (1 Cor. 14:9) describes talking in natural language, and contrasts with speech hard to be understood – language still, but language not understood by the hearer. In any case, to hold that non-linguistic tongues are nevertheless meaningful and translatable implies not only that angelic speech is unrecognizable as language, but also that the tongues recordings studied by linguists are all in angelic speech that happens to conform closely to the linguistic range of sounds accessible to the tongue-speaker.

Many Christians in the charismatic movement are sure that their own experience shows that tongues have not ceased. They are persuaded that the Spirit has given them the gift granted to the Corinthian church. They may feel that those who do not possess the experience are in no position to question the presence of the gift. Yet the question cannot be decided by appealing to experience. Other religions practise syllabic utterance, or 'free vocalization'.[26] Anyone can vocalize freely;[27] tongue-speakers have sometimes urged those who desire the gift to begin by a deliberate imitation of tongue-speaking, looking to the Spirit to take over when they have 'primed the pump'.

A Christian convinced that tongue-speaking is a precious gift of the Spirit may speak this way while engaged in prayer and praise, and be overwhelmingly grateful to God for a gift thought to be supernatural. The blessing of personal communion with God may be perfectly genuine, even if the worshipper should be mistaken about what is happening in the uttering of syllables. As Paul says, it is much better to say something you understand, so that your mind is engaged in worship (1 Cor. 14:14–15), but one can surely enjoy fellowship with God without the use of specific words to express devotion.

It is quite possible, therefore, that the apostolic gift of speaking in tongues has ceased, even though millions of Christians believe that they now possess it.

Does the New Testament predict the termination of the special gifts of the apostolic age? Some point to 1 Corinthians 13:8:

> Love never fails. But where there are prophecies, they
> will cease; where there are tongues, they will be stilled;
> where there is knowledge, it will pass away.

Tongues will cease, but the question is, when? Paul contrasts the partial and incomplete with the perfect. Knowledge and prophecy are partial and will be done away when the perfect comes, for then we shall see face to face and know fully as we are fully known. Paul compares the gifts to childish ways of speaking, thinking and feeling that pass away, superseded by adulthood. Some press the comparison; they reason that the church came of age as the apostles completed their founding work, so that we have now entered the perfected period of revelation, when we see the glory of God in the face of Jesus Christ (2 Cor. 3:18; 4:6). This explanation, however, does not do justice to the 'knowing in part' that Paul says is now his situation (13:12).

Rather, Paul seems to have Christ's second coming in view

when he speaks of being 'face to face'. As John says, 'But we know that when he appears, we shall be like him, for we shall see him as he is' (1 Jn. 3:2b). Paul does not declare that tongues must cease before Christ's return, or that they must continue until then. The apostle knows of certain events that must occur before Christ comes again (1 Thes. 2:1–5), but he does not know the time of Christ's coming, and he does not describe a situation in which centuries will elapse while the church continues to be built on the apostolic foundation.[28] He does, however, claim the uniqueness of his own apostolic office, and does recognize the miraculous gifts as signs of an apostle, thereby providing for the cessation of the gifts that certified the apostolic ministry.

There is no mention of tongues in the later Pauline letters, or in the other New Testament writings after the time of the Corinthian letters. Paul's letter to the Romans, most probably written in Corinth, does not mention the gift of tongues in the list of ministries and enduements (Rom. 12:4–8).[29]

Irenaeus, who had contact with the apostolic generation through Polycarp, a disciple of John, speaks of having heard, or heard of, speaking in tongues and prophesying.[30] Contemporary with Irenaeus was Montanus, who proclaimed himself the prophet of the imminent coming of the New Jerusalem, and claimed a new outpouring of the Spirit. He attributed his prophesying and ecstatic utterance to that new visitation.[31] The church rejected his claim, and in 230 AD the Synod of Iconium refused to recognize Montanist baptism.

Augustine, writing in the second decade of the fifth century, asks why no-one in his day speaks in tongues, and gives two answers. The first is that the 'testimony of temporal sensible miracles' was given in former days 'to be the credential of the first beginnings of the church'.[32] The second is that the church first spoke in the tongues of the nations as a sign that it would spread to all the nations and therefore speak those tongues.[33]

From the middle of the third century until the seventeenth, there is little if any evidence of the practice of speaking in tongues in the church. It appeared among persecuted Camisards in the Cevennes region of southern France after the revocation of the Edict of Nantes in 1695. After the few remaining pastors had been caught and martyred, men and women prophets rose up to reject the message of the pastors that the community should patiently endure suffering. They proclaimed instead armed vengeance against the works of the 'Beast'.

After the time of the Reformation, tongues appeared in connection with revival movements like the Shakers during the eighteenth century, and notably among the followers of Edward Irving in England in the nineteenth. The modern Pentecostal movement traces its origins to speaking in tongues at Bethel Bible College in Topeka, Kansas, in 1901 and at the Azusa Street revival in Los Angeles in 1906.[34]

If tongues did not cease with the apostolic age because of their function as an apostolic sign, why was the gift so long absent? Two explanations are offered from the charismatic perspective. One is that the signs died out with the loss of spirituality in the church, and that the efforts of Montanus and others to revive it were crushed by institutional imperialism. An alternative explanation is that the apostolic signs did cease, and that the modern tongues movement is a fresh gift of the Spirit marking the end times prophesied in Joel.

John MacArthur seeks to meet this last explanation by pleading that the cosmic phenomena in that same prophecy have not yet appeared, and that the Pentecostal outpouring was only a foretaste of what must yet happen in the Millennium.[35] It would seem, however, that Peter's message and Luke's account indicate that the 'last days' began when the Father fulfilled his promise, giving the Spirit, with the accompanying gifts (Acts 2:16, 33; 3:24). Cosmic signs will yet signal the coming of the great Day of the Lord, but the special signs at Pentecost were precisely the initiatory signs that marked the outpouring of the Spirit.

The practical question is whether what is now occurring is what occurred at Pentecost and later at Corinth. If it is the same gift of God's grace, it should be regulated as Paul has instructed, but it should not be forbidden, as the apostle has also instructed. If it is not, it cannot authenticate the presence of the Spirit or certify revelation as a sign. It must then be identified, not with the supernatural gift granted through the hands of the apostles, but with the devotional practice of free vocalization. Paul assigns little value to unintelligible words (1 Cor. 14:19). The same would apply to syllabic vocalizing.

It would be wrong, however, to assume that tongues are lying wonders from the powers of darkness. There is nothing inherently wrong in free vocalization, and a person practising it in an attitude of devotion, using the name of the Father and of the Lord Jesus, is shielded by the power of the One addressed and adored. The danger flows from misunderstanding, so that the exercise becomes a source of assurance, or of spiritual pride. The other danger lies in the interpretation of tongues, which is impossible if the tongue is not the gift of language as in the New Testament. The question of interpretation brings us to the issue of continuing prophecy, which is discussed in the next chapter.

Distinct from worship in tongues as a sign of the Spirit's presence are the physical phenomena appearing in contemporary revival movements. People fall over in a trance at a touch; they shake convulsively, or laugh uncontrollably. They may emit strange cries, or crow like a cock. Debate about such behaviour often refers to Jonathan Edward's reflections on the Great Awakening in New England, 1734–35 and 1740–42.[36]

Edwards argues that a work of the Spirit 'is not to be judged of by any effects on the bodies of men; such as tears, trembling, groans, loud outcries, agonies of body, or failing of bodily strength; and the reason is because the Scripture nowhere gives us any such rule'.[37] The rule of the Scripture, rather, is that 'By their fruit you will recognise them' (Mt. 7:16). Jesus gave that rule to warn against claims to the gifts of the Spirit that are not supported by a life of obedience to the Father (Mt. 7:21–23).

Jack Deere agrees with Edwards: 'We want to honor the work of the Spirit in convicting, forgiving, saving, healing, and delivering – not the physical reaction to his work.'[38] Yet Deere also thinks of these strange actions as from God, given from his hand.[39] They are then perceived as signs that God is at work, as John Wesley regarded them.[40] One may well hold that bizarre behaviour may or may not be a work of the Spirit, and that the fruit of the Spirit is the sign of his work. But that does not imply that the Scripture offers no ground for evaluating bizarre behaviour. Deere recognizes this when he recommends that pastoral leaders should gently but firmly stop 'truly bizarre and exhibitionist' behaviour.[41]

Edwards, too, speaks of excesses as exceptions, but goes much further by describing the origins of unusual behaviour in the converting power of the Spirit. He witnesses to two kinds of strange conduct: first, outcries and weeping under conviction of sin; and second, physical faintness before God's sovereign grace in Christ and the wonder of his presence.[42] He reports that the responses of distress arose from 'real proper conviction' in awareness of the truth. As they agonized, they were 'in perfect exercise of their reason' with a lively idea of the horrible pit of eternal misery.[43] He distinguishes from them a class of morbidly melancholy folk – we might call them the clinically depressed. He tells us that in the second phase of the awakening, those who were overcome with delight in the Lord spoke of it with a flood of tears. 'Thus those who laughed before weep now, and yet by their united testimony their joy is vastly purer and sweeter . . .'[44]

Edwards views physical expressions of emotion as understandable in consequence of the Spirit's work, but not in themselves God-given. In a service of worship, he says, those so affected should refrain to their utmost from manifestations that would disrupt the service, although he could wish that all the churches might know such conviction of the Spirit as to lead to such responses.[45]

The ardour of the Spirit never negates the order of the Spirit, who brought order from chaos at creation. To tremble before God's majesty, to weep over sin, or to rejoice in salvation: the Bible recognizes such responses. God's power may overwhelm his enemies: so he prevented Saul from capturing David by the power of the Spirit (1 Sa. 19:20–24); and so, in a different manner, he stopped Saul's namesake on the road to Damascus. Those who came to arrest Jesus fell backward as he identified himself (Jn. 18:6). Not until the parousia will the risen Lord be seen again, but awareness of his power may still overcome his creatures.

Yet the Spirit God gives us is the Spirit of love, power and discipline (2 Tim. 1:7). The Spirit bears fruit in self-control. He may humble us, but he will not debase the image of God in us. Frenzied and uncontrolled behaviour makes God's people a laughingstock to their enemies (Ex. 32:25). The spirits of the prophets are subject to the prophets (1 Cor. 14:32).

As we saw in considering the worship of the church in chapter 9, the Lord has revealed the worship that pleases him, and here the Lord's directions are clear. God is not a God of disorder, but of peace (1 Cor. 14:33). In worship, all things are to be done in a fitting and orderly way (14:40). Paul instructs us in the Lord's command (14:37) precisely with regard to the use of spiritual gifts. Good order will mean that the unbelieving visitor will not say that you are out of your mind, but, being himself convinced of sin, will fall down – yes, he may indeed fall down – and say, 'God is really among you!'

We must heed Edwards' warnings not to speak against, or fail to rejoice in and pray for, the work of the Spirit in bringing conviction of sin and opening the eyes of sinners to the glory of Christ. His plea carries weight when he says that the powerful working of the Spirit may at times make physical responses irrepressible, but it cannot excuse substituting continuing chaos for the order of reverent joy in the presence of the Lord.

17

THE GIFT OF
PROPHECY IN
THE CHURCH

Does prophecy in the New Testament sense continue in the church today? Are there Agabuses or daughters of Philip (Acts 11:28; 21:9–10) at the end of the second millennium of Christian history?

Prophecy and tongues are closely related. The apostle Paul prefers prophecy to tongues, unless tongues are interpreted, when they have the force of prophecy.[1] Why this is so appears from Paul's words in 1 Corinthians 14. The one who speaks in a tongue does not know what he (or she) is saying (14:14–15). Yet what he says is translatable, and may be interpreted by someone with that gift. What, then, is the source of his words? They do not originate in his mind, but are given to him of the Spirit. He speaks mysteries: the mysteries of the gospel, no doubt, but mysteries that are unknown to him as he utters them (1 Cor. 14:2). When these words are interpreted by one enabled by the Spirit to understand them, the church receives a message that originated with God.

Such revelation was given often at Corinth, and perhaps in other churches also; frequency could not diminish its significance. Some minimize the unique content of such revelation, observing that tongues usually utter praise to God, and that their interpretation employs the familiar language of praise. Praise was the content of the tongues spoken at Pentecost, and probably in Corinth also (addressing God; 1 Cor. 14:2, 28). Tongues might also be used to bless the church (14:16). Yet the Bible does not view praise as the routine recitation of liturgical formulas. God gave Moses his song as a witness against Israel (Dt. 31:19); the Psalms blend praise with instruction – we speak to one another as we sing to the Lord (Eph. 5:19). The breathtaking realization that the church is hearing a message from the Lord himself brings an awe that wonderfully concentrates the mind. Granted, the church should always hear Scripture as at the foot of Sinai, but prophetic praise brings the conviction that God is speaking in *this* hour to *this* gathering.

Can the interpretations of tongues, usually phrased in scriptural language, be considered fresh revelation? Simply note what the message does *not* say. Think of the Spirit's message through Paul to the churches of Galatia, or of the letters to the churches in the book of Revelation. Are these familiar words of comfort and doxology? If the Lord gives words (in a tongue), and provides at least the gist of the message (in an interpretation) it is of enormous importance to know whether the Lord seeks joyful praise or tears of repentance. Are there teachings of the Nicolaitans that he would condemn by name? Is there a Jezebel to be exposed? Such authority has been claimed in tongue-speaking and prophecy, but what is then claimed is new revelation.

Interpreted tongues are a form of prophecy, to be taken with full seriousness. The question is whether revealed messages are *now* communicated to the church by the Spirit as fresh revelation, beyond Scripture. Are prophets still speaking the word of the Lord? Not all prophecy, in Old or New Testament times, was recorded in Scripture. Does the claim to continuing prophecy, nevertheless, question the *sufficiency* of the canonical Scriptures? Some charismatic churches keep written records or recordings of the messages brought by their prophets. These messages are the latest word from the Lord, addressed to a particular church. Are they not the most specific revelation of God's will?

Prophecy today

Dr Wayne Grudem, of Trinity Divinity School in Illinois, has laboured to resolve this question in a way that would respect the final authority and sufficiency of Scripture, but would also open the doors of the church to the continuing ministry of contemporary prophets.[2]

He builds a case for two levels of prophetic ministry in the church: the apostle-prophet who speaks the very words of God by inspiration, and the congregational prophet, who does not speak words given him of God, but seeks to express a concept or impression given him by revelation, but which he may not adequately understand, and may distort in the telling. The apostle-prophets are therefore agents of revelation like Moses and the prophets of the Old Testament, but the prophets at Corinth, or the prophet Agabus in the book of Acts, are not so inspired. They utter prophecies to be critiqued by the church in order to distinguish true and false elements. Contemporary prophetic utterances are of the second class, according to Dr Grudem. The congregation should not only scrutinize prophecies, but use greater caution when they predict future events or provide specific guidance for individuals or the congregation.[3]

Dr Grudem's close linking of the apostles with the Old Testament prophets is well supported from Scripture, for example, in 2 Peter 3:2: 'I want you to recall the words spoken in the past by the holy prophets and the command given by our Lord and Saviour through your apostles.'

The same epistle warns against those who twist the writings of Paul as they do also the 'other Scriptures' (3:15–16). The apostles were chosen and called by Christ to be his witnesses, inspired of the Spirit to convey to the church the words and work of Jesus.

Dr Grudem, however, distinguishes sharply between the inspired apostles and the other New Testament prophets. He argues that the term 'prophet' became inappropriate to describe an inspired person because of its loose usage in the Hellenistic world.[4] 'Apostle' was therefore the term of choice.

But, as against this, the word 'prophet' was used in the Greek version of the Old Testament, and continues to be used in the New Testament for those who promised the coming of Christ. God sent prophets and apostles to his people from of old (Lk. 11:49), and Jesus will send prophets and wise men and scribes (Mt. 23:34). That promise of Jesus and the Pentecost sermon of Peter indicate how the Old Testament concept of prophecy carried over into the New Testament church. Agabus, a New Testament prophet, introduced his message with the Old Testament formula 'Thus says the Holy Spirit' (Acts 21:11, NKJV).

The apostles spoke with prophetic authority, but not all prophets were apostles, for they did not have Christ's call as witnesses to his words and deeds. Paul lists apostles first and prophets second in describing those Christ appointed in the church (1 Cor. 12:28). Just as Moses experienced direct contact with God that distinguished him from other Old Testament prophets, so the apostles experienced direct contact with Christ that distinguished them from other New Testament prophets. But in neither case did the distinction diminish the inspiration or authority of the prophets.[5]

Dr Grudem understands Paul to be claiming authority of a different order from that of prophets when he says, 'If anybody thinks he is a prophet or spiritually gifted, let him acknowledge that what I am writing to you is the Lord's command. If he ignores this, he himself will be ignored' (1 Cor. 14:37–38). But any true prophet who had received a command by revelation from the Lord could speak in the same way to all others, including other prophets.[6] Paul anathematizes an angel, another apostle, or even himself if he were to deny the gospel he had received (Gal. 1:8). He certainly condemned apostles who rejected his words, identifying them ironically as 'super-apostles' (2 Cor. 11:5; 12:11). Apostles who contradicted his inspired utterances were false apostles; prophets who contradicted him were false prophets. Paul's words in no way diminish the calling of the true prophet. He goes on to tell the Corinthians to 'be eager to prophesy' (1 Cor. 14:39).

To support his distinction between Old and New Testament prophets, Dr Grudem invokes the difference between revelation and inspiration. An Old Testament prophet, he agrees, was inspired, given actual words by the Lord; but New Testament prophets received revelation, not words. He argues that, in John 4, the Samaritan woman used 'prophet' as the term was understood by 'ordinary people', *i.e.* in the sense of his possessing supernatural knowledge, not that 'he could speak with divine authority in his actual words'.[7] The narrative certainly does not suggest this: Jesus offered more than an approximation of the number of her former husbands. She found his utterance uncomfortably precise, and asked for an authoritative statement about the place of worship, to settle the dispute between the Samaritans and the Jews.

Even less persuasive is Dr Grudem's effort to attach the lesser meaning of 'prophesy' to the demand of the soldiers striking the blindfolded Jesus. Were Jesus to name the one who had hit him, he would identify an assailant whose name he presumably would not have known even without the blindfold (Lk. 22:64).

Dr Grudem also appeals to Peter's quotation of Joel's prophecy (Acts 2:17–18). Joel promises that sons and daughters will prophesy as a result of the outpouring of the Spirit on 'all flesh'. Grudem argues that a gift so widely diffused cannot be the same as the prophetic gift that enabled Isaiah or Jeremiah to write Scripture.[8] If all of God's people may be called prophets, some stronger term must be used for Scripture-writers. That term, he says, is 'apostle'.

But not all believers are prophets (1 Cor. 12:29), and 'all flesh' cannot be pressed to mean every living individual. Joel's prophecy promises a vastly wider distribution of the gift, but in no way suggests that God will water it down for a mass market. The prophets foresee not an inflation of spiritual currency, but an inconceivably greater glory for the latter days.

Dr Grudem's distinction between receiving true revelation and communicating it infallibly is logically valid, but the Old Testament binds the two together, emphasizing the word. Samuel became a prophet, 'For the LORD revealed Himself to Samuel in Shiloh by the word of the LORD' (1 Sa. 3:19–21, NKJV; 1 Ki. 21:19; Am. 3:8).[9]

As George Vandervelde points out, the prophets function as the Lord's mouthpiece even when they are not quoting his words: 'At times the prophet inserts what may be called the actual divine words in the midst of a prophetic address, as in

Isaiah 5:8–10. Yet there is no suggestion that the authority of the prophet's message hinges on the direct quotation formula.'[10] The book of Revelation continues the Old Testament use of 'prophet' and 'prophecy', along with the command to 'write'. But the lack of a command to write would not lead us to think of the revelation as second-class prophecy: dreams and visions that might be erroneously reported by John.

For Dr Grudem's case, the exegesis of Ephesians 2:20 and 3:5 is critical. In the first passage Paul says that the church is 'built on the foundation of the apostles and prophets, with Christ Jesus himself as the chief cornerstone'. Paul then goes on to explain that the apostles and prophets are the foundation of the church because they are recipients of the mystery of the salvation of Jews and Gentiles in Christ: 'the mystery of Christ, which was not made known to men in other generations as it has now been revealed by the Spirit to God's holy apostles and prophets' (Eph. 3:4b–5).

That Paul is not speaking of Old Testament prophets in either passage seems clear from the close connection of the two passages, and from the fact that he is contrasting what has now been revealed with 'what was not made known to men in other generations'. Paul presses his own claim to divine revelation as an apostle, by joining it to that of other apostles and prophets of the New Covenant. These passages appear to bar demoting New Testament prophecy to a secondary role, or denying the role of New Testament prophets in bringing the fundamental revelation of the gospel.

Dr Grudem, however, urges a grammatical point that would change the meaning of Paul's expression. Neither text in Greek has the article 'the' repeated before 'prophets'. As Dr Grudem points out, when the article is not repeated, the two nouns may describe a single class. For example, in Galatians 1:21 'according to the will of God and our Father' the article is found before 'God' but not before 'Father'. Both nouns refer to the same subject. When two separate subjects or classes are in view, the article is often repeated: for example, 'May the God who gives [the] endurance and [the] encouragement . . . ' (Rom. 15:5). On the other hand, in the expression 'the God of [the] love and peace be with you' (2 Cor. 13:11), the article appears before 'love', but not before 'peace', although the two nouns are as distinct as 'endurance' and 'encouragement'. It is therefore difficult to determine from the use of the article how the relation of the two nouns connected by 'and' are to be understood.

An instance to which Grudem calls attention is 'and some to be [the] pastors and teachers' (Eph. 4:11), where he would find the meaning, 'pastors, that is, teachers'. That passage, however, makes a clear distinction between apostles and prophets: 'It was he who gave some to be apostles, some to be prophets, some to be evangelists, and some to be pastors and teachers.' Dr Grudem must insist that Paul is using the word 'prophets' in Ephesians 2:20 in the sense of apostles and the same word in Ephesians 4:11 in his sense of 'community prophets'. Yet in each passage both apostles and prophets are listed, and in the second, as in 1 Corinthians 12:28, prophets are placed second only to apostles and above teachers and preachers of the Word. The same ranking appears in Acts 13:1, where prophets are listed ahead of teachers in the description of the two groups of leaders in the church in Antioch (leaders who included Barnabas and Paul). Such a positioning of prophets does not fit with Grudem's characterization of congregational prophets as those whose words must be screened to decide what utterances are to be accepted. Paul's placing of prophets next to apostles in his lists fits rather with their position as recipients, together with the apostles, of the revelation of the mysteries of the gospel.

The absence of the article before 'prophets' in Ephesians 2:20 and 3:5 indicates, then, not that prophets are identical with apostles, but that they are closely linked with them since they, too, receive and communicate revelation. Such an understanding of the passage rules out Grudem's view, for the New Testament prophets are then declared to be second in office only to the apostles, and to share with them the foundational role that Grudem rightly defends.[11]

This high estimate of the prophetic gift, consistent with the Old Testament and Septuagint usage, accounts for the gifts of those who joined with the apostles in the authorship of Scripture. Silas (Silvanus) was a prophet, associated with both Paul and Peter in authoritative communication of the mysteries of the gospel (Acts 15:32; 1 Thes. 1:1; 1 Pet. 5:12). Others, like Luke and John Mark, while not apostles, may well have been recognized as prophets in a time when the gift was abundantly evident. In any case, Grudem's effort to reduce the prophetic gift removes the designation that could best be applied to those inspired authors of Scripture who were not apostolic eye-witnesses and 'ear-witnesses' of the Lord, but who, by the Spirit, laid down the foundational and final teaching of Christ for his church.

Grudem further argues for two levels of prophecy from his analysis of 1 Corinthians 14:29. His understanding concurs with the reading of the NIV: 'Two or three prophets should speak, and the others should weigh carefully what is said.'

The phrase 'should weigh carefully what is said' translates one word in Greek, the verb *diakrinō*. There is nothing in Greek corresponding to the words 'what is said'. The translators added the phrase to provide their interpretation of what was to be discriminated or judged.

Dr Grudem assumes this and more. He interprets the verb to mean that the others were to sift the content of the prophecy: 'Each prophecy might have both true and false elements in it, and those would be both sifted and evaluated for what they were.'[12] He then declares that no such evaluation, to pick and choose the good and useful from the false and useless, could possibly have been commanded in response to Old Testament prophecy.[13] He cites two other instances of what he regards as congregational evaluation: the response of the Bereans to Paul's preaching described in Acts 17:11; and the charge to 'prove the spirits' given in 1 John 4:1.[14] Neither reference is helpful to his interpretation of 1 Corinthians 14:29. Since Paul has apostolic authority equivalent to Old Testament prophets, the fact that the Bereans searched the Scriptures to see whether what he said was true seems to run counter to Grudem's argument that authoritative deliverances could not be examined. The Bereans actually examined not Paul, in order to pick and choose from his teaching, but the Scriptures that he explained, in order to discover the truth of his whole message, which they had enthusiastically received. The command of 1 John 4:1 runs counter to Grudem's description of evaluating prophets at Corinth, for he insists that the evaluation is not of the prophets (whether they are true or false), but of elements in their message. John, however, says, 'Test the spirits to see whether they are from God, because many false prophets have gone out into the world.'

As Grudem rightly says, the verb *diakrinō* has the meaning of separating or distinguishing. It is used in non-biblical Greek to describe the separating of two combatants. Paul uses it to ask, 'For who makes you different from anyone else?' (1 Cor. 4:7; literally, 'For who distinguishes you?'). To 'distinguish' someone in this sense, is to separate them out, set them apart. In this last passage, the verb has an object, 'you'. The verb has the object 'words' in the Greek version of Job: 'For the ear distinguishes words, the palate tastes grain' (Jb. 12:11, LXX). But in 1 Corinthians 14:29 the verb is used without an object. Does it refer to prophets or prophecies? The context must decide.

In 1 Corinthians 14, Paul is speaking of the preservation of order in the church. Spiritual gifts are for the upbuilding of the church, and disorder in their use would frustrate their purpose (14:26). Paul limits tongue-speaking to two or three participants, followed by interpretation. He then puts the same limit on prophecy: there are to be only two or three to deliver prophecies, and they are not to compete with one another for the floor. Rather, they are to prophesy one at a time, and if another prophet receives a fresh revelation, the one speaking is to defer to him, so that both are not speaking at once. Both before and after making his comment that the others are to discriminate, Paul is concerned with order.

He evidently expects that passing reference to discriminating by the others to be readily understood. What is the connection that is most easily made? Surely one that follows the pattern in which Paul relates tongues and prophecy. That pattern was stated earlier in his discussion of spiritual gifts (12:10). In that list of spiritual gifts, he says, 'to another [*allos*] prophecy, and to another [*allos*] discrimination of spirits, to a different one [*heteros*] a kind of tongues, and to another [*allos*] the interpretation of tongues'. (The word translated 'discrimination' is *diakrisis*, a noun cognate to the verb *diakrinō*.) Paul takes up the same two pairs when he turns his attention to orderly worship in chapter 14: with tongues goes interpretation, with prophecy discrimination. The 'others' (*alloi*) who are to discriminate, are, of course, those who have the gift of discrimination (12:10). (Other prophets presumably possessed that gift.) The object of discrimination, according to 1 Corinthians 12:10, is the *spirit* of the prophet. Is the Spirit of God, or of men (*cf.* I Jn. 4:1)? Is the prophet a true bearer of God's words?

The discriminating that Paul has in mind, therefore, is not separating between elements of the prophet's message, but the separation between 'spirits' that is the regular safeguard for prophetic speech in the assembly (12:10).

Dr Grudem objects that there would be no need to exercise the gift of discrimination to differentiate between true and false prophets in the Corinthian church. Such prophets, he says, would be well known, and discrimination would be necessary only for visitors who claimed the prophetic gift. But it is to the Corinthian church that Paul writes listing the gift of discrimination (12:10), a gift that obviously existed and was used. In any case, Corinth was a centre for trade and travel, and does not seem to have lacked visitors, including false apostles on tour. Further, Paul warns the Ephesian elders not only against wolves from without that will threaten the flock, but also against men from their own number who will arise to distort the truth (Acts 20:30).

Indeed, it is the very authority of prophecy that makes the discrimination of spirits so essential. This is reflected in the instructions given in the *Didache*, dating perhaps from as early as the first century. There testing or discriminating is forbidden when the prophet is speaking in the Spirit, for fear of being guilty of blasphemy against the Holy Ghost. A safer course, according to this handbook, is to make the determination by watching the prophet's behaviour. If, for example, he asks for money, or prophesies to order, he is a false prophet.[15] There is no suggestion here of picking or choosing among prophetic utterances. Since the word of the Lord is to be heard and heeded, the question is whether the speaker is a true prophet.

John Hilber has shown how important discerning true from false prophecy was in the Old Testament. At Corinth also, discerning prophecy was not picking and choosing among a prophet's words, but detecting any false word to reject the oracle and the prophet.[16]

Dr Grudem also appeals to 1 Thessalonians 5:19–22 to support his description of congregational prophecy of lesser authority, containing mistakes to weed out:

Do not put out the Spirit's fire; do not treat prophecies with contempt. Test everything. Hold on to the good. Avoid every kind of evil.

Grudem suggests that the possibility that prophecy might be despised argues for a lesser brand of prophecy. But the apostle to the Gentiles was himself treated with contempt. In the same chapter Paul begs the church to have a high esteem for those who are over them in the Lord (5:12). Despising prophecy is an instance of a broader danger of quenching the fire of the Holy Spirit. The question is whether 'test everything' means to evaluate prophetic messages, retaining what is good, and rejecting the rest. Grudem relies heavily on this passage to support his exegesis of 1 Corinthians 14:29. Since the latter passage refers not to differentiating prophecies but prophets, the Thessalonian passage cannot serve in a supporting role, but must bear the whole weight of the thesis.

It cannot bear that weight. For Grudem's point, Paul's words to 'test everything' must apply primarily to the content of the prophesyings just mentioned, so that the good to be held fast is the good in the prophetic utterance.[17] An immediate problem arises in the words that follow. If Paul were describing the process of sorting out the good from worthless elements, we would expect him to say, 'Keep the good and reject the worthless.' What he says is, 'Hold on to the good; abstain from every form of evil.' The negative command shows his meaning in the positive part of the sentence with which it is contrasted. We are to abstain from evil and hold fast to the good. The good, therefore is not a true element of prophecy, but the ethical good in our lives, as we follow after that which is good (*cf.* 5:15). The proving of all things is therefore not the proving of prophecy, but the proving so prominent in all of Paul's teaching: the discerning that enables us to discover what is the good and perfect and acceptable will of God (Rom. 12:2; Phil. 1:10; Eph. 5:10). Paul immediately continues: 'May God himself, the God of peace, sanctify you through and through' (5:23). At the conclusion of the letter, Paul's constant and burning desire for the holiness of the church again shines through.

For the Thessalonians to grow in holiness, they must respect those who rule over them (5:12), they must not quench the

Spirit, and they must not despise prophecy. They need the work of the Spirit for sanctification, and his help through prophetic revelation. This is how they know the will of God for their lives (5:18). The founding work of the apostles and prophets has now been completed. For us, Paul's word not to despise prophecy means not to despise the New Testament Scriptures, or those who expound them and help us apply them to our lives.

Grudem believes that the book of Acts offers a clear example of the imperfect prophecy he has defined. It is the prophecy of Agabus in Acts 21:10–11:

> A prophet named Agabus came down from Judea. Coming over to us, he took Paul's belt, tied his own hands and feet with it and said, 'The Holy Spirit says, "In this way the Jews of Jerusalem will bind the owner of this belt and will hand him over to the Gentiles."'

Dr Grudem compares this specific prophecy with Luke's account of Paul's arrest (Acts 21:27–33). Luke tells us that Paul was seized by the Jews in the temple and dragged outside. As they were trying to beat him to death, news of the riot reached the commander of the Roman troops in the Castle of Antonia adjacent to the temple. He came at once with officers and soldiers, arrested Paul and ordered him bound with two chains.

Since Paul was not bound by the Jews, but by the Romans, and since the Jews did not deliver him to the Romans, but the commander came and arrested him, there appears to be inconsistency between the prophecy of Agabus and Luke's history. Grudem judges the 'two small mistakes' in the prophecy serious enough to have condemned an Old Testament prophet.[18] One would scarcely need a prophetic gift to predict that Paul was headed for trouble by going to Jerusalem. The predictive element in Agabus' prophecy concerned the specifics of his being bound by his own people and handed over to the Romans.

Dr Grudem holds that the contradictions are so glaring that we must suppose that Luke expected us to note them, and to conclude that the prophecy of Agabus was correct in general, but wrong in specifics.[19] Do we then also suppose that Luke expects us to condemn Agabus for so clearly introducing his

266

prophecy as the words of the Holy Spirit? His formula 'The Holy Spirit says', like the prophecies of the Old Testament, claims to present the words of God.[20]

But we cannot suppose that Luke is making a point of mistakes in the prophecy of Agabus, for at the end of the book of Acts Luke puts the words of Agabus about being 'handed over to the Romans/Gentiles' into the mouth of Paul himself as he speaks to the Jews in Rome:

> 'Men and brethren, though I have done nothing against our people or the customs of our fathers, yet I was delivered as a prisoner from Jerusalem into the hands of the Romans' (Acts 28:17, NKJV).

Paul could be charged with similar inaccuracy in describing what happened. Since he pleads innocence of any offence against the Jews, but was handed over to the Romans, it is clear that he is speaking of the Jews as those who handed him over. Further, since Luke's report of Paul's words is not necessarily verbatim, we must conclude that Luke found nothing wrong with describing the 'handing over' of Paul in such terms.[21] Luke cannot expect us to think that Agabus had got it wrong in his prophecy.

Neither the prophecy of Agabus nor the report of Paul is in the least mistaken. The Jews seized Paul and may well have tied him – with his own belt for that matter. They also handed him over to the Romans, however reluctantly. Without the Jews, he would never have been delivered to the Romans.[22]

Both the prophecy of Agabus and Paul's repetition of its terms draw our attention to the similarity between Paul's suffering and his Saviour's. Jesus said that the chief priests and teachers of the law would condemn him to death and would 'hand him over to the Gentiles' (Mk. 10:33). Jesus was arrested, bound, and handed over to the Romans; so was Paul. Paul, like his Lord, had set his face to go to Jerusalem, knowing the things that must await him there. Like the Lord, Paul must be seized and handed over to the Gentiles.[23]

Prophecy and the sufficiency of Scripture

Dr Grudem wishes to foster understanding and unity between the ever-growing charismatic movement and other evangelicals committed to the historic orthodoxy of the Protestant Reformation. He also wishes to preserve a spirituality sensitive to the sovereign leading of the Holy Spirit in our daily lives, without in any way compromising the authority of Scripture. His goal is illustrated when he speaks of a Bible verse coming to mind in the early morning as being a 'small prophecy'.[24]

Surely the fullest recognition of the illumination of the Holy Spirit is essential, not only for the reading, study and preaching of the Bible as the Word of God, but also for the illumined wisdom we seek as God's gift in directing our daily lives. There is a sense in which our knowing the Lord is by revelation (Eph. 1:17–18), although that word is used in the New Testament almost exclusively in the sense of God's disclosure of his truth by the Spirit (Rom 2:5; 16:25; 1 Cor. 14:6, 26; 2 Cor. 12:1, 7; Gal. 2:2; Eph. 3:3). All Christians confess God's hand of direction, not only in the doors he opens and closes in his providence, but also in desires and impressions that arise while they meditate on how to serve him in their circumstances. The key here, if we are not to set aside the sufficiency of Scripture, is to recognize that the degree of certainty that we may have as to any course of action must always be directly proportional to the degree of clarity with which we can see how the word of God applies to our situation.

Dr Grudem can agree with that statement, but the view he has developed gives the authority of prophecy to impressions, notions or feelings that are no more revelation than the words in which they are expressed. He warns against using formulas like that used by Agabus in describing congregational prophecy,[25] and he has certainly emphasized the degree of error that may enter into such prophecy. Yet his view does not do justice to the finality of revelation given in Jesus Christ and to the sufficiency of Scripture in communicating to us God's last words through Christ's apostles and prophets. It is not through new revelations, but through the gift of wisdom that the Spirit leads the church into the understanding of the truth and the path of obedience.

18

THE
SACRAMENTS

'We live in a world of signs, and of signs about signs.' So begins the jacket blurb of a book about the 'science of signs' – semiotics.[1] The word 'sign' suggests traffic signs, advertising signs, neon lights. But our daily lives are woven with other signs: the signs of language, spoken and written; the other 'languages' we use – the dialect of a sportscaster, sign language for the deaf, 'body language'. There are systems of signs for auctions or financial trading, and for etiquette at the table. Every tourist sooner or later becomes aware of the sign systems that shape a different culture.

The Lord Jesus Christ addresses his church, not only in the language of Scripture, rich with the symbolism of revelation, but also through the sacramental signs he has appointed.

Is creation sacramental?

As we have seen in considering the catholicity of the church in chapter 7, Roman Catholic theologians have linked catholicity with sacramentality. The Protestant Reformation is said to have veered toward Gnostic 'spirituality' by rejecting the sacramental principle, the 'depth' dimension of catholicism, as Avery Dulles describes it. Not only would Catholics add five more sacraments to the two that the Reformers found biblical, they also extend the sacramental principle so that the church, as the body of Christ, becomes a sacrament, and all of creation is sacramental.

A prominent Catholic writer, arguing for a male priesthood, sees the priest as a vessel of sacramental power, bringing God to us:

> The most wonderful miracle in the world occurs at the priest's canonical bidding: The Son of Man, who already did a wondrous deed in assuming male flesh, now becomes again flesh and blood under the appearances of bread and wine.[2]

'Christianity', he says, 'is a sacramental religion, that is, a religion of the flesh.' The hierarchy of the church is a sacramental sign and the church today is a sacrament. Indeed, the 'very fleshy' G. K. Chesterton was affirming the sacramental sense of God's presence in creation when he said: 'Catholicism is a thick steak. a glass of stout, and a good cigar.'

Spreading the sacramental over the whole creation dilutes its force. If everything is sacramental, then bread and wine are already sacraments before their consecration, and the mystery of the Eucharist differs only in degree from the sacramentality of an incarnate creation.

Roman Catholic thought does well to stress the reality of the incarnation, and of Christ's resurrection body. It rightly condemns a Gnostic 'spiritualism' that pretends disdainfully to ignore the body, rise above the constraints of the physical world, and make its proud way as pure, disembodied spirit. But to affirm physical reality is not to sacramentalize it. All of God's works reveal him; they all bear witness to his power, wisdom, justice and goodness. Yet not all God's works in nature convey redemptive power.

Christ fills all things in the sense that his power controls all things, and that he is omnipresent as God the Son. But Christ is not incarnate in all things, nor does his incarnation give redemptive power to the elements of creation. To see all nature as sacramental does not affirm the good gifts of God, or

270

advance proper Christian 'worldliness'. Rather, it claims for the natural world what that world cannot offer: a means of saving grace.

There is a profound difference between the majesty of Mount Sinai as the people of Israel first glimpsed it and the majesty of God's glory revealed on it when he spoke from the cloud. God may use natural or supernatural phenomena as signs of his presence. The bush Moses saw, burning but not burnt, was itself part of creation, bearing witness to the Creator. But, aflame with God's glory, it became a sign, not only of his wisdom and power, but of his saving grace.

The distinctiveness of the sacraments

Even such an immediate use of nature as a sign of grace is not yet a sacrament in the specific sense of the word. A sacrament is not just something in nature created in order to be a sign of grace (the rainbow, for example). A sacrament is a sign of *participation* in *saving* grace.[3] It marks not simply the presence and work of God, but his application of salvation to sinners. The revelation of God in nature does display God's 'eternal power and divine nature' (Rom. 1:20), making all humankind accountable to him, but God's *special* revelation in word and deed provides the signs of his redeeming power. God's Word declares his saving grace; he has appointed particular signs to mark and accompany that saving Word. In the Old Covenant circumcision was the sign that marked participation in the covenant promises of God. The Passover and the daily sacrifices symbolized the ongoing participation of God's people in the blood of his atonement and at the table of his peace.

Through Christ's circumcision and baptism, his righteous life and his offering as God's Lamb, the shadows of the Old Covenant ceremonies became reality. Christ is our circumcision, our Passover (Col. 2:11; 1 Cor. 5:7). To replace those blood-shedding signs, he appointed new signs for the inclusion and fellowship of the renewed people of God. These sacramental signs are baptism and the Lord's Supper.

The Roman Catholic Church also considers confirmation, penance, extreme unction, ordination and marriage to be sacraments, sanctifying almost every event in the lives of church

271

members.[4] Since their institution is not clearly given in Scripture, appeal is made to tradition in order to support their legitimacy. The additional number links with the assumption that sacraments convey infused grace. Since the grace of baptism provides forgiveness only for past sins, penance must provide for further sins, and extreme unction is needed to prepare for meeting God in judgment. Ordination conveys the grace that qualifies the priest to offer the eucharistic sacrifice.[5]

Are the sacraments unspiritual?

At the opposite extreme from Catholic sacramentalism is the view that the New Covenant can no longer be marked by signs, but must be entirely spiritual and invisible in its form and practice. The simplest answer to this misunderstanding is that Christ appointed these signs. His command was explicit: to make disciples of all nations, baptizing them in the triune Name. He gave the bread and the cup at the Last Supper with the commandment to remember his death until he comes.

These outward signs mark out a visible fellowship; they structure Christ's church as a community with membership. Baptism requires a decision about admission to the community. The Supper, a sign of continuing fellowship, implies the exclusion of those who have turned away from the Lord. Those who scorn the church as an institution may rightly rebuke the secularizing of the church on the model of imperial Rome or entrepreneurial Wall Street, but the sacraments testify that the church must have organized form as well as an organic life.

We revere the wisdom of the Lord's commands as he builds his church. Creatures of dust we are, but our common clay bears God's image, and our Lord became a man, not an angel. Such ordinary actions as washing, eating and drinking remind us of the humanity we share with him. Daily we thank the Lord for bread; at the Lord's Table, remembering his death, we thank him for the grain from the wheatfields, given to us as the Bread of heaven.

The sacraments also remind us of our fellowship with one another as we receive the Lord's blessing: they require *corporate* worship. The Lord's Supper is not a self-served, frozen TV dinner, enjoyed alone before the television screen. Baptism is not to be celebrated in the privacy of one's bath or shower. Western culture has made religion a private matter, tolerating Christian faith that does not go public or behave in ways that are politically incorrect. The sacraments, however, require us to confess Christ's name before others, even in hostile societies where we risk persecution.

Evangelical Christians sometimes forget that sacramental blessing is to be found in the company of God's people. For them, real fellowship with God, real intimacy in prayer, can take place only when all distractions have been removed – and fellow-Christians are included among the distractions. To be sure, there is no distinct brand of God's grace that can be conveyed only by the sacraments. The Spirit of God pours out his love in our hearts and makes Christ present with us as we meditate on the Scriptures and pray alone as well as in our gatherings together. The fellowship of the sacraments, however, provides the setting in which the body of Christ is not only present but active, functioning together. The sacraments are the Word made visible; they are joined to the preaching and teaching of the Word, and the Word gives them their authority. Just as there is blessing in hearing the Word together (as it is addressed),[6] so, too, the blessing of the sacraments is shared. The Scriptures do not teach that only the legitimate ordained priesthood can convey sacramental grace. They do support the claim that God's grace is ministered within the fellowship of Christ's body.

The joy that we share in the sacraments lies in their immediate reference to our real Lord: his name, his body and blood. Although sacraments are symbols, they are authenticated by the presence of the Lord. Contemporary thinkers, who pay great attention to systems of symbols, have concluded (or assumed) that the medium is the message: the only 'reality' we know is the one we keep constructing as we play with signs and symbols. They seek to 'liberate' us from these systems we have created, since they have no objective reality, but are fictions, mythologies created to organize experience. They are especially eager to liberate us from Christian 'mythology' in European culture.

At issue, of course, is the truth claim of Jesus Christ and of God's revelation in Scripture. Reality and communication are grounded in God's creation and revelation. The profound simplicity of the incarnation anchors our existence in the ultimate meaning of God's design. The sacraments are reminders of the historical reality of Christ's redemption. They embody concretely the reality of our faith. They are signs, but not mere signs, or only signs in a construct of religious mythology. They are signs given the force of God's own promise, so that our participation in them is not an exercise in fantasy nor in transformation of consciousness. The sacraments certify *reality* for us, by the assurance of God's own Word. Our participation differs from the awareness of God's presence that we might have in smelling a rose or viewing a sunrise. By faith the sacraments present to our senses the touch of the unseen, the foretaste of heaven's feast with the Lord.

Are the sacraments magic?

While it is hard to exaggerate the blessing given by the Spirit in the sacraments, it is easy to misunderstand how the blessing comes. In his *Institutes,* John Calvin first describes the value of the sacraments, then turns to their abuse, particularly the error that the sacraments 'justify and confer grace, provided we do not obstruct their operation by any mortal sin'.[7] Such a position, Calvin laments, leads people to believe that the sacraments can justify them without faith, and encourages superstitious attachment to the sacramental elements rather than to the Lord himself. Calvin affirms that 'Christ is the matter, or substance of all the sacraments; since they all have their solidity in him and promise nothing out of him'.[8]

To those who argue that the effective power of the sacraments cannot be frustrated by the unworthiness or unbelief of those who receive it, Calvin answers in the words of Augustine, 'If thou receive it carnally, still it ceases not to be spiritual; but it is not so to thee.'[9] The function of the sacraments is 'precisely the same as that of the word of God: which is to offer and present Christ to us, and in him the treasures of his heavenly grace; but they confer no advantage or profit without being received by faith . . .'[10]

The sacraments are not sacred magic, the elements themselves containing the blessing, as if the Holy Spirit could be dispensed from a font, or Christ contained in a cup. God does not surrender his work of grace to external symbols, controlled

274

by the manipulation of men. The prophets of Israel condemned the formalism that trusted in the sacrifices of the temple, but did not tremble at his word.[11]

There remains only a negative efficacy for the one who receives the signs of salvation in unbelief and disobedience. Paul warns of the danger of eating and drinking condemnation to ourselves (1 Cor. 11:29).

The historic controversies about the sacraments are still with us. The World Council of Churches has given more than a decade of attention to the report of the Faith and Order Commission (Lima, 1982): *Baptism, Eucharist and Ministry* (*BEM*). That document declares of baptism that 'It is incorporation into Christ . . . It unites the one baptized with Christ and with his people.'[12] In answer to responses received from the churches, the Commission seeks to explain such formulations by saying: 'The church is neither independent of its divine master nor do baptism and eucharist have their role and efficacy in themselves independently of God's action.'[13]

In view of the persisting tendency to view the sacraments as having efficacy in themselves, explanation is certainly needed.[14] The explanation given, however, does not set the matter straight. In the controversy following the Protestant Reformation, the Roman Catholic Church never endorsed a magical view of the sacraments. The formula '*ex opere operato*' in the Council of Trent never claimed that the sacraments worked of themselves apart from God.[15] The point was that they operated without the need for faith in the recipients. This point, as *BEM* acknowledges, remains unresolved among the participating churches. The continuing disagreement appears in the following statement on faith and the sacraments, particularly about the efficacy of a sacramental act that may have no discernible relation to personal faith 'either before, concurrent with or subsequent to the act'.[16]

The Roman Catholic theology of the sacraments thinks of them as infusing grace into the recipients. Catholic theologians criticize Protestants for missing the reality of the sacraments, their immediate and objective imparting of grace. The emphasis of the Reformers on faith is seen as making the grace of the sacrament subjective, dependent on the recipient. It might seem that Roman Catholic sacramentalism seeks to secure God's sovereignty in the sacraments, so that he infallibly infuses grace by sacramental power. There is a qualification, however. While the sacraments are said to 'contain the grace that they signify', they grant this grace 'to all who do not place obstacles in the way'. This is not a small qualification, even if mortal sin were rare. Put more positively, as has been done by Catholic writers defending against the accusation of 'magic', this means that the participant must have a certain disposition in receiving the sacrament. The objectivity of the sacrament must then be combined with a reception that is not altogether unworthy. Such a disposition is said not to merit the infused grace or make it effective.[17]

The difference between the Catholic and Reformed views remains crucial, however. For the Reformed, faith is in no sense a human given, a disposition that at least does not interpose obstacles to the inflow of grace. Faith, God's gift, is never meritorious. It only lays hold on Christ. The objectivity of the sacrament is the work of God in blessing us as he promised; that promise is embraced by faith. In the sacraments faith receives the blessing that is signified by the authority of God's Word and given according to his promise. The gift is nothing less than Christ himself, present with his people. Apart from faith, the sacrament may be deemed 'objective' as though it operated entirely by itself, or 'subjective' as though the sign had no meaning apart from our experience. But faith holds the sign and the blessing signified together.

Since the sacraments are addressed to believers, and are used by the Lord for their blessing, they stand in the closest relation to the blessings given in the Word of God. Like a benediction of the Word, pronounced upon the people of God, so the sacraments are a word of divine power, given in visible form. Faith accepts the benediction and receives the grace pronounced for what it is. So, too, must the sacraments be received for what they are. Receiving does not create the blessing of Christ's presence, but accepts it, all through the Holy Spirit.

Christian baptism

The ceremony of baptism points us to the symbolism of water. The Old Testament makes 'cleanness' a foundational figure for the holiness demanded in the presence of the Lord. Both water and blood cleansed from sin as defilement. The author of Hebrews reminds us of the 'various ceremonial washings' (Heb. 9:10; cf. Lv. 8:5–6; 14:8–9; 15:5), and particularly of cleansing by blood: 'In fact, the law requires that nearly everything be cleansed with blood . . .' (Heb. 9:22).

The washing of baptism was required of proselytes to Judaism. Male converts were also circumcised. The Qumran community made daily washing a sign of the superior cleanness the sect professed.

John's baptism made new use of the familiar symbol. His was not a repeated washing, like those of the Dead Sea community. Rather, John proclaimed a 'baptism of repentance for the forgiveness of sins' (Mk. 1:4). The coming One would bring righteousness and judgment, destroying the wicked and ushering in the rule of God. John baptized in water, but the Lord to come would baptize in the Spirit and fire. To receive his baptism in repentance was to flee the wrath to come, and to prepare for the coming of the Lord.

Jesus, the Lord, came to John for baptism, the sinless one identifying himself with sinners. He then took up John's announcement of the kingdom, and his disciples baptized those who heeded the message. Their baptizing did not pass over into the Christian sacrament without change, however. After his death, resurrection and ascension, Jesus did what John had predicted: he sent the promise of the Father and baptized the disciples in the Spirit. The requirement of repentance and the promise of the forgiveness of sins remained. But baptism became the sign, not merely of preparation for the kingdom, but of entrance into it.

The risen Lord commanded his disciples to baptize into his name, marking by baptism those who belong to him. Indeed, to be baptized into his name is to be baptized into the name of the Father and of the Holy Spirit. The divine name is one, for the Son of God is one with the Father and the Spirit (Mt. 28:18–19).

Important as the water symbol is, we must remember that we are baptized, not into water, but into the name of the Father, the Son and the Holy Spirit. Christian baptism uses the cleansing sign of water so that sinners may bear the holy Name in blessing, not in judgment.

Christian baptism is a naming ceremony. The baptized person is given a name, not the name on a baptismal certificate, but the name of the triune God. A flustered pastor performing an infant baptism may address little Martha as Margaret, but he is not giving her that name. The name that he gives her is the name of the triune God. Baptism gives Christians their family name, the name they bear as those called the children of God (Is. 43:6b–7).

Again we see the close relation of the sacraments to the Word, and particularly to the blessings of the Word. The Lord says of the Aaronic benediction: 'So they will put my name on the Israelites, and I will bless them' (Nu. 6:24–27).

For the priests to bless the people of God was to give them God's name. Christian baptism puts the blessing of God on those he has claimed in Christ. For this reason, baptism is connected with the making of disciples (Mt. 28:19). It is the initiating sacrament that marks belonging to the family of God.

The apostle Paul says: 'For this reason I kneel before the Father [patēr], from whom his whole family [patria] in heaven and on earth derives its name' (Eph. 3:14–15). When Paul met disciples in Ephesus who had received only John's baptism, he explained the difference, and baptized them into the name of the Lord Jesus (Acts 19:5–6).

If we understand the giving of God's name, we will recognize how fully baptism centres on Jesus Christ, the Son of God. To bear his name is to be united to him, who gives us his righteousness and bears our sins; it is to share his glory. Our union with Christ, marked in baptism, means forsaking our sins, the world, the flesh and the devil in order to be consecrated to him as our Lord.

God gave Abraham circumcision as a sign of his covenant. In the background was God's awesome, self-maledictory oath to be faithful to his covenant promise (Gn. 15:8–21; Je. 34:18).[18] The immediate context was God's renewal of his promise that he would give a son to Abraham and Sarah, establishing the line of the promise from which Christ would come (Gn. 17:1–22).

Circumcision was a ritual of cleansing, for the uncircumcised are unclean. It is a cleansing of dedication, for it marks the acknowledgment of God's lordship.[19] In the context of covenant-making, this bloody rite performed on the male organ also included the sign of judgment against the covenant-breaker, with reference to his descendants. The threat of the sanction is expressed: any uncircumcised male will be *cut off*, because 'he has broken my covenant' (Gn. 17:14). The 'cutting' of the covenant, with the cutting off of the foreskin, symbolizes that curse.[20] Further, Abraham is responsible for his household. Male children are to be circumcised on the eighth day. When Moses was returning to Egypt to begin his mission, the threat of destruction was brought against his uncircumcised son.[21]

When God made his covenant with Israel at Sinai, blood was sprinkled on God's altar and on the people. This blood, however, was not simply that of covenant-making, picturing its sanction, the death of the covenant-breaker. It was the blood of atoning sacrifice, offered on God's altar. In Jesus Christ, the true and final sacrifice was made. Entrance to God's kingdom is now by way of his cross, by his blood (Eph. 1:7; Col. 1:20; Heb. 9:18). Instead of the blood of sacrifice, we are purified by the water that speaks of the coming of the Spirit.

Peter compares baptism to the flood, and speaks of our being saved *through* water, bringing the threatening symbolism of water into view (1 Pet. 3:21). In harmony with this image, Meredith Kline has built a convincing case for seeing the water of baptism not only as water of cleansing, but as water of judgment. Paul wrote of Israel's being baptized in the cloud and the sea (1 Cor. 10:2). Like Peter, he compares the water of baptism to the threat of the waters of death: like the water of the flood, the water of the sea overwhelmed the Egyptians. In baptism we are united to Christ in his death (Rom. 6:3–4). That is, baptism also symbolizes the judgment that Christ has endured for us, his entering the waters of death for us, and bringing us with him to the shores of eternal life.

The baptism that saves us is not 'the removal of dirt from the body', Peter says, but the spiritual transaction in which we bring 'the pledge of a good conscience toward God' (1 Pet. 3:21). The word *pledge* implies an undertaking made in response to formal questions. In that pledge, Christians agree with God's judgment on sin, including their own sinful past (1 Pet. 4:3). They acknowledge that to turn from their commitment would be to bring upon themselves God's just judgment. Yet Peter's words stress the wonder of the sacrament even more than its solemnity.

Noah's physical deliverance from the flood symbolized the final deliverance of Christ. Christ has saved us, for he died for our sins and gave us life through his resurrection (3:18–21).[22]

Baptism, then, is a ceremony of cleansing, of naming, of the gift of the Spirit and of covenantal commitment. The Lord claims us, and we him as our Lord and God. Although the water of baptism represents the judgment Christ bore for us, it also represents the life he gives us. Jesus used the symbolism of water (as well as wind and fire) to speak of the Spirit. In his conversation with Nicodemus, Jesus expressed surprise that Nicodemus did not understand the teaching of the Old Testament about the new birth. Our Lord's description of being born of water and the Spirit (Jn. 3:5) should have reminded Nicodemus of the passage in Ezekiel where God said that he would sprinkle his people with clean water, give them a new heart and spirit, and put his Spirit in them (Ezk. 36:25–27).

Jesus also speaks of his gift of the water of the Spirit as springing up to eternal life (Jn. 4:14), and calls to those who thirst to come to him (Jn. 7:37–38). As we have seen, Jesus fulfils the Scriptures that spoke of the water flowing from the Rock and from the temple. From his side on the cross flowed water as well as blood, symbolizing the water of the Spirit.

Paul, in his letter to Titus, speaks of 'the washing of rebirth and renewal by the Holy Spirit, whom he poured out on us generously through Jesus Christ our Saviour' (Tit. 3:5). This statement does not describe baptism, but does allude to it.

Since the Holy Spirit is God's seal on our salvation (Eph. 1:13; 4:30), baptism serves as an outward sign of the inward seal, and by grace through faith becomes itself a sacramental seal that we receive.

Other figures associated with baptism are being clothed with Christ (Gal. 3:27), and awakening from death to the light of Christ (Eph. 5:14). This rich imagery suggests much more: the blessings God bestows in the baptism of his Spirit include not only the gift of life, but the gift of union with Christ and fellowship with the triune God.

That only confessing believers are to be baptized seems to many Christians to be the clear teaching of the New Testament. The continuation of infant baptism in the Lutheran and Reformed churches is viewed as a failure of the Reformation to make a clean break with Roman Catholic practice. Surely the only reason for baptizing infants must be the doctrine of baptismal regeneration, teaching that the sacrament infuses grace in an infant who has no awareness of what is occuring. In contrast, the reply of Philip to the Ethiopian eunuch's request for baptism (found only in later manuscripts) expresses the requirement: 'If you believe with all your heart, you may' (Acts 8:37, NIV margin). If a sacrament is not effective apart from faith, on what ground may infants who are not capable of faith be baptized?

Since infants eight days old were circumcised in the Old Covenant, it is evident that we must consider the relation of the Old Testament to the New in order to address the question. As we have seen, the Lord declared that a male who was not circumcised was cut off from the covenant. Circumcision marked inclusion in the people of God; it was applied to males as representative of females as well, and its symbolism referred to the seed or descendants of those who bore the sign.[23]

Was circumcision, then, a sign only of Israel as a nation, marking an outward relation to God that was replaced by an inward and personal relation in the New Covenant? In our study of the biblical teaching about the church as the people of God, we have seen that such an opposition cannot be made. In the Old Covenant form of the people of God, the core of the covenant is the same: that God will be our God, and we his people. Fulfilment in Christ does not destroy that relation, it brings it to accomplishment. We Gentiles who once were far off are now made fellow-citizens with the Old Testament saints (Eph. 2:19). The Old Testament saints were believers, no less than we, and Paul tells us that circumcision was the sign of the faith that Abraham had before he was circumcised (Rom. 4:11). Circumcision marked the claim of God on his children. They were his by creation and by redemption: by creation, because they bear his image (Gn. 1:27; Mt. 22:20–21); by redemption, because God claims them in the first-born (Ex. 13:1, 13; Nu. 3:40–41; 18:12; Ps. 127:3). When idolatrous Israel offered children to Moloch, the Lord protested, 'You took your sons and daughters whom you bore to me and sacrificed them as food to idols . . . You slaughtered my children and sacrificed them to the idols' (Ezk. 16:20–21).

It is this claim of God upon the children of his covenant that Paul alludes to when he says that our children are holy (1 Cor. 7:12–14).[24]

When Christ came to fulfil the promises of God's covenant, he was circumcised on the eighth day, and presented to God in the temple as a first-born son, consecrated to the Lord (Lk. 2:23). Simeon took the child in his arms and blessed God (2:29–32). Already in his circumcision, Jesus suffered for us, and his blood was spilled. In him, circumcision was fulfilled. Paul applies Christ's circumcision to what was done at the cross:

> In him you were also circumcised with a circumcision not made with hands, in the putting off of the body of flesh, by the circumcision of Christ. You were buried with him in baptism; in him you were also raised with him through faith in the power of God that raised him from the dead (Col. 2:11–12).[25]

Paul thinks of a circumcision that cut off not a bit of flesh, but Christ's whole body in violent death. Christ endured what circumcision symbolized: the cleansing of judgment in death, the 'cutting off' of the sinner. Baptism signifies union with Christ in his death, burial and resurrection. The circumcision done by men no longer avails, for the circumcision of the Christian is now God's doing, bringing us out of the death that our sins deserve into the life that Christ provides. We are circumcised by union with Christ in his death, and baptism is the sign of that union.

In the Old Covenant, children were given the sign of God's covenant promise. In the New Covenant the sign of its fulfilment is not denied them. The covenant promise is expressly claimed for households. When Peter calls on his hearers at Pentecost to repent and be baptized in the name of Jesus Christ, he holds forth the promise of the Holy Spirit, since 'The promise is for you and your children and for all who are far off – for all whom the Lord our God will call' (Acts 2:39). Peter refers to the promise that his hearers knew well: the promise that God made to Abraham and to the patriarchs, that he would bless them and their seed (Gal. 3:14). The book of Acts speaks of households being baptized (Acts 16:15, 33; 18:8). House churches were first of all family churches, and the place of children in the families of God's people was well understood. It is difficult for us, in our culture of isolated individualism, to understand what was self-evident at the time of the apostolic church.

Descriptions of family baptisms are not the only clue that children were included in the number of God's people and entitled to the sign of belonging to him. Jesus settled the matter by taking children in his arms and blessing them (Mt. 19:13–15; Mk. 10:13–16; Lk. 18:15–17).

If the disciples thought children too small or too unimportant for the serious work of the kingdom, they were wrong. Jesus welcomes children, takes them in his arms and declares that of such is the kingdom of heaven. The force of his words is clear. He does not say merely that the kingdom of heaven is for the childlike. He says that the kingdom belongs to them; it is made up of children and of those who come as children. 'Of such as these is the kingdom.' The little ones are highly privileged: their angels have access to the face of the Father in heaven.[26]

Jesus then takes the children, including infants (Lk. 18:15), and blesses them. As we have seen, blessing is not simply praying for them, it is pronouncing God's name upon them. Blessing is always in the divine name. Since Christian baptism is a naming ceremony (baptism into the name of the Father, the Son and the Holy Spirit, Mt. 28:19), the question about infant baptism compares to the benediction at the end of a worship service. Does it include the infants in the arms of the believing parents who hold them? Jesus did not baptize the children in water, for the day of Pentecost had not yet come. Those children had received the sign of cleansing already through circumcision. To pronounce the holy name of God upon fallen creatures without a sign of cleansing would not be a blessing at all, for it would call down judgment.

May our children be named with the name of our heavenly Father? May we teach them to pray, 'Our Father, which art in heaven . . .'? Or must we keep them outside the family of God until they are old enough to make a creditable profession of faith? The circumcised Jesus was presented in the temple. When we present our children to the heavenly Father, may we pronounce the name of the Father, the Son and the Spirzit upon them? If we may, then we must do so with the sign of water.

283

To be sure, we must bring them up in the nurture and admonition of the Lord (Eph. 6:4). His nurture is nurture that he conducts and directs, in which parents are but his instruments. Through his blessing and his promise, we look for our children to confess the Lord for themselves, but they will confess him who knew them from the beginning and whose name has been on their lips from their first babbled words. The confession of faith at the baptism of infants is made by their parents, who claim for them the promise of God's name, and pledge faithfulness in nurturing them. Early in the third century, Hippolytus, a presbyter at Rome, described the order of a daybreak baptismal service, beginning with children, then men and women. If the children are capable of responding for themselves, they are to answer the baptismal questions. If they are incapable, their parents or someone from their family is to respond for them.[27]

Should baptized children also partake of the Lord's Supper? This has been urged, on the ground that weaned children participated in the Passover (Ex. 12:26; *cf.* Heb. 5:12–14). The decisive difference between the two sacraments is that the Supper requires active and discerning participation. Indeed, communicants who take and eat in remembrance of Christ's death are performing the sacrament as well as receiving it. Paul warns against eating without discerning the meaning of the sacrament (1 Cor. 11:23–34). The Westminster Larger Catechism therefore limits participation 'to such as are of years and ability to examine themselves'.[28]

The Lord's Supper

The Lord's Supper is a covenantal meal. Jesus said, 'This cup is the new covenant in my blood, which is poured out for you' (Lk. 22:20; 1 Cor. 11:25). It is a meal of the New Covenant instituted by Jesus in the course of the celebration of a meal of the Old Covenant, the Passover.

Jesus, the Lord incarnate, sat down with his disciples to eat the Passover. The Old Covenant prepared for this. The Lord provided food for his people: manna and quail in the wilderness, rich harvests in the land. Moreover, he brought them to his table at the feasts. From his altar the Lord provided the meat of sacrifice for the fellowship-offering. God was the Host, but sinners could come to his table only when the blood of atonement had been poured out.

The covenant-making ceremony at Sinai concluded with a fellowship meal where Moses was joined by the priests and elders (Ex. 24:11). Remembering the feasts of the covenant, the prophets promised God's great feast in the latter days (Is. 25:6–8; Ho. 12:9; Zc. 14:16). Jesus spoke of God's dinner in his parables; he promised that the Gentiles would be brought in to sit down with Abraham, Isaac and Jacob in the feast of the kingdom (Mt. 8:11). At the supper in the upper room, he said that he would not drink again of the fruit of the vine until he drank it new in the kingdom of God (Mt. 26:29; Mk. 14:25). The Lord's Supper looks forward to the final feast because it marks the atoning blood of Christ through which that feast is made ready and its guests brought in.

The death of a substitute was at the heart of the Passover, too. The lamb was slain in the place of the firstborn of Israel, and the blood put on the doorposts (Ex. 12:13). The lamb set aside for the Passover, like the sacrificial lambs, had to be perfect, without defect (Ex. 12:5; Lv. 22:17–25). Peter writes to God's elect in Asia Minor that they were redeemed 'with the precious blood of Christ, a lamb without blemish or defect' (1 Pet. 1:19). Christ's broken body and shed blood are sacrificial, not only because he went to his death in willing love, but because he was the Lamb of God, offered as a substitute for sinners. 'He himself bore our sins in his body on the tree . . . by his wounds you have been healed' (1 Pet. 2:24).

The Lima statement of the WCC on the Lord's Supper speaks of 'propitiatory sacrifice' and 'expiation' only when it comments on Catholic theology and the sense in which the Eucharist is spoken of as a sacrifice.[29] The text declares that 'The eucharist is the sacrament of the unique sacrifice of Christ, who ever lives to make intercession for us. It is the memorial of all that God has done for the salvation of the world.'[30] This broadening of the reference, not only to 'the incarnation, life, death, resurrection and ascension of Christ' but to all that might be viewed as God's saving acts may seem to heighten the significance of the sacrament. Instead, it loses sight of the specific charge to 'remember the Lord's death till he come'. We do remember the

Lord, in relation to the future as well as the past, but we remember him in terms of his broken body and his 'blood of the covenant, which is poured out for many for the forgiveness of sins' (Mt. 26:28). The broadening language of *BEM* loses what is crucial: the specific purpose and accomplishment of Christ's sacrifice on the cross – his substitutionary atonement. To partake of the sacrament means to confess that we deserve death for our sins, and that God gave his Lamb, his Son, in our place. The Lamb is God's Lamb, not ours, and Jesus Christ is both Priest and Sacrifice who offered up himself for us, once for all, on the cross.[31]

At the sacrament of Christ's atoning sacrifice, the Lord calls us to his table to receive the seals of the New Covenant, attesting his finished work on the cross, and sealing our faith. As baptism into the triune Name marks union with God, and membership in his family, so, too, does the Supper mark union with Christ. Baptism is the sacrament of initiation; the Supper is the sacrament of continuing communion in the family of God. Both reflect our status before God because we are joined to Christ, and both also reflect the life we receive from Christ. In baptism that life appears as the life of the new birth in the Spirit; with Christ we are buried and raised to new life. The Supper portrays our receiving of life from Christ as we feed on him.

Jesus used the figure of feeding on him in his claim to be the bread of life, given from heaven. 'If anyone eats of this bread, he will live for ever' (Jn. 6:51). When his hearers were offended, he pressed the figure:

> Whoever eats my flesh and drinks my blood has eternal
> life, and I will raise him up at the last day. For my flesh
> is real food and my blood is real drink (Jn. 6:54–55).

That his language is figurative is clear, for he added, 'The Spirit gives life; the flesh counts for nothing. The words that I have spoken to you are spirit and they are life. Yet there are some of you who do not believe' (6:63–64).

Partaking of Christ by faith is eating the true manna, the bread of heaven given for the life of the world. At the same time, the work of the Spirit in opening the heart to believe gives life by enabling the believer to feed on Christ, the only Source of life.

Our Lord's teaching makes it clear that he gives us life not only by what he has done for us, but by his being united to us. He is the true Vine, and we are the branches. We feed on him, draw life from him, and this vital connection appears in the eating and drinking of the Lord's Supper. The sacrament brings both assurance of the saving power of his death and joy in the renewal of his life.

The vividness of the sacramental symbolism, however, has been the centre of controversy through the centuries. Gary Macy makes the case that variant views were tolerated until the Reformation: 'What was lost in the reformation was not just Christian unity, but the toleration of pluralism.'[32] He notes that in the ninth century, the abbey of Corbie in Normandy housed monks with two opposite views about the physical presence of the body of Christ in the Eucharist.

Paschasius Radbertus, the abbot, taught that the body of Christ present was the physical body born of Mary, and that we live on account of him because we eat him.[33] Ratramnus, also at the abbey, answered a query from Charles the Bald, the royal grandson of Charlemagne, to say that the reality of the body of Christ in the Eucharist was spiritual, and that the physical body of the Lord could not be present on the altar. How well the two brother monks got on we do not know, but when, after two chaotic centuries, Berengar of Tours revived the teaching of Ratramnus, he was forced by the Synod of Rome in 1059 under Pope Nicholas I to take an oath declaring that the body and blood of Christ 'are physically taken up and broken in the hands of the priest and crushed by the teeth of the faithful, not only sacramentally but in truth.'[34] That did not end the controversy, but the reaction to the Reformers on the part of the Popes and of the Council of Trent gave ample evidence of intransigent commitment to a hierarchical sacramentalist system, a system that rested on the power of the priest to make the Mass the offering of the body of Christ.

How is Christ present in the Supper? In what sense did he declare, 'Take, eat, this is my body'? The question is distinct from the efficacy of the sacraments, although related to it. (The efficacy of baptism is also at issue, but there is no question about the water *becoming* the Holy Spirit.)

The literalism of Paschasius, as enforced under Pope

Nicholas, was certainly not the prevailing view of the church fathers. Augustine spoke of the need of distinguishing the sign from the thing signified. Further, as Dr Macy points out, the old catholic church discussed the reality of Christ's body and blood in the setting of Neoplatonic philosophy, which understood reality as the participation of things in the ideal as the real. To speak of the reality of the body of Christ in that framework would not raise the question that later caused so much distress: if the host was really the body of Christ, what about the mouse who nibbled the bread? Was Christ also present in the stomach of the mouse?

Many insisted on the presence of the actual body of Christ in the Eucharist because they were convinced that the benefit of union with Christ's body could be obtained in no other way. Since the Lord was incarnate, and shared with us a human body, our human bodies can partake of eternal life only by feeding on him.

Thomas Aquinas drew his solution from his understanding of Aristotle, and the distinction between substance and accident. Cows may come in different colours, sizes and shapes, but the differing outward aspects are accidental: they may change radically, yet the animal still remains substantially a cow. Using that distinction, Thomas could maintain that the Eucharist was really and substantially the body of Christ, even though the accidental outward appearances remained those of bread and wine.

The Protestant Reformation rejected this doctrine of transubstantiation, along with the view that the sacraments operated apart from the faith of the recipient. John Calvin, in his *Institutes*, wrote a carefully reasoned account of the doctrine of the Supper, in which he responded not only to the position of the Roman Catholic church, but also to other Reformers. He disagreed with those who denied transubstantiation but who insisted with Luther that the risen body of Christ was present in, with, or under the bread. He particularly objected to the idea that the physical body of Christ was omnipresent, since Calvin believed that this confused the divine and human natures of Christ. The risen body of Christ, he said, is located in a particular place, at the right hand of God.

On the other hand, Calvin also rejected the teaching that the

Supper is a mere symbol of a spiritual reality. Ulrich Zwingli in Zurich appealed to the words of Jesus in the passage cited above (Jn. 6:63) to argue that the Spirit gives life and the flesh profits nothing. To Calvin and the other Reformers, however, to say that the flesh of Christ profited nothing was unthinkable. Calvin reasons:

> If, by the breaking of the bread, the Lord truly represents the participation of his body, it ought not to be doubted that he truly presents and communicates it.[35]

He agrees that the symbols are symbols, but holds that they must mean what Christ says they do. In faith we must receive what they symbolize, the body of Christ. How can the body of Christ, at the right hand of the Father, be present to faith in the Supper? 'Let our faith receive, therefore, what our understanding is not able to comprehend, that the Spirit really unites things which are separated by local distance.'[36]

Calvin compels our agreement when he says that the sacrament must mean what Christ says that it means. Yet when Jesus broke the bread and said, 'This is my body', he surely was not saying that in giving it he was distributing his physical flesh. What they ate was what they were given, bread. Yet in eating it they were accepting him and his sacrifice for them. Jesus gave the bread and the wine at the table in reference to his giving his body and blood on the cross. In asking them to partake of it Jesus is not offering two parts of his physical constitution but himself. He had predicted his death, and they had not understood. Now he would seal to them the meaning of his death: that it was for them. Not just the elements, but the action of eating and drinking are part of the final parable that he gives them. What it means is that he gives himself for them, and they live in union with him. We must respect Calvin's awe before the mystery he so long pondered and found so overwhelming. Though he may have forced a needless problem about the distance of Christ's physical body from us, he is surely right about the meaning: incorporated into one body with Christ, we rest assured that whatever is his is ours. Eternal life can no more be lost by us than by him; we cannot be condemned by our sins, for he has borne them as though they were his own.[37]

The seal of Christ's New Covenant could not be more concrete and specific. He gives himself to us as our Surety and our Life. No less does his sacrament bind us to each other. We participate, Paul says, in the blood of Christ and in the body of Christ. Because we are united to Christ, we cannot be joined to idols. But because we are united to Christ, we must be joined to one another: 'Because there is one loaf, we, who are many, are one body, for we all partake of the one loaf' (1 Cor. 10:17). Baptized into the name of Christ, partaking of the body of Christ, the church is the Lord's. The doctrine of the church is the teaching of the Lord himself, who loved the church and gave himself for it. The unchanging Christ still gives the bread and the cup, sealing his presence until the day when the mission of the church is finished, and with that host from every family and nation we will see him whom we love, and he will eat with us again in resurrection glory.

Notes

Preface

[1] Stephen J. Paterson, associate professor of New Testament, Eden Theological Seminary, St Louis, Missouri, quoted by Ira Rifkin, *San Diego Union Tribune*, 10 March 1995.

1. The colony of heaven

[1] Paul Johnson, *Modern Times: The World from the Twenties to the Eighties* (New York: Harper Colophon Books, 1983), p. 698.

[2] Robert L. Wilken, 'No Other Gods', *First Things* 37, November 1993, p. 13.

[3] Due to the bomb damage and subsequent renovation programme, services were shifted to other churches, including nearby St Andrew's, Undershaft.

[4] The Chancellor's judgment in November 1993, following the Consistory Court in June and July, authorized the major changes, with the exclusion of moving the reredos.

[5] Vatican II, *Gaudium et Spes*, 7 December 1965: *Pastoral Constitution on the Church in the Modern World*, para. 22, in Austin Flannery, OP, ed., *Vatican Council II: The Conciliar and Post Conciliar Documents* (Northport, NY: Costello; Dublin: Dominican Publications, 1975), p. 924. Francis A.

Sullivan, SJ, sets the problem by documenting the contrast between the unqualified papal and conciliar statements of earlier centuries, and the formulations of Vatican II and of recent Popes (*Salvation Outside the Church? Tracing the History of the Catholic Response* (New York: Paulist Press, 1992). He writes to demonstrate development rather than contradiction, pleading the rejection of the Augustinian doctrine of original sin and election in mainstream Catholic doctrine, and defending Karl Rahner's view of 'anonymous Christians' and the saving potential of non-Christian religions (p. 172).

[6] John Hick, 'The Non-Absoluteness of Christianity', in *The Myth of Christian Uniqueness: Toward a Pluralistic Theology of Religions*, ed. John Hick and Paul F. Knitter (Maryknoll, NY: Orbis Books, 1987; London: SCM Press, 1988), p. 23.

[7] So Wilfred Cantwell Smith, 'Idolatry in Comparative Perspective', in Hick and Knitter, *op. cit.*, pp. 58f.

[8] J. C. Hoekendijk, 'The Church in Missionary Thinking', *The International Review of Missions* XLI, 1952, p. 325.

[9] Mt. 16:18.

[10] See Wolfhart Pannenberg, *The Church*, trans. Keith Crim (Philadelphia: Westminster, 1983), pp. 15–17.

[11] 1 Pet. 2:9–12.

[12] See Edward Schillebeeckx, *The Church: The Human Story of God* (London: SCM Press; New York: Crossroad Publishing, 1990). 'Nothing is determined in advance: in nature there is chance and determinism; in the world of human activity there is the possibility of free choices. Therefore the historical future is not known even to God; otherwise we and our history would be merely a puppet show in which God holds the strings. For God, too, history is an adventure, an open history for and of man and woman' (p. 91). Jesus, too, is contingent, and 'cannot in any way represent the full riches of God'; he cannot shut off or deny other ways to God, or appropriate ethics exclusively to himself (p. 9).

[13] 1 Tim. 3:15.

[14] Jn. 18:36.

[15] Rev. 22:2 describes, however, twelve *crops* of fruit from the tree of life.

[16] O. S. Tomkins, *The Third World Conference on Faith and Order* (London: SCM Press, 1953), p. 22.

[17] Claude Welch, *The Reality of the Church* (New York: Charles Scribner's Sons, 1958). See, for example, 'The Unity of the Person', pp. 97ff.

[18] Gonzalo Cardenas, 'The Challenge of the Latin American Revolution', in John C. Bennett, ed., *Christian Social Ethics in a Changing World* (New York: Association Press, 1966), pp. 212f.

[19] *Ibid.*, p. 33.

[20] Wesley Granberg-Michaelson (Director of the WCC's sub-unit on

Church and Society), 'Editorial', *The Ecumenical Review*, 42.2, April 1990, pp. 89–91.

[21] *Ibid.*, p. 90.

[22] See *The Ratzinger Report: An Exclusive Interview on the State of the Church*, Joseph Cardinal Ratzinger with Vittorio Messori, trans. Salvator Attanasio and Graham Harrison (San Francisco: Ignatius Press, 1985).

[23] Schillebeeckx, *op. cit.*, p. 230. See note 12 above.

[24] See Gustavo Gutiérrez, *A Theology of Liberation* (Maryknoll, NY: Orbis Books, 1973; London: SCM Press, 1974), Part 1, pp. 3–42, and the extensive footnotes.

[25] Richard P. McBrien, *Do We Need the Church?* (New York: Harper & Row, 1969), p. 16.

[26] *Ibid.*, p. 228.

[27] *Ibid.*, pp. 14f.

[28] Avery Dulles, *The Resilient Church: The Necessity and Limits of Adaptation* (Garden City, NY: Doubleday & Co., 1977), p. 11 (see also pp. 17–21).

[29] Avery Dulles, *The Reshaping of Catholicism: Current Challenges in the Theology of the Church* (San Francisco: Harper & Row, 1988), pp. 13f.

[30] Maurice Blondel, *History and Dogma* (1904), discussed by Dulles in *The Reshaping of Catholicism*, pp. 83–92.

[31] See Gregory Baum, *The Credibility of the Church Today: A Reply to Charles Davis* (New York: Herder & Herder, 1968).

[32] James Davison Hunter, *Evangelicalism: The Coming Generation* (Chicago and London: University of Chicago Press, 1987).

[33] George Marsden has pointed this out, showing the importance of distinguishing evangelicalism as a doctrinal position from evangelicalism as a movement, and as a community. 'In this respect evangelicalism is most like a denomination' ('The Evangelical Denomination', in G. Marsden, ed., *Evangelicalism and Modern America* [Grand Rapids: Eerdmans, 1984], p. xi).

[34] 'A church member or an individual church that will not give to promote the officially authorized missionary program of the Presbyterian Church is in exactly the same position with reference to the Constitution of the Church as a church member or individual church that would refuse to take part in the Lord's Supper or any other of the prescribed ordinances of the denomination' (*1934 Minutes of the General Assembly, the Presbyterian Church, USA* [Office of the Stated Clerk], p. 110).

[35] The General Assembly did not require that all giving be channelled through the church, but that no giving be directed to Presbyterian missions not managed by the denomination. The basic issue was the nature of the gospel. Machen had appealed against the support of liberal missionaries by the denominational Board. When all relief was denied, he organized the Independent Board so that Presbyterians could support missionaries who would be true to the Bible and the doctrinal position of the church.

[36] This position was taken by some at a combined meeting of the Inter-denominational Foreign Mission Association (IFMA) and the Evangelical Foreign Mission Association (EFMA) at Green Lake, Wisconsin, in 1971.

2. The people of God

[1] Robert W. Jenson, 'How the World Lost Its Story', *First Things* 36, October 1993, pp. 19–24.

[2] See E. P. Clowney, *The Unfolding Mystery: Discovering Christ in the Old Testament* (Colorado Springs, CO: NavPress, 1988; Leicester: Inter-Varsity Press, 1990).

[3] Lesslie Newbigin, *The Household of God* (London: SCM Press, 1953), pp. 30f.

[4] Herwi Rikhof, *The Concept of the Church: A Methodological Inquiry into the Use of Metaphors in Ecclesiology* (London: Sheed & Ward, 1981), pp. 13–38. See E. P. Clowney, 'Interpreting the Biblical Models of the Church', in D. A. Carson, ed., *Biblical Interpretation and the Church: Text and Context* (Exeter: Paternoster Press, 1984), pp. 64–109.

[5] That Peter is writing to churches composed mainly of Gentiles is evident from his descriptions of their past manner of life (1:18; 4:3–4).

[6] Paul Minear, *Images of the Church in the New Testament* (Philadelphia: Westminster Press, 1960).

[7] See J. Y. Campbell, 'The Origin and Meaning of the Christian Use of the Word EKKLESIA', *JTS* 49, 1948, pp. 130–142; and James Barr, *The Semantics of Biblical Language* (London: Oxford University Press, 1961), pp. 119–129.

[8] Peter T. O'Brien, *Colossians, Philemon*, Word Biblical Commentary 44 (Waco, TX: Word Books, 1982), pp. xlv, xlvi, 57–61.

[9] See chapter 8.

[10] God chose and called Abraham (Gn. 12:1–2); he chose Isaac and not Ishmael (Gn. 21:12); Jacob, not Esau (Mal. 1:2–3; Rom. 9:11–13).

[11] The NIV translates 'a servant of the Jews', using 'Jews' for 'circumcision'. In the context, however, Christ is the Servant of circumcision, not in the sense that he ministered to Jews while Paul ministers to Gentiles (*the* circumcision, Gal. 2:8); but in the sense that he serves the covenant of circumcision, fulfils the calling of circumcision, and accomplishes the function of circumcision so that God's purpose in giving the sign to Abraham might be fulfilled: that the Gentiles might glorify God for his mercy.

[12] That the Servant is an individual is clear from the parallel with Cyrus, the Gentile king, who is declared to be anointed as the Lord's servant for bringing back God's people (Is. 45:1–7). The contrast is also clear from the repeated statement that Cyrus has not known the Lord.

[13] Henri Blocher, *Songs of the Servant* (London: Inter-Varsity Press, 1975), pp. 39f.

3. The church of Christ

[1] Lk. 7:22; Is. 35:5–6.

[2] If Jesus spoke Aramaic, further words would have been necessary since in that language there is no gender difference between the personal name and the generic term for 'rock'.

[3] The term *skandalon* may refer to anything that causes one to trip. In Israel stones and outcroppings of rock were the commonest causes of stumbling. The Greek translation of Is. 8:14 uses *petra* to describe the rock that causes stumbling. In the Aramaic translation of the passage, the word used is *keph*, the Aramaic name of Peter (Cephas). Peter uses the phrase from Is. 8:14 in 1 Pet. 2:4–8.

[4] The names of the twelve apostles of the Lamb are on the twelve foundations of the New Jerusalem, come down from heaven (Rev. 21:14).

[5] Psalm 18:4–5 puts 'the cords of Sheol' in parallel with 'the floods of Belial' and 'the waves of death' (*cf.* Jon. 2:2, 6). The Dead Sea Scrolls use this figure: in the *Hymns* from the Qumran community, the drowning man in a storm is sinking down to the gates of death, but is delivered by God and set on a rock (1 QH 3:17; 6:24).

[6] To speak of the church as the new and true Israel is now often said to be anti-Semitic, since it implies that Christianity has superseded Israel as God's covenant people. (Hershel Shanks, 'Silence, Anti-Semitism and the Scrolls', *BAR* XVII.4, July/August 1991, p. 57).

Eugene J. Fisher, Director for Catholic–Jewish Relations, expounds the Vatican II declaration *Nostra Aetate* (1965) as ending for Catholics 'any theory that the Christian Church has "superseded" or "replaced" the Jewish people as God's Chosen People in the history of salvation' ('The Church's Teaching on Supersessionism', *BAR* XVII.4, p. 58). He declares, 'Jewish refusal to convert to Christianity is not to be understood as anything less than a faithful witness to God.'

The solemnity of God's judgment, announced by Jesus (Mt. 21:43), has nothing to do, however, with racist hatred. Jesus wept over Jerusalem, and prayed for those who crucified him. The apostle Paul was ready to be cursed and cut off from Christ for the sake of his own race, the people of Israel (Rom. 9:3).

The apostle deals at length with this issue in Romans 9 – 11. He follows the Old Testament in distinguishing an Israel within Israel. Not all descendants of Abraham are children of the promise, the believing remnant that is saved (Rom. 9:6, 27). Against an unbelieving people, the prophets pronounced judgment (Acts 13:41, 46, 51; 28:25–28).

On the other hand, the apostasy of many in Israel does not mean that God has forgotten his promise to Abraham. Their very fall brings in the Gentiles; Paul evangelizes the Gentiles in the hope that Israel will in holy jealousy claim its own promises (Rom. 11:11–14). God's people of old are 'beloved for the fathers' sake'. Jew and Gentile alike have been disobedient and deserve the judgment of God, but to both God extends his mercy in Jesus Christ, in whom all the promises are fulfilled (Rom. 11:32). At last the full number of believing Israel and of the nations will be gathered to him.

[7] Jn. 2:4; 5:25, 28; 7:30; 8:20; 12:23, 27; 13:1; 16:32; 17:1.

[8] See Allison A. Trites, *The New Testament Concept of Witness* (Cambridge and New York: Cambridge University Press, 1977) for a thorough treatment of the subject.

4. The fellowship of the Spirit

[1] Heribert Mühlen says that the church is not a continuation of the incarnation, but 'a continuation in the history of salvation, of the anointing of Jesus by the Holy Spirit' (*L'Esprit dans l'église* [Paris: du Cerf], vol. 1, p. 106).

[2] For a defence of the RSV translation 'what person or time', see Wayne Grudem, *The First Epistle of Peter*, Tyndale New Testament Commentaries (Leicester: Inter-Varsity Press; Grand Rapids: Eerdmans, 1988), pp. 74f.

[3] B. B. Warfield gives a clear statement of the continuity of the Spirit's work in the Old Testament and the New, showing that he worked in the hearts of God's people no less prevalently then than now, and that all the good in the world was then as now due to him ('The Spirit of God in the Old Testament', in *Biblical and Theological Studies* [Philadelphia: Presbyterian and Reformed, 1968]). No less clearly, he says of the Old Covenant: 'The object of the whole dispensation was only to prepare for the outpouring of the Spirit upon all flesh . . . The dispensation of the Spirit, properly so called, did not dawn until the period of preparation was over and the day of outpouring had come' (p. 155).

[4] Hans Küng, *The Church*, trans. R. and R. Ockenden (New York: Sheed & Ward, 1968; London: Search Press, 1969), p. 175. Küng later says, 'The Church cannot take over the Spirit, or in any real sense "possess" him, control or limit, direct or dominate him.' That is true, except that there is a real sense of possessing the Spirit that is in no sense a domination, but is the marvellous outcome of God's giving himself and his grace to us. Yves Congar also states that the Spirit does not come only to animate an institution totally determined in its structures, but that he is properly 'co-institutor' (*Je Crois en L'Esprit Saint*, vol. 2 [Paris: du Cerf, 1980], p. 19). As against Luther and the Reformers, Congar affirms the Roman Catholic position that the Spirit revealed elements essential to the doctrine of the

church and the sacraments in historical developments after the New Testament period.

[5] Küng, *op. cit.*, p. 176.

[6] *Ibid.*, p. 177.

[7] *Ibid.*, p. 177.

[8] Küng raises the point in a series of questions proposing a more 'restrained' manipulation of the canons and tenets of the church, and a more cautious attitude toward the preaching and sacraments of non-Roman Christian churches (*ibid.*, p. 178).

[9] *Ibid.*, p. 176.

[10] *Institutes*, IV.1.4 (John Calvin, *Institutes of the Christian Religion*, trans. and ed. John Allen, 2 vols. [Philadelphia: Presbyterian Board of Christian Education, 1936], vol. 2, p. 273).

[11] *Institutes*, IV.1.5 (p. 275).

[12] Stanley Hauerwas has defined Christianity as discipleship, likening it to a craft to be learned in a tradition (*After Christendom?*, Nashville, TN: Abingdon Press, 1991, pp. 101ff.). He condemns 'individualistic accounts of Christian salvation' (p. 96). He shows how the church has found tolerance in the modern world by accepting its assumption that religious belief is private opinion. In opposing that view, however, he also pushes aside the initiative of the Spirit in conversion, and the incorporation of the believer in Christ by the new birth. Becoming a disciple does mean becoming 'part of a different community with a different set of practices' (p. 107), but it is union with Christ that creates the community. Hauerwas even challenges '"sacrificial" atonement theories' as favouring the individualism of civil religion (p. 179, n. 25).

[13] 'According to the Protestant distinction, as it has been happily formulated, it is the believer's relation to Christ that puts him in connection with the Church; not his connection with the Church that puts him into a saving relation to Christ' (George Smeaton, *The Doctrine of the Holy Spirit* [London: Banner of Truth reprint, 1958], p. 235).

[14] See William Chillingworth (1602–44), 'Scripture the only rule whereby to judge of controversies', in *Works* (Philadelphia: Herman Hooker for Robert Davis, 1840), secs. 13, 22, pp. 112, 114f.

[15] Westminster Confession, I.x.

5. The gift of the Spirit

[1] 'Big Brother Education, 1994', *The Phyllis Schaffly Report* 27.10, May 1994, p. 1.

[2] Recall the 'Head' in C. S. Lewis, *That Hideous Strength* (London: Pan, 1955). The meaning of the relation of head and body in Eph. 4:16 is much discussed; in any case, the head is viewed as the source of life.

[3] See chapter 7.

[4] Adam was to fill the earth and subdue it (Gn. 1:28). Christ has subdued all things to himself and he fills all things (Eph. 1:22–23).

[5] The present imperative verb in Greek describes a continuing or repeated action rather than a simple action, expressed by the aorist (F. Blass, A. Debrunner and R. W. Funk, *A Greek Grammar of the New Testament* [University of Chicago Press, 1961], 334.C, p. 172). See Frederick Dale Bruner, *A Theology of the Holy Spirit* (Grand Rapids: Eerdmans, 1970), p. 172.

[6] John R. W. Stott, *Baptism and Fullness: The Work of the Holy Spirit Today* (Leicester: Inter-Varsity Press; Downers Grove, IL: InterVarsity Press, [2]1975), p. 50.

6. 'I believe . . . the holy catholic church'

[1] Paul S. Minear, *Images of the Church in the New Testament* (Philadelphia: Westminster Press, 1960).

[2] The Westminster Confession wisely enriches its direct description of the church as visible and invisible with appropriate scriptural figures. On the use of figures in describing the church, see E. P. Clowney, 'Interpreting the Biblical Models of the Church', in D. A. Carson, ed., *Biblical Interpretation and the Church: Text and Context* (Exeter: Paternoster Press, 1984), pp. 64–109.

[3] Although only Luke explicitly says that Jesus called the twelve 'apostles', the parallel accounts in Matthew and Mark name the twelve as a distinct group, and Matthew also calls them 'apostles'. Paul speaks of the apostles in Jerusalem at the beginning of his ministry (Gal. 1:19), and tells us that the risen Jesus appeared to the twelve (1 Cor. 15:5), spoken of, it would appear, as apostles (1 Cor. 15:7). In spite of the questions that have been raised about the apostleship of the twelve, it must be acknowledged that Jesus' choosing of twelve fits exactly with his announcing of the coming of the kingdom, and of the New Israel of the latter days (Mt. 19:28; *cf.* Rev. 21:24. See Hans Küng, *The Church* [New York: Sheed & Ward, 1968; London: Search Press, 1969], p. 349).

[4] The reconstructive surgery of critical scholarship on the apostleship has been reported and elaborated by Walter Schmithals, *The Office of Apostle in the Early Church*, trans. John E. Steely (Nashville, TN: Abingdon Press, 1969). Schmithals maintains that the 'twelve' were not apostles, but a later invention; only if Jesus had known himself to be the Messiah would he have gathered twelve disciples as eschatological rulers (Mt. 19:28; Schmithals, *ibid.*, p. 68, n. 49). The betrayal of Judas, he says, cannot be used to support the existence of the twelve, because the betrayal was also a later fiction, invented to condemn Judas for subsequent apostasy. Critical scholarship,

committed to its notion of scientific history, can outdo the flair for inventive fiction that it attributes to biblical authors.

[5] See Herman Ridderbos, *The Coming of the Kingdom*, trans. H. de Jongste (Philadelphia: Presbyterian & Reformed, 1962), pp. 363–365.

[6] See Karl Heinrich Rengstorf, art. '*apostolos*', *TDNT* I, pp. 414–420; Schmithals, *op. cit.*, pp. 103–110. Schmithals vigorously rejects the Jewish institution of the *šālîah* as the origin of the concept of the apostolate.

[7] Herman Ridderbos, *Redemptive History and the New Testament Scriptures* (Presbyterian & Reformed, [2]1988), p. 22. The scripture citation is 1 Cor. 15:2. Ridderbos defends this translation and interpretation.

[8] In John's Gospel, the phrase 'these things are written' is used of his Gospel, as well as of the Old Testament passages so often cited (Jn. 20:30–31; see 2:17; 6:31, 45; 10:34; 12:14; 15:25).

[9] Ridderbos, *op. cit.*, p. 23.

[10] 'If the Bible as a whole and in all its parts is not also read backwards in light of the Holy Spirit at work in the early catholic church and subsequently, the Bible will have no more authority that any other primitive document from antiquity.' Carl Braaten, director of the Center for Catholic and Evangelical Theology, cited by Richard John Neuhaus, who dismisses the evangelical view that 'the old-time religion is secured by a nineteenth century Protestant dogma of biblical inerrancy' ('Protestantism Then and Now', *First Things* 44, June/July 1994, p. 72).

[11] Küng, *op. cit.*, p. 281.

[12] Irenaeus, *Adversus Haereses* III.iii.3, cited in Eric G. Jay, *The Church: Its Changing Image Through Twenty Centuries* (Atlanta: John Knox Press, 1980), p. 45.

[13] Jay, *ibid.*, p. 48; Irenaeus, *Adv. Haer.* IV.xxvi.21.

[14] Küng, *op. cit.*, p. 355.

[15] Peter R. Jones, '1 Corinthians 15:8: Paul the Last Apostle', *Tyndale Bulletin* 36, 1985, pp. 3–34.

[16] Rudolf Schnackenburg, 'Apostles Before and During Paul's Time', in W. Ward Gasque and Ralph P. Martin, eds., *Apostolic History and the Gospel* (Exeter: Paternoster Press, 1970), pp. 287–303. Schnackenburg seeks to mediate the long controversy among critical scholars about the origin of the apostolate. Discounting Luke's description as late, he suggests that in Paul's time there were already two conceptions of apostles current: one in Jerusalem that included the requirement of having seen the Lord, and one among the Gentile churches that described a travelling missionary. He argues that Paul allowed for both, and was ready to press his own claim on any or all descriptions of an apostle. This proposal also assumes that Ephesians was not written by Paul, but reflects a still later time when the calling of the evangelist came to be recognized. An easier solution would be to assume that the word, like other terms in the New Testament, could

be used in more than one sense, whether or not they might be taken to be technical (as is the case with *diakonos*, for example).

[17] Paul's reference to his having 'seen Jesus our Lord' (1 Cor. 9:1) makes it likely that he thinks of the foundational apostolate in this passage, an interpretation that is supported by 9:5, where 'the rest of the apostles' are linked with the brethren of the Lord and Cephas, members of the original community around Jesus.

[18] The NIV happily translates the phrase 'God's fellow-workers', not 'fellow-workers with God'; Paul speaks of God as the owner of the field where the workers sow and water, or of the building on which they labour. God gives the task and blesses it, but he is not a colleague in the work-force.

[19] William Carey, *An Enquiry into the Obligation of Christians to Use Means for the Conversion of the Heathen* (1792, London: Baptist Missionary Society, 1942), reprinted in *Faithful Witness: The Life and Mission of William Carey* (Birmingham, AL: New Hope Press, 1991; Leicester: Inter-Varsity Press, 1992).

[20] 'The Church is that part of mankind which is conscious of the fact that it is moving towards the final goal' (*The Church for Others and the Church for the World* [Geneva: WCC, 1967], p. 13). J. C. Hoekendijk writes, 'The *nature* of the church can be sufficiently defined by its *function*, i.e., its participation in Christ's apostolic ministry' ('The Church in Missionary Thinking', *The International Review of Missions* 41, 1952, p. 354). See also Hoekendijk, *The Church Inside Out* (Philadelphia: Westminster Press, 1964).

[21] J. Robert Nelson, a former chairman of the Faith and Order division, has ridiculed the 'timeworn and now worn-out belief . . . that the Church, like the floating zoo of Noah, was launched by God on the surly insidious sea of history in order to be the lifeboat of the lucky few' ('Toward an Ecumenical Ecclesiology', in Martin E. Marty and Dean G. Peerman, eds., *New Theology* 9 [New York: Macmillan, 1972], p. 272).

[22] 'This is the unique Church of Christ which in the Creed we avow as one, holy, catholic and apostolic. After His Resurrection our Saviour handed her over to Peter to be shepherded (Jn. 21:17), commissioning him and the other apostles to propagate and govern her (*cf.* Mt. 28:18ff.)' (*Dogmatic Constitution on the Church*, I.8, in Walter M. Abbott and J. Gallagher, eds., *The Documents of Vatican II* [London: Chapman; New York: Guild Press, 1966], p. 23).

[23] See chapter 5, p. 65.

7. Holiness and catholicity

[1] J. I. Packer, *Among God's Giants: The Puritan Vision of the Christian Life* (Eastbourne: Kingsway, 1991 = *A Quest for Holiness*, Wheaton, IL: Good News Publishers, 1990), p. 11.

[2] Hans Küng, *The Church* (New York: Sheed & Ward, 1968), pp. 322ff.

[3] Yves Congar, *Sainte Eglise* (1963), pp. 144ff. Cited in G. C. Berkouwer, *The Church* (Grand Rapids: Eerdmans, 1976), p. 341.

[4] Pope Paul VI, *Ecclesiam Suam*, para. 46: 'This reform cannot concern either the essential conception of the Church or its basic structure.'

[5] Berkouwer, *op. cit.*, p. 341. See *Decree on Ecumenism*, in Walter M. Abbott and J. Gallagher, eds., *The Documents of Vatican II* (London: Chapman; New York: Guild Press, 1966), p. 346.

[6] Küng, *op. cit.*, p. 323.

[7] Vittorio Subilia has traced the nature and origins of the Catholic claim that the church is the continuing incarnation, exercising Christ's authority on earth. He shows why this dogma is fixed beyond debate. See *The Problem of Catholicism*, trans. Reginald Kissack (London: SCM Press; Philadelphia: Westminster Press, 1964).

[8] Küng, *op. cit.*, p. 323.

[9] The Westminster Shorter Catechism, Qs. 33–35.

[10] 'But it is a fact too frequently overlooked that in the N.T. the most characteristic terms that refer to sanctification are used, not of a process, but of a once-for-all definitive act' (John Murray, 'Definitive Sanctification', in *Collected Writings*, vol. 2, Edinburgh: Banner of Truth, 1977, p. 277).

[11] See chapter 3, pp. 44f.

[12] John Owen, *Works*, ed. William Goold (Edinburgh: Johnstone and Hunter, 1850–53; Banner of Truth Trust, 1965-68), vol. III, p. 370. Cited in Packer, *op. cit.*, p. 198.

[13] Peter Toon, art. 'Simeon the Stylite', in J. D. Douglas, ed., *The New International Dictionary of the Christian Church* (Grand Rapids: Zondervan, [2]1978), p. 905.

[14] Westminster Shorter Catechism, Q. 89.

[15] As the verbal use is a departure in English usage, so the transitive use of the verb *mathēteuō* differs from usage outside the New Testament (*TDNT* IV, p. 461).

[16] The adverb *katholou* is used in Acts 4:18 to express a universal negative. The Sanhedrin commands Peter and John not to speak or teach *at all* in the name of Jesus.

[17] J. B. Lightfoot, ed., *The Apostolic Fathers* (London: Macmillan, 1893), 'To the Smyrnaeans' vii, p. 129.

[18] Küng, *op. cit.*, p. 298.

[19] Westminster Confession, XXV.ii.

[20] Henry B. Parkes, *A History of Mexico* (Boston: Houghton Mifflin, [3]1960), p. 94.

[21] F. L. Cross and E. A. Livingstone, eds., *The Oxford Dictionary of the Christian Church* (Oxford: Oxford University Press, [2]1974), p. 800.

[22] Küng, *op. cit.*, p. 303.

[23] *Ibid.*, p. 301.

[24] Avery Dulles, *The Catholicity of the Church* (Oxford: Clarendon Press, 1985), ch. 2, 'Catholicity from Above: The Fullness of God in Christ', pp. 30–47. Dulles also presents the dimensions of depth, breadth and length: 'Catholicity from Below: The Aspirations of Nature'; 'Catholicity in Breadth: Mission and Communion'; 'Catholicity in Length: Tradition and Development'.

[25] Dulles notes the interpretation that Christ is filled by all in all; this seems unlikely in the light of Eph. 4:10.

[26] Dulles, *op. cit.*, p. 39.

[27] J. A. Heyns, *The Church*, trans. D. R. Briggs (Pretoria: N. G. Kerkboekhandel, 1980), pp. 136f.

[28] Dulles, *op. cit.*, p. 33.

[29] *Ibid.*, p. 34.

[30] Dulles describes the position of Teilhard de Chardin and cites James A. Lyons, *The Cosmic Christ in Origen and Teilhard de Chardin* (Oxford: Oxford University Press, 1982).

[31] Dulles, *op. cit.*, p. 37. In respect to Paul's use of the body-of-Christ figure exclusively for the church, Dulles acknowledges: 'Pauline usage is in this respect narrower than that of Teilhard de Chardin, who spoke of the entire cosmos as the body of Christ' (p. 39).

[32] Dulles refers to the *Pastoral Constitution on the Church in the Modern World* and cites the sentence, 'By His incarnation the Son of God has united Himself in some fashion with every human being' (Dulles, *op. cit.*, p. 38). The citation is from ch. 1, sec. 22 (Austin Flannery, OP, ed., *Vatican Council II: The Conciliar and Post Conciliar Documents* [Northport, NY: Costello; Dublin: Dominican Publications, 1975], p. 923). The section goes on to declare, 'For since Christ died for all, and since all men are in fact called to one and the same destiny, which is divine, we must hold that the Holy Spirit offers to all the possibility of being made partners, in a way known to God, in the paschal mystery' (*ibid.*, p. 924). See ch. 1 above, p. 15. This universalism seems to be salvific rather than cosmic. The document cited affirms orthodox Christology and footnotes the formulation of the Council of Chalcedon on the divine and human natures of Christ: sec. 22, n. 22 (*ibid.*, p. 923).

[33] *Redemptor Hominis* (London: Catholic Truth Society, 1979), para. 14. See citation in John Hick, 'The Non-Absoluteness of Christianity', in John Hick and Paul Knitter, eds., *The Myth of Christian Uniqueness: Toward a Pluralistic Theology of Religions* (Maryknoll, NY: Orbis Books, 1987; London: SCM Press, 1988), p. 21.

[34] Vatican II, *The Dogmatic Constitution on the Church*, secs. 3, 10, 11 (Flannery, ed., *op. cit.*, pp. 351, 361f.). Note the *Instruction on the Worship of the Eucharistic Mystery*, from the Sacred Congregation on Rites, 25 May 1967: 'Hence the Mass, the Lord's Supper, is at the same time and

inseparably: a sacrifice in which the sacrifice of the cross is perpetuated; a memorial of the death and resurrection of the Lord . . . a sacred banquet . . .' (Flannery, ed., *ibid.*, p. 102). And again: 'For in it Christ perpetuates in an unbloody manner the sacrifice offered on the cross' (*ibid.*, p. 103).

[35] Vatican II, *On the Church*, sec. 1 (Flannery, ed., *ibid.*, p. 350).

[36] Dulles cites J. A. Möhler, who called the church 'the permanent incarnation of the Son of God everlastingly manifesting himself, perpetually renewed and eternally young' (*Symbolism* [New York: E. Dunigan, 1844], p. 333). Dulles, *op. cit.*, p. 44.

[37] Subilia, *op. cit.*, cites Congar, Journet, Thils, Schlier and others to show the Catholic insistence on the 'continuous presence of eternity in time', 'ensuring Christ's uninterrupted presence in space and time' as constituting the 'mystery of Catholicity'. Subilia adds, 'Then there is no question of any break, there is continuity between Christ and the Church' (p. 177).

[38] Dulles, *op. cit.*, p. 44.

[39] *Ibid.*, ch. 3.

[40] *Ibid.*, p. 50. The Reformers appealed to the teaching of the apostle Paul, who regarded his legalistic righteousness as rubbish, 'that I may gain Christ and be found in him, not having a righteousness of my own that comes from the law, but that which is through faith in Christ – the righteousness that comes from God and is by faith' (Phil. 3:8–9).

[41] Augustine fought a battle on two fronts. He rejected the Manichaeanism to which he had once been attracted, and taught that evil was not created by the God of the Old Testament, but came from the free choice of the creature's will. When Pelagius, who denied original sin, quoted from Augustine to establish his doctrine of the free will, Augustine replied (in his 'Retractions') by quoting passages that Pelagius had ignored, such as: 'Since man cannot rise of his own will as he fell by his own will, let us hold with firm faith the right hand of God, Jesus Christ our Lord, which is stretched out to us', and 'When we speak of the will that is free to do right, we speak of the will with which man was [first] made' (*On Free Choice of the Will*, trans. A. S. Benjamin and L. H. Hackstaff [Indianapolis: Bobbs-Merrill, 1964]; pp. 156, 157f.).

[42] Paul Minear, ed., *Faith and Order Findings* (Minneapolis: Augsburg, 1963), Report of the Theological Commission on Christ and the Church (North American Section), p. 10.

[43] *Ibid.*, pp. 12–13.

[44] *Dogmatic Constitution on the Church*, I.8, in Flannery, ed., *op. cit.*, p. 357.

[45] Cross and Livingstone, eds., *op. cit.*, p. 393. David Kingdon has reminded me of the refusal of William Carey and his Serampore colleagues to compromise with caste, noting the account of the baptism of Krishna Pal in Timothy George, *Faithful Witness: The Life and Mission of William Carey*

(Birmingham, AL: New Hope Press, 1991; Leicester: Inter-Varsity Press, 1992), p. 131.

8. The marks of the church

[1] For example, Calvin's *Institutes*, IV.2.3.

[2] *Institutes*, IV.2.1.

[3] *Ibid.*

[4] *Institutes*, IV.2.3.

[5] Roberto M. Unger, *Knowledge and Politics* (New York: Free Press, 1975).

[6] *KPBS On Air Magazine*, 23.6, April 1992, p. 27.

[7] See the clear exposition of the change in Edward A. Dowey, Jr, *A Commentary on the Confession of 1967 and an Introduction to the 'Book of Confessions'* (Philadelphia: Westminster Press, 1968), chs. 7 and 10.

[8] See above, ch. 1, n. 36. In a case originating in the objection to the acceptance of Mansfield Kasemann in the Presbytery of National Capital Union, the Judicial Commission of the Assembly stressed the change that had taken place with the new form of subscription that accompanied the adoption of the *Book of Confessions* and the Confession of 1967. No longer was a candidate for the ministry of the church to be judged by subscription to a credal statement but only by his willingness to be instructed and guided by the Confessions of the church. No doctrinal belief (not even, apparently, in the deity of Christ) is in itself necessary (*193rd General Assembly, The United Presbyterian Church, 1981*, Part I, *Journal*, p. 115). The decisive change as to scriptural authority was explained in the 'United Presbyterian Report on Biblical Authority and Interpretation': see *The Presbyterian Outlook*, 164.22, May 1982, pp. 6–8.

[9] Conservatives succeeded in gaining token concessions. The phrase 'word of God written' was used for Scripture, although, as Edward Dowey pointed out, this phrase, taken in context, could not mean what it meant in the Westminster Confession (Dowey, *op. cit.*, pp. 101, 103).

[10] Cited in Hans Küng, *The Church* (New York: Sheed & Ward, 1968; London: Search Press, 1969) p. 37. Küng says that no Catholic who believes in the real church would make such a blunt statement today.

[11] As illustrated in the disastrous 'Bay of Pigs' decision of the J. F. Kennedy cabinet. See Irvine L. Janis, *Victims of Groupthink* (Boston: Houghton Mifflin, 1972).

[12] Vatican II acknowledges the right of local groups to be called churches, as they are in the New Testament, because the Church of Christ is present in them, 'in so far as they are united to their pastors'. The last clause is a key one, for the Church 'derives its life' from the Eucharist which the bishop 'offers or insures that it is offered', since he is invested with the full sacrament of Holy Orders as the 'steward of the grace of the

supreme priesthood' (*Dogmatic Constitution on the Church*, II. 26, in Austin Flannery, OP, ed., *Vatican Council II: The Conciliar and Post Conciliar Documents* [Northport, NY: Costello; Dublin: Dominican Publications, 1975], p. 381).

[13] *Kat' oikon* is the phrase in Rom. 16:5; 1 Cor. 16:19; Col. 4:15; Phm. 2, and has this meaning in Acts 20:20, probably also in the plural in Acts 8:3 where Saul presumably seized his victims from house-church groups, or from houses where the groups met.

[14] L. Praamsma, in G. C. Berkouwer and G. Toornvliet, eds., *Het Dogma der Kerk* (Groningen: Jan Haan, 1949), p. 488.

[15] 'Decree on the Apostolate of Lay People', in Flannery, ed., *op. cit.*, pp. 766-798. *Cf.* Avery Dulles, *The Resilient Church: The Necessity and Limits of Adaptation* (Garden City, NY: Doubleday & Co., 1977), p. 13.

[16] *Decree on the Apostolate of Lay People*, III. 10, in Flannery, ed., *op. cit.*, p. 777. The apostolate of the laity is expounded also in the *Dogmatic Constitution on the Church*, ch. IV, in *ibid.*, pp. 388–402. Included in the calling of the laity is 'a share in his [Christ's] priestly office to offer spiritual worship for the glory of the Father and the salvation of men'. Christ is also said to fulfil his prophetic office through the laity. He 'establishes them as witnesses and provides them with the appreciation of the faith (*sensus fidei*) and the grace of the word (cf. Acts 2:17-18; Apoc. 19:10) so that the power of the Gospel may shine out in daily family and social life.' Christ's kingdom power also finds expression as lay people labour in their secular callings as leaven in the world.

[17] *Constitution on the Church*, II.26, in *ibid.*, p. 381.

[18] *Constitution on the Church*, ch. III, 'The Church is Hierarchical', sec. 22, in *ibid.*, p. 375.

9. The service of worship

[1] 'The quality of Israel's worship is inevitably conditioned by the Object of worship, the Sovereign Lord of heaven and earth, righteous and gracious in all His ways, who in His inmost being is Holy' (A. S. Herbert, *Worship in Ancient Israel* [London: Lutterworth Press, 1959], p. 9).

[2] Westminster Confession of Faith, XX.2. Note the semicolon after 'Word' and the reading '*if* matters of faith, or worship'. From the S. W. Carruthers edition of the original manuscript of the Confession, 1646.

[3] *Ibid.*, XXI.1.

[4] J. I. Packer, 'The Puritan Approach to Worship', in *Diversity in Unity* (papers read at the Puritan and Reformed Studies Conference, December 1963), pp. 4–5. For this section see D. A. Carson, ed., *Worship: Adoration and Action* (Carlisle: Paternoster Press; Grand Rapids; Baker Book House, 1993).

[5] John Calvin, *Tracts and Treatises on the Doctrine and Worship of the Church*,

vol. 2 (Edinburgh: Calvin Translation Society, 1849; reprint, Grand Rapids: Eerdmans, 1958), p. 118, *cf.* p. 122. See also Article 32 of the Belgic Confession.

[6] *Institutes*, IV.10.8 (ed. J. T. McNeill, trans. F. L. Battles [Philadelphia: Westminster; London: SCM Press, 1961], vol. 2, p. 1187).

[7] *Institutes*, IV.10.27.

[8] See above, chapter 3, pp. 44ff.

[9] Westminister Confession, I.6.

[10] Harry S. Stout, *The Divine Dramatist: George Whitefield and the Rise of Modern Evangelicalism* (Grand Rapids: Eerdmans, 1992).

[11] Apart from scriptural indication, the practice of Israel would not be normative. The question is how much we may infer from the language of the Psalms.

[12] *Constitution on the Sacred Liturgy*, sec. 28, in Flannery, ed., *op. cit.*, p. 11.

[13] *Third Instruction on the Correct Implementation of the Constitution on the Sacred Liturgy* (5 September 1970) 3g, in *ibid.*, p. 215. *Cf. Parish Mass Book and Hymnal* (New York: Catholic Book Publishing, 1965), p. 282.

[14] See William D. Maxwell, *An Outline of Christian Worship: Its Development and Forms* (London: Oxford University Press, 1949), pp. 73–80.

[15] See the citation from a young French student's letter in *ibid.*, p. 98.

[16] Acts 2:1, 15; 3:1; 10:3, 9, 30. See *ibid.*, pp. 163-170.

[17] David Bryant, *Concerts of Prayer* (Ventura, CA: Regal Books, 1988).

[18] For example, by Professor John Frame, in class notes on worship at Westminster Theological Seminary, Escondido, California.

[19] In Rom. 15:8, the NIV translates 'a servant of the Jews' rather than, more literally, 'a servant (or 'minister') of the circumcision'. The genitive should be taken as subjective: Jesus is made a minister who is of the circumcision, for the sake of the truth of God. Jesus served the calling of the circumcision and thereby fulfilled the promises made to the circumcision, that they would lead the praises of the Gentiles.

10. The nurture of the church

[1] Roland de Vaux, *Ancient Israel*, vol. 1, *Social Institutions* (New York: McGraw-Hill Book Co., 1961), p. 49.

[2] This was the thrust of the television series *Millennium*, aired on public television stations in the United States in 1992.

[3] The NIV translation of Eph. 4:12 expresses a general consensus favouring it above the ASV, 'for the perfecting of the saints, for the work of ministering'. The latter rendering makes the work of ministering, spoken of in 4:12, to be the work of the apostles, prophets, evangelists, pastors and teachers. With either translation, the ministry of the teachers and of every believer (4:16) is recognized.

[4] C. S. Lewis, *The Abolition of Man* (London: Oxford University Press, 1943).

[5] For this explanation of the text, see Peter T. O'Brien, *Colossians, Philemon*, Word Biblical Commentary 44 (Waco, TX: Word Books, 1982), pp. 79–82.

[6] W. Michaelis, art. '*mimeomai*', *TDNT* IV, pp. 666–673.

[7] For a warning against a less bizarre example of this tendency, see Richard N. Ostling, 'Keepers of the Flock': 'Indeed the Boston Movement shows the effectiveness of getting each church member devoted to evangelistic effort – as well as the dangers of identifying the dictates of man with the will of God' (*Time*, 18 May 1992, p. 62).

[8] John Leo, 'The Seven Video Sins', *US News and World Report* 115.8, 23 August 1993, p. 19.

[9] Resolution B-60 of the NEA convention, New Orleans, July 1994, as reported in *The Phyllis Schaffly Report* 28.2, September 1994, p. 2.

11. The mission of the church

[1] The World Missionary Conference in Edinburgh in 1910 led both to the International Missionary Council (1921) and, through Bishop Charles Brent, to the World Conference of Faith and Order (Lausanne, 1927). The IMC was joined to the WCC at its third assembly in New Delhi in 1961.

[2] Hendrik Kraemer, *The Christian Message in a Non-Christian World* (Grand Rapids: Kregel/International Missionary Council, 1956).

[3] See *The Church for Others and the Church for the World: A Quest for Structures for Missionary Congregations* (Geneva: WCC, 1967), p. 18: 'We may say that the Church is only required to be separate in order to be prepared for engagement, that is, the Church exists for the world . . . This is not election to privilege but to serving engagement. The Church lives in order that the world may know its true being.' See also Thomas Wieser, ed., *Planning for Mission* (New York: The US Conference for the WCC, 1966).

[4] Richard Shaull writes: 'The God who is tearing down old structures in order to create the conditions for a more human existence is himself in the midst of the struggle . . . In this context, the Christian is called to be fully involved in the revolution as it develops . . . From within this struggle we discover that we do not bear witness in revolution by preserving our purity in line with certain moral principles, but rather by freedom to be *for man* at every moment.' 'Revolutionary Change in Theological Perspective', in John C. Bennett, ed., *Christian Social Ethics in a Changing World* (New York: Association Press; London: SCM Press, 1966), p. 33.

[5] Gustavo Gutiérrez, 'Freedom and Salvation: A Political Problem', in *Liberation and Change* (Atlanta: John Knox Press, 1977), p. 86.

[6] G. Gutiérrez, *A Theology of Liberation* (Maryknoll, NY: Orbis Books, 1973; SCM Press, 1974).

[7] Harvie Conn summarized the ways in which this approach departed from biblical teaching: praxis set over revealed truth; works added to grace; a humanistic eschatology; the 'poor' seen only in the socio-economic sense; sin seen as corporate to the exclusion of personal; and its commitment to Marxism. See 'Theologies of Liberation: Toward a Common View', in *Tensions in Contemporary Theology*, ed. Stanley Gundry and Alan Johnson (Chicago: Moody Press, 1976), p. 413.

[8] 'Report of the Report Committee', *Ecumenical Review* 43.2, April 1991, IV:85, p. 274, *cf.* II:39, p. 268.

[9] *Ibid.*, IV:97.

[10] *Ibid.*, II:41.

[11] Robin Boyd cites the statement in the Report that 'Not every spirit is of the Holy Spirit' and that the Spirit must be the Spirit of Christ (IV:93). He takes comfort in this after the platform presentation by Professor Chung of Korea that included invoking the spirits of the dead who had been victims of violence, and her use of the terms of Korean spiritism '*Han*' and '*Kwan In*' as terms for the Holy Spirit. ' "Come, Holy Spirit!" and We Really Mean "Come!" ', in *Ecumenical Review*, 43:2, p. 181.

[12] 'Report', III:71.

[13] *Ibid.*, I:16 (italics added). The verb '*ābad* can mean to 'serve', including to serve the Lord in worship; it also means to 'work', and is here used as elsewhere in Genesis for 'working' or 'tilling' the ground (Gn. 2:5; 3:23; 4:2, 12).

[14] *Ibid.*, I:21.

[15] *Ibid.*, III:75.

[16] *Ibid.*, IV:92.

[17] *Ibid.*, I:22, 23.

[18] *Ibid.*, III:78.

12. The church in the world's cultures

[1] R. Daniel Shaw, *Transculturation: The Cultural Factor in Translation and Other Communication Tasks* (Pasadena, CA: William Carey Press, 1988), p. 67.

[2] H. Richard Niebuhr, *Christ and Culture* (New York: Harper & Row, 1951; Torchbook ed., 1956). See also Charles H. Kraft, *Christianity in Culture* (Maryknoll, NY: Orbis Books, 1984).

[3] Don Richardson, *Eternity in Their Hearts* (Ventura, CA: Regal Books, 1981).

[4] Niebuhr, *op. cit.*, pp. 85ff.

[5] Peter Jones, *The Gnostic Empire Strikes Back: An Old Heresy for the New Age* (Phillipsburg, NJ: Presbyterian & Reformed, 1992).

[6] Bengt G. M. Sundkler, *Bantu Prophets in South Africa* (London: Lutterworth Press, 1948); *Zulu Zion and Some Swazi Zionists* (London: Oxford University Press, 1976).

[7] On the 'Chinese Rites' controversy, see Kenneth Scott Latourette, *A History of Missions in China* (New York: Macmillan, 1932), pp. 131–155; Louis J. Gallagher, *China in the Sixteenth Century: The Journals of Matthew Ricci 1583–1610* (New York: Random House, 1953), pp. 93–105; Robert C. Jenkins, *The Jesuits in China and the Legation of Cardinal de Tournon* (London, 1894), pp. 59–74; Arnold H. Rowbotham, *Missionary and Mandarin: The Jesuits at the Court of China* (Berkeley: University of California Press, 1942).

[8] Luther, *Works*, IV, pp. 265f., cited in Niebuhr, *op. cit.*, pp. 171f.

[9] Niebuhr, *op. cit.*, pp. 173ff.

[10] Niebuhr gives a succinct account of Augustine's views on this subject, but feels at a loss to account for Augustine's looking for the eschatological kingdom in which the elect will inherit eternal life, rather than embracing an earthly kingdom of universal salvation, to which he could easily have accommodated the biblical teaching, as Niebuhr sees it (*ibid.*, pp. 215f.).

[11] *Ibid.*, p. 215.

[12] Paul J. Achtemeier, *An Introduction to the New Hermeneutic* (Philadelphia: Westminster Press, 1969), p. 16.

[13] *Cf.* Cornelius Van Til, *The Defense of the Faith* (Philadelphia: Presbyterian & Reformed, 1955).

[14] The ground of ethics cannot be merely formal, but must be theistic. See David W. Clowney, *Virtues and Divine Commands: An Essay in Ethics and the Philosophy of Religion* (Ann Arbor, MI: University Microfilms International, 1986).

[15] Niebuhr, 'At the edges of the radical movement the Manichean heresy is always developing' (*op. cit.*, p. 81).

[16] *Institutes*, II.3.3.

[17] *Ibid.*, I.17.7.

[18] *Ibid.*, II.3.3, 4.

[19] *Ibid.*, II.3.4.

[20] See Ruth Benedict, *Patterns of Culture* (New York: New American Library, 1946).

[21] Richardson, *op. cit.*, p. 103. See *idem*, *Peace Child* (Ventura, CA: Regal Books, 1974).

[22] J. H. Bavinck, *An Introduction to the Science of Missions* (Philadelphia: Presbyterian & Reformed, 1960), p. 253.

[23] Hans-Georg Gadamer, *Truth and Method* (New York: Seabury Press, 1975), pp. 388ff.

[24] Bruce J. Nicholls, *Contextualization: A Theology of Gospel and Culture* (Downers Grove, IL: InterVarsity Press; Exeter: Paternoster Press, 1979), p. 54.

[25] Stephen Neill, 'Religion and Culture', in Robert Coote and John Stott, eds., *Gospel and Culture* (Pasadena, CA: William Carey Library, 1979).

[26] Stephen Neill, *A History of Christian Missions* (Harmondsworth, Middlesex: Penguin Books, 1964), p. 75.

13. The kingdom, the church and the state

[1] Robert Payne, *The Dream and the Tomb: A History of the Crusades* (New York: Stein & Day, 1985), p. 34.

[2] See E. P. Clowney, 'The Politics of the Kingdom', *WTJ* 41.2, Spring 1979, pp. 291–310. See also C. E. B. Cranfield, 'The Christian's Political Responsibility According to the New Testament', *SJT* 15, 1962, pp. 176–192; Charles W. Colson, *Kingdoms in Conflict* (New York: Morrow; Grand Rapids: Zondervan, 1987), pp. 81–94.

[3] Jacques Ellul, *The False Presence of the Kingdom* (New York: Seabury Press, 1972), pp. 92f.

[4] T. L. Underwood, 'The Inquisition', in J. D. Douglas, ed., *The New International Dictionary of the Christian Church* (Grand Rapids: Zondervan, [2]1978), p. 511.

[5] This is the position of Herman Dooyeweerd, *The Christian Idea of the State* (Nutley, NJ: Craig Press, 1978), p. 10.

[6] The 'Anti-revolutionary' party led by Abraham Kuyper in the Netherlands was established as a Christian political party. Kuyper advocated the principle of 'sphere sovereignty', marking out distinct spheres of life in which the kingdom came to expression. See his *Calvinism* (Grand Rapids: Eerdmans, 1931). Because of proportional representation in the Netherlands, political power was shared in practice, although in principle one party could come to power.

[7] When Christians act together in works of compassion or witness they do so as members of the church ('general' officers). When they act together to exert political power, they may not act as a specifically Christian group, excluding unbelievers. That would be in principle to reach for the sword in the name of Christ's kingdom. The use of the sword and political power may advance justice, and relieve oppression, but this is not the calling of Christ's kingdom of salvation (Jn. 18:36).

[8] Cited by Dewi Morgan, *The Church in Transition: Reform in the Church of England* (London: Charles Knight, 1970), p. 89.

[9] Canon Selwyn Gummer quotes an Anglican priest, 'The Church of England is the only Free Church in England', in D. Morgan, ed., *They Became Anglicans* (Oxford: Mowbray, 1959), p. 57, cited in Morgan, *op. cit.*, p. 90.

[10] John R. W. Stott, *Christian Mission in the Modern World* (London: Falcon Books; Downers Grove, IL: InterVarsity Press, 1975), p. 30.

[11] *Ibid.*, p. 88.

[12] *Ibid.*, pp. 26f. On the debate about the relation between evangelism and social action, see Timothy Chester, *Awakening to a World of Need: The Recovery of Evangelical Social Concern* (Leicester: Inter-Varsity Press, 1993).

[13] Stott, *op. cit.*, p. 29.

[14] *Ibid.*, p. 30.

[15] *Ibid.*, p. 99.

[16] 'Salvation by faith in Christ crucified and risen is moral, not material, a rescue from sin not from harm, and the reason why Jesus said "your faith has saved you" to both categories is that his works of physical rescue (from disease, drowning and death) were intentional signs of his salvation, and were thus understood by the early church' (*ibid.*, p. 87).

[17] *Ibid.*, p. 34.

[18] *Ibid.*, p. 30.

14. The structure of Christ's church

[1] Strangely, so biblical a theologian as Thomas Witherow, after describing the 'divine right' of church government, adds that 'To affirm this, is little more than to say of the Church what is true of any voluntary society . . .' (*The Form of the Christian Temple*, Edinburgh: T. & T. Clark, 1889, p. 159).

[2] Vatican Council II, *Dogmatic Constitution on the Church*, II.10 (in Austin Flannery OP, ed., *Vatican Council II: The Conciliar and Post Conciliar Documents* [Northport, NY: Costello; Dublin: Dominican Publications, 1975], p. 361).

[3] *Ibid.*

[4] *Ibid.*, III.22 (in *ibid.*, p. 375).

[5] For a classic presentation of the case for episcopacy, see Richard Hooker (*c.* 1554–1600), *Treatise on the Laws of Ecclesiastical Polity* (Manchester: Carcanet Press, 1990).

[6] Robert Wuthnow has reported on a five-year project relating religion to the use of money in America. The survey reveals the stewardship of many committed Christians, but also shows that most people have some explaining to do about serving God *and* mammon (*God and Mammon in America* [New York: Free Press, 1994].

[7] Yves Congar, *Lay People in the Church: A Study for a Theology of Laity*, trans. Donald Attwater (Westminster, MD: Newman Press, [2]1965).

[8] This association of the prophets with the apostles will be defended in chapter 17.

[9] Günther Bornkamm, '*presbus*', *TDNT* VI, p. 659, n. 47.

[10] For this section, see 'Biblical Guides for Mercy Ministry in the Presbyterian Church in America', *Minutes of the Fifteenth General Assembly of the PCA, 1987*, pp. 506ff. (a committee report that utilized a draft by the author).

15. The ministry of women in the church

[1] This is true, although most of the major Protestant denominations now ordain women. The Episcopal Church in the United States took the step in 1976, and the General Synod of the Church of England voted to ordain in 1992. Many aspects of the Measure passed by the Synod continue to be debated. See Philip Turner, 'Communion, Order, and the Ordination of Women', in *Pro Ecclesia*, vol. 2, no. 3, Summer 1993.

[2] Krister Stendahl, for example, argues that the male image of God has become oppressive to many women, and by implication also to men. To avoid picturing God in our own image, Stendahl counsels thinking of the Holy Spirit as 'It'. 'It is equally true to say about God that she is black as it is to say he is white. Or equally false. To meditate upon God as Spirit is an indispensable corrective' (*Energy for Life* [Geneva: WCC, 1990], p. 8). Paul Jewett uses masculine or feminine pronouns for deity interchangeably: 'She who reigns is none other than the Lord our God Almighty, Rev. 19:6' (*God, Creation and Revelation: A Neo-Evangelical Theology* [Grand Rapids: Eerdmans, 1991], p. 352). See Susanne Heine, *Matriarchs, Goddesses, and Images of God: A Critique of Feminist Theology* (Minneapolis: Augsburg, 1989), p. 28.

[3] Paul K. Jewett, *Man as Male and Female: A Study of Sexual Relationships from a Theological Point of View* (Grand Rapids: Eerdmans, 1975), pp. 137–140. Jewett argues that Paul was ambivalent about slavery, and that he could not escape his 'historical limitations' in speaking of male headship as he does in Eph. 5:22–33.

[4] Howard Keir, in *Evangelical Quarterly* LV, January 1983, p. 33, suggests that 1 Cor. 11:13–17 is not Pauline. Gordon D. Fee argues that 1 Cor. 14:34–35 is a later gloss (*The First Epistle to the Corinthians* [Grand Rapids: Eerdmans, 1987]). See Donald A. Carson, ' "Silent in the Churches": On the Role of Women in 1 Corinthians 14:33b–36', in John Piper and Wayne Grudem, eds., *Recovering Biblical Manhood and Womanhood: A Response to Evangelical Feminism* (Wheaton, IL: Crossway Books, 1991).

[5] Craig Keener alleges that Paul used arguments that he felt would be persuasive to his readers, and that we do not know what he would write today; indeed, that Paul himself could not have imagined a culture so different as ours (*Paul, Women and Wives: Marriage and Women's Ministry in the Letters of Paul* [Peabody, MA: Hendrickson Publishers, 1992], pp. 21f., 134).

[6] See, in addition to the commentaries, the book by Keener, just cited, and Stephen B. Clark, *Man and Woman in Christ: An Examination of the Roles of Men and Women in Light of Scripture and the Social Sciences* (Ann Arbor, MI: Servant Books, 1980); Mary J. Evans, *Woman in the Bible* (Exeter: Paternoster Press, 1983); Mary Hayter, *The New Eve in Christ: The Use and*

NOTES

Abuse of the Bible in the Debate about Women in the Church (London: SPCK, 1987); James B. Hurley, *Man and Woman in Biblical Perspective: A Study in Role Relationships and Authority* (Leicester: Inter-Varsity Press, 1981); George W. Knight III, *The New Testament Teaching on the Role Relationship of Men and Women* (Grand Rapids: Baker Book House, 1977); Alvera Mickelsen, ed., *Women, Authority and the Bible* (Downers Grove, IL: InterVarsity Press, 1986); Piper and Grudem, eds., *op. cit.*

[7] Paul's use of the metaphor 'head' in this passage is further illumined by Eph. 1:22, 'all things under his feet', and Colossians 2:10, 'the head of all rule and authority'. Paul says that the church is subject to Christ who is its head (Eph. 5:23–24). See Wayne Grudem, 'The Meaning of *Kephalē* ("Head"): A Response to Recent Studies', in Piper and Grudem, eds., *op. cit.*, pp. 425–468.

[8] John M. Frame, 'Men and Women in the Image of God', in Piper and Grudem, eds., *op. cit.*, pp. 225–232. Note the refutation of Barth's view, and also the defence of the sense in which both individually and corporately the divine image is apparent in human beings.

[9] As Keener supposes, '*Nothing* in this passage suggests wives' subordination' (*op. cit.*, p. 47).

[10] Richard Oster, 'When Men Wore Veils to Worship: The Historical Context of 1 Corinthians 11:4', *New Testament Studies* 44, 1988, pp. 481–505.

[11] Keener's description of Paul's multiplying of arguments indicates, I believe, the culturally variable aspect of head-covering that Paul is addressing (pp. 22–31). Keener, however, fails to recognize the distinction between a practice that Paul is arguing *for* and a principle that he is arguing *from* (established in creation). Paul applies the principle to the Corinthian situation. Our situation is different, but we, too, must take account of the principle.

Keener objects to the translation 'the woman ought to have a sign of authority on her head' (11:10, NIV), pointing out that there is no word for 'sign of' in Greek. He explains the meaning of 'the woman has authority over her own head' as 'it is the woman's right to choose what she will wear' (pp. 21, 38). He sees Paul as asking the woman to forgo her rights for the sake of others. Although it is true that Paul has been speaking of giving up one's rights (1 Cor. 8 – 10), there is no statement to that effect here. A translation that fits the context is suggested by Plummer: 'the woman ought to have control over her head', *i.e.* by covering it (A. Robertson and A. Plummer: *A Critical and Exegetical Commentary on the First Epistle of St Paul to the Corinthians* [Edinburgh: T. & T. Clark, ²1914], p. 232). Plummer cites the same Greek expression with this sense in Rev. 11:6; 14:18; 20:6).

[12] Raymond C. Ortlund, Jr, 'Male–Female Equality and Male Headship: Genesis 1 – 3', in Piper and Grudem, eds., *op. cit.*, p. 108.

[13] 'While we cannot be sure about this, there is good reason to think

that the problem in both situations [Ephesus and Corinth] was rooted in a false belief that Christians were already in the full form of God's kingdom and that they had accordingly been spiritually taken "out of the world" so that aspects of this creation, like sex, food, and male / female distinctions, were no longer relevant to them' (Douglas Moo, 'What Does it Mean Not to Teach or Have Authority over Men? 1 Timothy 2:11–15', in Piper and Grudem, eds., *op. cit.*, p. 181). (See literature cited, *ibid.*, p. 497, n. 18.) See also David M. Scholer, '1 Timothy 2:9–15 and the Place of Women in the Church's Ministry', in Mickelsen, ed., *op. cit.*, pp. 198f.

[14] See S. Lewis Johnson, Jr, 'Role Distinctions in the Church: Galatians 3:28', in Piper and Grudem, eds., *op. cit.*, pp. 154–156.

[15] Jewett, *op. cit.*, p. 142.

[16] For a brief but clear development of this point, see Vern S. Poythress, 'The Church as Family: Why Male Leadership in the Family Requires Male Leadership in the Church', in Piper and Grudem, eds., *op. cit.*, pp. 233–247.

[17] See the summary in Poythress, 'The Church as Family', *ibid.*, pp. 233f.

[18] Keener, *op. cit.*, pp. 186f. His argument for excepting the subjection of parents to children urges various distinctions between that relationship and the other two. But the exception shows that 'submit to one another' cannot, *as an expression*, demand an absolute mutuality of submission without respect to relationship.

[19] *Ibid.*, p. 170.

[20] *Ibid.*, p. 168.

[21] See my exposition of 1 Peter 3:1–7 in *The Message of 1 Peter*, The Bible Speaks Today series (Leicester: Inter-Varsity Press; Downers Grove: InterVarsity Press, 1988), pp. 126–135.

[22] Peter T. O'Brien, *Colossians, Philemon*, Word Biblical Commentary, 44 (Waco, TX: Word Books, 1982), pp. 296–299.

[23] Keener's point, *op. cit.*, p. 206.

[24] Douglas Moo argues for construing 'man' (*andros*) as the object of 'teach' as well as 'have authority'. He also defends the meaning of *authentein* in this text as 'have authority' rather than 'domineer' ('What Does it Mean Not to Teach or Have Authority over Men? 1 Timothy 2:11–15', in Piper and Grudem, eds., *op. cit.*, pp. 186f.). See the literature cited, *ibid.*, p. 497, n. 18.

[25] See the thorough treatment of this text by Donald A. Carson, ' "Silent in the Churches": On the Role of Women in 1 Corinthians 14:33b-36', in Piper and Grudem, eds., *op. cit.*, pp. 140–153, especially the bibliography on p. 489, n. 42.

[26] This is in disagreement with the thesis of Wayne Grudem, alluded to in *Recovering Biblical Manhood and Womanhood* and defended in *The Gift of Prophecy in the New Testament and Today* (Westchester, IL: Crossway Books;

Eastbourne: Kingsway, 1988). For a discussion of this question, see chapter 17 below.

[27] Paul's phrase is that they were 'noteworthy among the apostles'. James D. G. Dunn explains: 'That is, they belonged most probably to the closed group of apostles appointed directly by the risen Christ in a limited period following his resurrection . . .' (*Romans 9–16*, Word Biblical Commentary 38b [Dallas: Word Books, 1988], p. 895). Dunn bases this on his interpretation of 1 Corinthians 15:7, where he holds that the 'apostles' of that verse are not the same as the 'twelve' of verse 5. He then further holds that these apostles are the foundation of the church in Ephesians 2:20, so that his 'most probably' strengthens to the concluding statement, 'We may firmly conclude, however, that one of the foundation apostles of Christianity was a woman and a wife.' The conclusion that Junia is 'noteworthy' among these foundational apostles would be rejected by a different analysis of the New Testament teaching about the apostleship. The class of 'apostles' as missionaries is also recognized by Dunn, and fits much better with other teams of 'fellow-workers' whom Paul names.

[28] This position is taken in the majority report of a Committee to Study the Role of Women in Church Office presented to the 1988 General Assembly of the Orthodox Presbyterian Church in the United States. A careful examination of this question is given by Robert B. Strimple in a dissenting minority report, *Minutes of the Fifty-Fifth General Assembly* (Philadelphia: OPC, 1988), pp. 356–373. I am indebted to Dr Strimple's exposition.

[29] C. E. B. Cranfield, *A Critical and Exegetical Commentary on the Epistle to the Romans* (Edinburgh: T. & T. Clark, 1986), vol. 2, p. 781.

[30] The word *kai*, 'also', is supported by P^{46}, B and C*.

[31] Cranfield, *op. cit.*, vol. 2, pp. 626f.

[32] John Calvin, *The Epistles of Paul the Apostle to the Romans and to the Thessalonians*, trans. Ross MacKenzie (Grand Rapids: Eerdmans, 1961), pp. 320f. (on Rom. 16:1).

[33] The seven chosen to assure equitable provision for the Grecian Jewish widows (Acts 6:1–6) were all men, but this seems to be the first differentiation of office beyond the apostles. The men were elders and evangelists supervising diaconal ministry, rather than deacons in distinction from elders / bishops.

16. The gifts of the Spirit in the church

[1] David B. Barrett, 'Statistics, Global', in Stanley M. Burgess and Gary B. McGee, eds., *Dictionary of Pentecostal and Charismatic Movements* (Grand Rapids: Zondervan, 1988), p. 816 (hereafter refered to as *DPCM*). Barrett

projects 562.5 million by the year 2000, making up 28.6% of Christian church members (p. 813). The difficulty of reaching even approximate figures is illustrated by two Gallup polls reported in the 1980s. One claimed that 19% of American adults identified themselves as Pentecostal-charismatic (29 million adults). Another poll asked about involvement or participation in the charismatic movement, and netted a positive response from 3%, or 5.8 million adults. This last figure conformed to the earlier survey that showed 4% who had spoken in tongues.

[2] C. Peter Wagner, 'Church Growth', in *DPCM*, p. 192.

[3] See Wagner, 'Third Wave', in *DPCM*, pp. 843f., and his article on 'Church Growth'. For a critical evaluation, see John F. MacArthur, Jr, *Charismatic Chaos* (Grand Rapids: Zondervan, 1992), pp. 128ff. For survey articles, see *DPCM*, including G. Wacker, 'Bibliography and Historiography of Pentecostalism (US)'. See also Robert G. Clouse, 'Pentecostal Churches', and Watson E. Mills, 'Glossolalia', in J. D. Douglas, ed., *The New International Dictionary of the Christian Church* (Grand Rapids: Zondervan, 1974), and J. W. Ward, 'Pentecostal Theology' in S. B. Ferguson and David F. Wright, eds., *New Dictionary of Theology* (Leicester: Inter-Varsity Press; Downers Grove, IL: InterVarsity Press, 1988).

[4] C. Peter Wagner, 'Third Wave', in *DPCM*, p. 844. Before Wagner, the late David Watson took basically the same position. He vividly describes his own experience of the filling of the Spirit in his life, and his struggle in evaluating Martyn Lloyd-Jones's description of the 'baptism of the Spirit' in contrast to John Stott's teaching that the baptism of the Spirit refers to Christian initiation. See David Watson, *You Are My God* (London: Hodder & Stoughton, [2]1986) pp. 56–61.

[5] See John R. W. Stott, *Baptism and Fullness: The Work of the Holy Spirit Today* (Leicester: Inter-Varsity Press: Downers Grove, IL: InterVarsity Press, [2]1975); Anthony A. Hoekema, *Holy Spirit Baptism* (Grand Rapids: Eerdmans; Exeter: Paternoster Press, 1972); James D. G. Dunn, *Baptism in the Holy Spirit* (London: SCM Press, 1970).

[6] Stott, *op cit.*, p. 25.

[7] Luke's usual expressions would be that they believed *in* Jesus Christ or the gospel, affirming the commitment of faith. See Dunn, *op. cit.*, p. 65. Dunn's explanation is also accepted by Hoekema, *op. cit.*, pp. 34–37.

[8] Dunn, *op. cit.*, pp. 83–89.

[9] *Ibid.*, p. 85.

[10] Peter R. Jones, '1 Corinthians 15:8: Paul the Last Apostle', *Tyndale Bulletin* 36, 1985, pp. 3–34.

[11] Jack Deere argues that the 'signs, wonders and miracles' in this passage do not authenticate Paul's apostleship. He says, correctly, that Paul does not put 'signs, wonder and miracles' in the nominative case, in apposition to 'apostolic signs', to give the meaning, 'apostolic signs . . .

(namely) signs and wonders and miracles' (*Surprised by the Power of the Spirit* [Grand Rapids: Zondervan, 1993; Eastbourne: Kingsway, 1994, p. 104].

Paul does not equate apostolic signs with the signs and wonders because his apostolic signs were more inclusive. The Corinthian Christians themselves, as the fruit of his ministry, were seals of his apostleship (1 Cor. 9:1–10). Paul's ministry, exercised in 'all patience', showed the integrity of his claim to apostleship. But as Philip Hughes points out, the accompanying 'signs, wonders and powers', taken together, 'constitute one of the signs of an apostle' (*Paul's Second Epistle to the Corinthians*, The New International Commentary on the New Testament [Grand Rapids: Eerdmans, 1962], pp. 457f.).

The dative case of the signs and wonders expresses the manner in which the apostolic signs were done among the Corinthians. The same use of the dative appears in Rom. 15:18–19, where Paul describes his apostolic ministry as 'by the power of signs and miracles through the power of the Spirit'. (See also 2 Thes. 2:9.)

Signs and wonders did accredit the apostles, even as they accredited their Lord (Acts 2:22, 43). They confirmed those who had heard the words of the Lord, and witnessed to his salvation (Heb. 2:3–4). To say, as Deere does, that the Word of God did not need miraculous confirmation (p. 106) is as pointless as to say that the words of Jesus did not need miraculous confirmation. It pleased God to authenticate the foundational witness of the apostles and the prophets. Paul reminds the Corinthians that the gifts they received had come through his ministry – no doubt through the laying on of his hands (*cf.* Acts 8:17; 19:6). That the gifts God granted through the apostles were themselves miraculous (healing and prophecy, for example) does not lessen their authenticating of the apostles, since they were given through the laying on of their hands.

[12] For example, in Benjamin B. Warfield, *Counterfeit Miracles* (1918; Banner of Truth edition, London, 1972), pp. 25f.: 'Miracles do not appear on the pages of Scripture vagrantly, here, there, and elsewhere indifferently, without assignable reason. They belong to revelation periods, and appear only when God is speaking to his people through accredited messengers, declaring his gracious purposes.' For an exposition of the view that the working of miracles is not to be regarded as restricted to the apostles and their associates, see Wayne Grudem, *Systematic Theology: An Introduction to Christian Doctrine* (Leicester: Inter-Varsity Press; Grand Rapids: Zondervan, 1994), pp. 361–368.

[13] For a classic refutation of linking revival with the manifestation of prophecy and other gifts of the apostolic age, see Jonathan Edwards, 'The Distinguishing Marks of a Work of the Spirit of God', Section III.iii, in *Jonathan Edwards on Revival* (Edinburgh and Carlisle, PA: Banner of Truth Trust, 1965), pp. 137–141.

[14] See the articles on 'Initial Evidence' by B. C. Aker and K. Kendrick in *DPCM*, pp. 455-460.

[15] Kendrick, *DPCM*, p. 459.

[16] 'It would be absurd to approach the story as a literal, matter-of-fact report' (Frank W. Beare, 'Speaking With Tongues: A Critical Survey of the New Testament Evidence', in Watson E. Mills, ed., *Speaking in Tongues: A Guide to Research on Glossolalia* [Grand Rapids: Eerdmans, 1986], p. 117).

[17] J. G. Davies has shown the close connection between the account of the division of languages at Babel in Gn. 11:1–9 and the account of Pentecost in Acts. The same vocabulary is used in the Septuagint of Gn. 11 and Dt. 32:8, and in Acts 2 ('Pentecost and Glossolalia', *JTS*, new series 5, 1952, pp. 228–231).

[18] This link is made on the assumption that Israel had come to Sinai fifty days after the Passover and their departure from Egypt ('in the third month', Ex. 19:1).

[19] See I. Howard Marshall, *The Acts of the Apostles*, Tyndale New Testament Commentaries (Leicester: Inter-Varsity Press; Grand Rapids: Eerdmans, 1980), p. 68; and see *Tanhuma* 26c, cited in F. F. Bruce, *The Acts of the Apostles* (Grand Rapids: Eerdmans; Leicester: Apollos, [3]1990), p. 116.

[20] It has been objected that the disciples would not have been accused of drunkenness if they had been speaking in known languages. See Cyril G. Williams, *Tongues of the Spirit: A Study of Pentecostal Glossolalia and Related Phenomena* (Cardiff: University of Wales, 1981), and the reply by D. A. Carson, *Showing the Spirit: A Theological Exposition of 1 Corinthians 12 – 14* (Grand Rapids: Baker Book House, 1987), pp. 80ff. Surely the use of so many different languages by disciples in the grip of such spiritual exaltation could be taken as ground for a sceptical evaluation.

[21] Carson, *op. cit.*, p. 87.

[22] See also Dt. 28:49; Is. 33:19; Je. 5:15.

[23] Williams, *op. cit.*

[24] A thorough examination and summary are found in William J. Samarin, *Tongues of Men and Angels: The Religious Language of Pentecostalism* (New York: Macmillan; London: Collier-Macmillan, 1972).

[25] Vern S. Poythress, 'Linguistic and Sociological Analyses of Modern Tongues-Speaking: Their Contributions and Limitations', in Mills, ed., *op. cit.*, pp. 469–489. See also Carson, *op. cit.*, pp. 84–87.

[26] L. Carl May, 'A Survey of Glossolalia and Related Phenomena in Non-Christian Religions', in Mills, *op. cit.*, pp. 53–82. May also gives examples of xenoglossia, speaking in other languages, allegedly unknown to the speaker.

[27] As Samarin reminds us. He defines glossolalia as 'strings of syllables, made up of sounds taken from among all those the speaker knows, put together more or less haphazardly but which nevertheless emerge as word-

like and sentence-like units because of realistic, language-like rhythm and melody' (*op. cit.*, p. 227).

[28] John MacArthur (*op. cit.*, p. 230) argues that there is a significant difference in meaning between the middle voice of the verb *pauō* ('cease') affirmed of tongues, and the passive form of the verb *katargeō* ('do away with') affirmed of prophecy and knowledge. He suggests that tongues are said to come to a stop of themselves, while prophecy and knowledge are brought to an end. But the verb *katargeō* is used in 1 Cor. 13:11, where Paul says that with maturity he put away childish ways. The thought would seem to be the same in application to prophecy, tongues and knowledge. MacArthur also regards prophecy and knowledge as being continuing gifts to the church, in distinction from tongues. It seems more likely that Paul is referring to all three in their heightened, miraculous sense.

[29] The interpretation of the 'groanings' of the Spirit (Rom. 8:26) as referring to speaking in tongues, while ancient, does not take adequate account of the fact that Paul is describing the groanings of the Spirit, in contrast to our groanings (8:23). See C. E. B. Cranfield, *A Critical and Exegetical Commentary on the Epistle to the Romans* (Edinburgh: T. & T. Clark, 1975, vol. 1, p. 423).

[30] Irenaeus, *Adversus Haereses*, V.VI.1, cited in E. Glenn Hinson, 'The Significance of Glossolalia in the History of Christianity', in Mills, ed., *op. cit.*, pp. 184f.

[31] Henry Bettenson, ed., *Documents of the Christian Church* (London: Oxford University Press, 1963), p. 77, cited in MacArthur, *op. cit.*, p. 74.

[32] Augustine, *On Baptism*, III.xviii.16–21.

[33] See Augustine, Homily 6 on 1 John, sec. 10, in Philip Schaff, ed., *The Nicene and Post-Nicene Fathers*, First Series (New York: Christian Literature Co., 1888), p. 497, cited in MacArthur, *op. cit.*, p. 233. Augustine is explaining why the sign of tongues is not to be expected in the laying on of hands in baptism in his day. He speaks to encourage Christians not to suppose that they do not have the Spirit because they have not received the gift of tongues described in the New Testament. Joseph Bentivegna argues that Augustine teaches the continuance of the miraculous charismatic gifts, including tongues. He misconstrues, however, Augustine's analysis of Paul's teaching about praying in tongues in 1 Cor. 14. Augustine is developing the relation of the human spirit to the mind and is supporting his view from the text. He is not affirming the continuance of a practice which he says has ceased. Bentivegna, 'The Witness of St Augustine on the Action of the Holy Spirit in the Church and the Praxis of Charismata in his Times', in Elizabeth A. Livingstone, ed., *Studia Patristica* XXII (Leuven: Peeters Press, 1989), pp. 188–201. The citation is from Augustine, *De Genesi Ad Literam* XII.8 (J. H. Taylor, trans., *St Augustine: The Literal Meaning of Genesis*, vol. 2 [New York: Newman Press, 1982], pp. 188f.

[34] See 'Bibliography and Historiography of Pentecostalism (US)', in *DPCM*; also articles on 'European Pietist Roots of Pentecostalism', 'European Pentecostalism', 'Edward Irving', 'Charismatic Movement', 'Azusa Street Revival', *etc.*

[35] MacArthur, *op. cit.*, p. 236.

[36] Note the endorsement of Edwards in the December 1994 Joint Statement of the British Evangelical Alliance, *Evangelicals Now*, February 1995, p. 3. See *Jonathan Edwards on Revival: A Narrative of Surprising Conversions; The Distinguishing Marks of a Work of the Spirit of God; An Account of the Revival of Religion in Northampton 1740–1742* (Edinburgh and Carlisle, PA: Banner of Truth Trust, 1965).

[37] Edwards, *op. cit.*, p. 91. Cited in Deere, *op. cit.*, p. 96.

[38] Deere, *ibid.*, p. 96.

[39] *Ibid.*, pp. 96f.

[40] *Ibid.*, p. 88.

[41] *Ibid.*, p. 98.

[42] Edwards, *op. cit.*, pp. 123f.

[43] *Ibid.*, p. 125.

[44] *Ibid.*, p. 130.

[45] *Ibid.*, pp. 126–127.

17. The gift of prophecy in the church

[1] Tongues and prophecy may be distinguished in that tongues are addressed to God (1 Cor. 14:2, 28), and prophecy to man. The distinction is not sharp, for Christians speak to one another in hymns that are also addressed to the Lord (Eph. 5:19). Peter applied Joel's promise of prophecy to tongues at Pentecost (Acts 2:17–18).

[2] Wayne A. Grudem, *The Gift of Prophecy in the New Testament and Today* (Westchester, IL: Crossway Books; Eastbourne: Kingsway, 1988).

[3] Grudem approves 'a cautious and hesitant view towards receiving guidance through prophecy'. The primary function of prophecy is not guidance or prediction but 'upbuilding, encouragement, and comfort' (*ibid.*, p. 248).

[4] Grudem cites Paul's reference to Epimenides as an example of this loose usage. Writing to Titus about the people of Crete, Paul calls Epimenides 'a prophet of their own' (Tit. 1:12). But to apply the term to a pagan context requires only that an analogy exists: that the Cretans, too, would think of individuals as inspired, whose words would be thought to carry divine authority.

[5] See John W. Hilber, 'Diversity of OT Prophetic Phenomena and NT Prophecy', *WTJ* 56.2, Fall 1994, pp. 243–258. Hilber shows that 'The ministry of all OT prophets meets the criteria set forth by the prophet

Moses in Deut 18:15–22' (p. 244). He also defends the continuity of NT prophets with OT expectations.

[6] 1 Ki. 13:20–22; Hilber, *ibid.*, p. 252.

[7] Grudem, *op. cit.*, p. 39.

[8] *Ibid.*, p. 32.

[9] Hilber, *op. cit.*, p. 244.

[10] George Vandervelde, 'The Gift of Prophecy and the Prophetic Church', in *idem*, ed., *The Holy Spirit: Renewing and Empowering Presence* (Winfield, BC: Wood Lake Books, 1988), p. 103; *cf.* Abraham J. Heschel, *The Prophets*, vol. 1 (New York: Harper & Row, 1955), p. 21, cited in *ibid.*, p. 105.

[11] Grudem acknowledges that his interpretation of these Ephesian texts is crucial for his position (*op. cit.*, p. 46).

[12] *Ibid.*, p. 78.

[13] *Ibid.*, p. 79.

[14] *Ibid.*, p. 72.

[15] *Didache* XI:7ff.

[16] Hilber, *op. cit.*, pp. 253, 257.

[17] Grudem rightly calls attention to the particle *de* in 1 Thes. 5:21, which, after negative statements, may be translated 'but' or 'but rather'. We are not to quench the Spirit or despise prophecies, but rather prove all things, hold fast the good, and abstain from every form of evil. The contrast, however, is not between despising prophecies and testing prophecies, but between, on the one hand, quenching the Spirit and despising what the Spirit says (prophecies) and, on the other hand, instead of rejecting the Spirit (4:8), proving all things with the aid of the Spirit, so as to abstain from every form of evil.

[18] Hilber shows that prophecy uses ordinary language, not pedantic precision, citing Abijah's prophecy that Rehoboam would be left with one tribe (1 Ki. 11:32, 36), the doom oracle against Jeroboam, Baasha and Ahab (1 Ki. 14:11; 16:4; 21:24), and other instances (*op. cit.*, p. 250, n. 31.

[19] Prophecy is given not simply to provide information in advance, but to put predicted events in the setting of God's purposes and the continuity of his redemptive work. Malachi is not a false prophet because he predicted the coming of Elijah, although that prophecy was fulfilled by John the Baptist (Mal. 4:5–6; Mt. 11:14). A prophecy naming John-ben-Zachariah would not have conveyed the role of John in his ministry. As noted below, there is a rationale in the prophecy of Agabus, for it puts the sufferings of Paul into the framework of the sufferings of Christ.

[20] J. A. Alexander, *The Acts of the Apostles* (Philadelphia: Presbyterian Board of Publication, 1857; repr. Edinburgh: Banner of Truth Trust, 1980). It is 'a formula equivalent to *Thus saith the Lord* in ancient prophecy, and claiming for the words of Agabus direct divine authority' (pp. 265f).

[21] The Gk. phrases in Acts 21:11 and 28:17 are parallel. In each case the verb for 'deliver' or 'hand over' and the phrase 'into the hands of' are the same, while the word 'of the Gentiles' is replaced in Paul's language with 'of the Romans'.

[22] Grudem interprets Paul's words to apply to his being handed over from the Jewish judicial system at Jerusalem to the Roman judicial system at Caesarea. But if the same literal exactness were demanded of Paul that Grudem demands of Agabus, Paul, too, could be accused of misrepresentation. The Romans permitted the Jewish court to examine Paul, but, knowing him to be a Roman citizen, they never delivered him to Jewish authority. Actually, it was the Romans who delivered him out of Jerusalem in a night ride to foil an assassination attempt (Acts 22:30 – 23:35).

[23] The same verb, *paradidōmi*, is used in Mk. 10:33; Acts 21:11; 28:17. F. F. Bruce comments: 'The parallel between the Master's last journey to Jerusalem and the servant's is closely drawn by Luke (*cf.* v. 11). Like his Lord, Paul refuses to be diverted from the path of duty and suffering by the pleas of well-meaning friends, but "sets his face" to go to Jerusalem (*cf.* Lk. 9:51)', *The Acts of the Apostles: Greek Text with Introduction and Commentary* (Grand Rapids: Eerdmans; Leicester: Apollos, [3]1990), p. 442. He also notes the phrase 'The will of the Lord be done', *cf.* Lk. 22:42 with Acts 21:14.

[24] Grudem, *op. cit.*, p. 36.

[25] *Ibid.*, p. 262: 'Gently teach people and encourage them not to say, "Thus says the Lord," before they report a prophecy to the church.'

18. The sacraments

[1] Terence Hawkes, *Structuralism and Semiotics* (Berkeley, CA: University of California Press, 1977).

[2] Michael Novak, 'Women, Ordination, and Angels', *First Things* 32, April 1993, p. 31.

[3] Calvin defines *sacrament* as comprehending generally 'all the signs which God has ever given to men, to certify and assure them of the truth of his promises' (*Institutes*, IV.xiv.18). He explains that these signs may be natural or miraculous. Using this broader definition, he includes the rainbow among the sacraments, as well as the tree of life in the Garden of Eden. Under the narrower definition, as proposed by Meredith Kline, the tree of life would be a sacrament, but not the rainbow.

[4] *The Constitution on the Sacred Liturgy* II.61 (Austin Flannery, OP, ed., *Vatican Council II: The Conciliar and Post Conciliar Documents* [Northport, NY: Costello; Dublin: Dominican Publications, 1975], p. 20).

[5] On the relation of the number of the sacraments to the theology of the sacraments, see G. C. Berkouwer, *The Sacraments* (Grand Rapids: Eerdmans, 1969), pp. 27–42.

[6] The Pastoral Epistles are addressed to individuals, and Luke addresses his two volumes to Theophilus, yet even these have broader audiences in view. They are not private letters.

[7] *Institutes*, IV.xiv.14.

[8] *Institutes*, IV.xiv.16.

[9] *Institutes*, IV.xiv.16.

[10] *Institutes*, IV.xiv.17.

[11] Is. 1:13; 66:3.

[12] *Baptism, Eucharist and Ministry*, Faith and Order Paper No. 111 (Geneva: WCC, 1982), p. 2.

[13] *Baptism, Eucharist and Ministry 1982–1990: Report on the Process and Responses*, Faith and Order Paper No. 149 (Geneva: WCC, 1990), pp. 144f.

[14] The Westminster Confession of Faith speaks of the 'spiritual relation, or sacramental union, between the sign and the thing signified', so that the sacrament may be spoken of in the terms of the grace that it symbolizes (XXVII.2). The Confession gives this explanation to account for New Testament passages that speak of the sacramental sign in terms of what it signifies (Rom. 6:3; 1 Pet. 3:21). The context of the scriptural passages, however, guards against misunderstanding in a way that brief credal formulations may not. The emphasis on the necessity of faith in Romans is unmistakable.

[15] H. Denzinger, C. Bannwart, *et al.*, *Enchiridion Symbolorum, Definitionum et Declarationum de Rebus Fidei et Morum* (Barcinone: Herder, 1963), pp. 849–851.

[16] Deeper issues are raised by the place of the church in relation to the sacraments, and by the basis of *BEM*, which is not only Scripture plus tradition, but Scripture as contributing to tradition, in the context of contemporary experience.

[17] *The Constitution on the Sacred Liturgy* of Vatican II speaks of the sacraments as 'sacraments of faith', in the sense that they presuppose faith, and nourish, strengthen and express it. It is added that 'They do, indeed, confer grace, but, in addition, the very act of celebrating them most effectively disposes the faithful to receive this grace to their profit, to worship God duly, and to practise charity' (III.59). Note the care with which the formulation maintains the conferring of grace by the sacrament, so that the conferred grace may dispose the faithful to receive it. Faith is still not required for the reception of the sacramental grace.

[18] Meredith G. Kline, 'Oath and Ordeal Signs', *WTJ* 27.2, May 1965, pp. 115–119; see his *By Oath Consigned: A Reinterpretation of the Covenant Signs of Circumcision and Baptism* (Grand Rapids: Eerdmans, 1975). Kline has called attention to the death sanction in the ritual for a covenant oath in an eighth-century-BC treaty.

[19] Kline calls attention to the symbolism of consecration in the figurative

language used of fruit trees in Lv. 19:23–25. For the first three years, the fruit was 'uncircumcised' and might not be eaten. After the fruit was consecrated to the Lord in the fourth year, that consecration served as a 'circumcising' of the tree, in a manner of speaking. The fruit could then be eaten in the fifth year and beyond.

[20] Kline, *op. cit.*, p. 119.

[21] Or perhaps against Moses himself (Ex. 4:24).

[22] E. Clowney, *The Message of 1 Peter: The Way of the Cross*, The Bible Speaks Today series (Leicester: Inter-Varsity Press; Downers Grove, IL: InterVarsity Press, 1988), pp. 166f.

[23] Circumcision had corporate significance for Israel, male and female, as the sign of God's covenant with his people (Gn. 17:11); it is therefore a sign of faith (Rom. 4:11–12). The circumcision that was performed on the generation that entered the land is called the circumcision of 'all the nation' (Jos. 5:8). The coming renewal of the covenant is described as circumcision of the heart (Dt. 10:16; 30:6; Je. 4:4).

[24] Paul is showing why New Testament believers are not required to separate themselves from unbelievers as was the case in the Old Covenant (*e.g.* Ezr. 10:10–11; Ne. 13:23–27). Under the Old Covenant, the 'clean' Israelite was defiled by sexual union with one not in the covenant. But under the New Covenant, Paul explains, this does not occur. In marital intercourse between a believer and an unbelieving spouse, the believer is not defiled, but the unbeliever is sanctified. The believer is not compelled, therefore, to divorce an unbeliever in order to avoid the desecration of his or her body as a temple of the Holy Spirit. The 'sanctification' in view is not that of salvation, but of setting apart for the sexual union (*cf.* 1 Cor. 6:15–16). The significance of the passage for infant baptism is that Paul reasons from the recognized position of the child as holy, belonging to the Lord, to the fact that the unbelief of the spouse has not rendered the child conceived of the union to be outside the covenant.

[25] For this translation and its interpretation, see Peter T. O'Brien, *Colossians, Philemon*, Word Biblical Commentary 44 (Waco, TX: Word Books, 1982), pp. 114–118.

[26] Whether this refers to their guardian angels or to their own spirits as having such access is not clear. See Jean Héring, 'Un texte oublié: Matthieu 18.10', in *Aux sources de la Tradition chrétienne*, Mélanges offerts à M. Maurice Goguel (Neuchâtel: Delachaux & Niestlé, 1950, pp. 95–112. In either case, the claim of such access indicates full privilege for the little ones in the kingdom.

[27] Dom Gregory Dix (ed.), *The Treatise on the Apostolic Tradition of St Hippolytus of Rome* (London: SPCK; New York: Macmillan, 1937); Ph. M. Menoud, 'Le baptême des enfants dans l'église ancienne', *Verbum Caro* 2, 1948, pp. 15–26.

[28] Westminster Larger Catechism, Q. 177. For both sides of this question see 'Report of the Ad-Interim Committee to Study the Question of Paedocommunion', *Minutes of the Sixteenth General Assembly of the Presbyterian Church in America* (Atlanta: Committee on Christian Education and Publication, 1990), pp. 516–527.

[29] *BEM*, Commentary on Eucharist II, B (8), p. 11.

[30] *Ibid.*

[31] D. N. Power, in his essay 'How we can speak of the Eucharist as sacrifice', seeks to reconcile *BEM* with the essentials of the doctrine of Trent. Part of his effort is to redefine the doctrine of propitiation as applied to Christ's atonement. (See *Baptême–Eucharistie Ministère* [P. G. Farnedi, OSB, ed., *Studia Anselmiana* 74; *Sacramentum* 4, Rome: Editrice Anselmiana, 1977], pp. 153–176.)

[32] Gary Macy, *The Banquet's Wisdom: A Short History of the Theologies of the Lord's Supper* (New York: Paulist Press, 1992), p. 14.

[33] Gary Macy, *Theologies of the Eucharist in the Early Scholastic Period* (Oxford and New York: Oxford University Press, 1984), p. 27; *The Banquet's Wisdom*, pp. 70f.

[34] Macy, *The Banquet's Wisdom*, p. 77; Calvin, *Institutes*, IV.xvii.12.

[35] *Institutes*, IV.xvii.10.

[36] *Institutes*, IV.xvii.10.

[37] *Institutes*, IV.xvii.2.

Index of Biblical References

331

Index of Subjects and Names

333